W9-BXP-606

Brighter Leaves

Brighter Leaves

CELEBRATING THE ARTS IN DURHAM, NORTH CAROLINA

Edited by a Company of Friends of Patrick D. Kenan, M.D.

Historic Preservation Society of Durham ▓ Durham, North Carolina, 2008

Historic Preservation Society of Durham
Post Office Box 25411
Durham, NC 27702-5411

5   4   3   2   1

Design and production by Chris Crochetière,
BW&A Books, Inc., Durham, NC

Printed in the United States of America.

ISBN 978-0-9615577-4-4

Library of Congress Control Number: 2008927410

*D*edicated to the memory of Patrick Dan Kenan, M.D. (1930–2002), whose imagination conceived this project and whose inspiration has guided its compilers in bringing it to fruition

Contents

Color plates follow page 130

Foreword

When the trumpet sounds the notes of Aaron Copland's *Quiet City* somehow the city of Durham comes to mind—a crescendo from quietness, with undertones of growth.

This is a call to awareness that a cultural transformation has happened in this area! From a country village, through the years as a mill town, to busy years as a small factory city, there has been a gradual awakening to the need for a cultural dimension in Durham. This was not due to one person's cultural introspection; nor was it one person's vision. There were many forays made into the world of the arts—splendid attempts to start arts projects—but they were sporadic, disconnected, and without wide participation. They were mostly led by small dedicated groups. Then, as Durham's arts constituencies multiplied and many segments of the community were attracted to cultural programs, the arts gained their foothold at last. Durham's two educational institutions, Duke University and North Carolina Central University, brought in worldwide student bodies and facilities, injecting into Durham's population an international flavor and ethnic diversity. This ideal medium for the flowering of the arts has been building and has become one of the vital parts of the community.

One can say that Durham people working together, slowly but firmly, have built this strong arts position. Added to this is the creativity of Duke University and North Carolina Central University, whose artistic presentations have beckoned to the community with the hope of attracting its participation.

The response has been striking, and beautiful collaborations are blossoming. People in every part of Durham are involved. This equality of participation is typical of how Durham's interests have evolved and is one of the many reasons why Durham has become such an attractive place in which to live. The greatest demonstration of this was Durham's glowing tribute to Ella Fountain Pratt in 2000. She had been director of the Artists Series at Duke University for many years, serving on arts committees and promoting the arts in every possible way. Since her retirement, she has poured her talents into the Durham Community—working tirelessly for the Arts Council. She has made friends in literally every part of the community. The City of Durham and the Durham Arts Council honored Mrs. Pratt with a sparkling gala. Many of us remarked that it was the perfect example of Durham's spirit. It brought together the ideal ensemble of the churches, the city and county communities, the arts communities, and the university communities, all in the name of the arts. It was a triumph for Durham, a symbol of what it stands for.

As we advance into future years, let us not forget that the arts are what bring beauty to our lives. Look about and notice that the churches, gardens, buildings, and parks which have survived over the years are those which have lifted our community and surrounded us with beauty. We must be relentless in fighting unsightliness and we must continue in our pursuit of beauty and the arts, pouring our energies into that mission and cherishing each moment together.

Mary D. B. T. Semans

Preface

When the late Dr. Patrick Kenan recognized a need for a history of the arts in Durham, he envisioned a volume that would encompass all the arts, crafts, and culture of our town. He wanted to record their remarkable efflorescence during the last fifty years of the twentieth century. To help him realize this conception, he asked a group of friends and acquaintances to act as advisors and a board of directors for the project—hence the committee that has produced *Brighter Leaves*. For all it has been a labor of love.

Our first collective decision was to define the parameters of the book. We realized immediately that his original conception would have to be reduced if it were to fill only one volume. We therefore limited the scope to the fine arts, omitting culture in general and literature in particular because of the much larger treatment they would have required. With that decided we went ahead with the problem of finding capable and willing authors for the chapters.

At this stage in the book's planning, we were confronted by the sudden death of Dr. Kenan. While we were uncertain of our ability to proceed without him, loyalty compelled us to try. The result, we hope, would please him.

Brighter Leaves is not intended to be a comprehensive treatment of the arts in Durham. We have tried instead to indicate the broad outlines of their history and to highlight their special achievements, including some information about the more prominent artists and organizations that have contributed to their luster.

To help us and the authors of the chapters decide what was essential to include, we have had the advice of those interested and experienced in the various arts. Despite these precautions, we shall have inevitably omitted someone or something of importance. We apologize for any such omissions as well as for errors of fact that may have been made. We are breaking new ground, and information has not been easy to obtain or evaluate. We have been dependent in many instances on oral history and the artists themselves for much of our information.

In each chapter and in the book as a whole, we have tried to achieve a balance between the allotted space and the importance of the information. Obviously subjective judgments have been made throughout, an operation inherent in the task. Critics may cavil at the results; we can only assure them that we have tried to be objective and fair and as inclusive as possible within the scope of the project.

The first chapter tells the history of Durham's development in conjunction with its first artistic stirrings. Then follow chapters on the fine arts and crafts, and one on facilitating organizations, all focusing primarily on the last fifty-five years. Some pick up in the nineteenth century; some run over into the present century. Almost two hundred photographs enhance the book's contents. We are indebted to John Kenan for his efforts in making this possible. An appendix (arranged alphabetically by names of artists, organizations, and places) supplements material in the chapters and introduces additional information.

We have been helped in this large undertaking by many persons and organizations. First we are indebted to the Historic Preservation Society of Durham (now Preservation Durham), under whose aegis we have operated. Generous donors have made the project possible by their monetary gifts and have validated our efforts at crucial points. We thank the following organizations and individuals: the Mary Duke Biddle Foundation, Central Carolina Bank (now SunTrust), Duke Medical Center, Duke University Office of the President, the Durham Choral Society, the Kenan Family Foundation, the North Carolina Mutual Insurance Company, the Randleigh Foundation, the Barrie Wallace Fund for the Arts (Triangle Community Foundation), Wachovia Bank, Keith and Brenda Brodie, Susan Coon and Conrad Weiser, Pepper Fluke, Jan Harris, Jean S. Kahler, Mrs. Julia Kenan and the late Patrick Kenan, Kim Walsh and Daniel Kenan, Thomas S. Kenan III, Sylvia Kerckhoff, Randy and Cathy Lambe, Dr. David and Anna A. Martin, Phillip McMullan, Billy Olive, Norman E. Pendergraft, Hildegard Ryals, Nan and the late Max Schiebel, Kelly Matherly and the late John Setzer, Marian Frances Wallace Smith, Kim Stasheff, Mary Maddry Strauss, Elvin and Anne Strowd, the late Wesley Wallace, Robert Ward, George Williams, the late Elizabeth Willis, and one anonymous donor. We are also indebted to many persons who have selflessly given their time, expertise, and encouragement. Keith and Brenda Brodie, Mary and Jim Semans, E'Vonne Coleman, Thomas S. Kenan III, and Ella Fountain Pratt gave us a special perspective from their long involvement with the arts in Durham. We are equally indebted and deeply grateful to the authors of each chapter. We also thank Cynthia Satterfield for coordinating the project through many phases.

The following artists and citizens granted interviews, shared their important perspectives, supplied information, and facilitated or obtained photographs: Dr. Johnny Alston, Greg Bell, Paul Bryan, Kelly Bryant, Melvin Carver, John Compton, Peter Coyle, Morris Davis, Ernie Dollar, Jennifer Duffy, Jessie Thompson Eustice, Pepper Fluke, Gallery C, Amanda Gladin-Kramer, Jason Gotta, Hilton Goulson, Heidi Halstead, Samuel Hammond, Joan Hanks, Lee Hansley, Thomas Harkins, Bryant Holsenbeck, Edward Hunt, Dean Jeffrey, Jereann King, Peter Kramer, Barbara Lau, Robert Lawson, Christy Lentz, Ronnie Lilly, Lynn McKnight, Brooklyn McMillon, Mrs. Samuel McPherson, Nancy Tuttle May, Amy Milne, Jacqueline Morgan, Chris Morris, Linda Norflett, Julie Olson, Norman Pendergraft, Matt Pennachi, Ruth Phelps, Nancy Pinckney, Dianne Pledger, Warren Pope, Deborah Pratt, Andrew Preiss, Ann Prospero, Phyllis Randall, Charlie and Kathy Register, Carol Richards, Lynn Richardson, Lucien Roughton, Earl Sanders, Miriam Sauls, Brian Schroeder, Kathy Silbiger, Vincent Simonetti, Kay Sullivan, Clay Taliaferro, Tim Terry, William F. Twaddell Jr., Tyndall Galleries, Ranny Umberger, Amanda van Scoyoc, Eli Van Zoeren, Francis Vega, Zannie Voss, Lee Vrana, Robert Ward, Nancy Wardropper, Barbara Williams, Ella Williams, George Williams, Anna Wilson, Linwood Wilson, Jill Winter, David Wray, and Rodney Wynkoop.

Finally, as the board members who oversaw the project we take responsibility for errors of omission or commission. We hope that our perseverance will be vindicated by the usefulness of this book. If it spurs others to further investigation and more comprehensive efforts, we shall be gratified. If it also informs and gives pleasure to those who read it, we shall be delighted.

Jean Bradley Anderson   *Jane Goodridge*   *Louise Maynor*
E'Vonne Coleman   *Daniel Kenan*   *Marion Salinger*
Frank DePasquale   *William King*   *Benjamin Speller*

Overture

GEORGE W. WILLIAMS

Some time ago, when I was asked to remember my good friend Pat Kenan with some remarks preliminary to this book, the Durham Savoyards Ltd. was planning to celebrate its fortieth year of continuous and successful production of the operas of Gilbert and Sullivan. And how did the members of this society celebrate? How else? With a party, of course, for the organization began at a party. And that was at the home of Pat Kenan. Originator, energizer, and constant supporter, as well as resident medical officer, Pat was always one of the first and foremost heroes of the enterprise.

Furthermore, at that same time the Savoyards were holding auditions for the forty-first annual offering, *Ruddigore*, the company's fourth production of that operetta, in the spring of 2004. In the first production, in 1969, "Patrick D. Kenan"—as he always styled himself on stage—was cast in the role of "Old Adam Goodheart, Robin Oakapple's Faithful Servant." No one in 1969 could have imagined how prophetic that name and description would prove to be. Pat was certainly a goodhearted member of the society; he described it as "the source" of some of his "most significant friendships." And he was also a faithful servant of all the arts in Durham.

His first love was music. From the time of his student days at the Duke Medical School, he sang in the choir of St. Joseph's Episcopal Church in Durham, serving as choirmaster from 1977 to 1988, and continuing as a choir member until he sang a full Easter schedule the day before he died. And then at that party in 1963, he became a Savoyard, singing in the annual operas with unparalleled devotion over the years, and serving as president of the society from 1970 to 1972. But comic operas were not enough. He was also active in the Choral Society of Durham and in the chorus of the Street Operas of Durham, and he sang with the Durham choruses that went abroad to Russia and to Israel. It was from his musical experiences in Israel that he came to appreciate the setting of the Twenty-third Psalm, later sung at his funeral in the Duke Chapel. For the church choir, the Savoyards, the Choral Society, the Street Operas, and for visiting opera singers, he served faithfully and selflessly as the friendly doctor; many a throat gargled un-

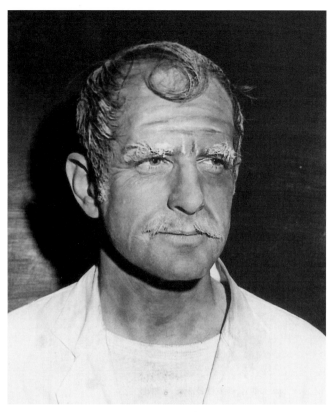
Pat Kenan as 'Old Adam Goodheart' in *Ruddigore*, 1969
(Courtesy of Daniel Kenan and John Kenan)

der his instructions was able to sing in the next performance.

But his specific and primary interest in the voice and in medicine for the voice extended to the inflammation and the muscles of the other arts as well. He became one of the pioneers in the practice of arts medicine in this region and was recognized as such by being invited to serve as guest editor of an issue of the *North Carolina Medical Journal* (1993), "Turning Pointe: Arts Medicine." For this issue he compiled and presented reports of medical personnel specializing in dance, the vocal arts, instrumental music, literature, painting, and drama. This compilation extended from top to toe: from the violinist's neck to the ballerina's pointe, and was a sign of Pat's broad interest in all the arts.

It is hardly surprising then to find that Pat was president of the board of the Durham Symphony, and president of the Arts Council of Durham, a position which he found challenging but which he served with dedication. More surprising was his emergence as a composer in 1999, when he wrote two Christmas anthems which were presented by the choirs of St. Joseph's Episcopal Church that year, St. Stephen's Episcopal Church in 2000, and Duke Chapel in 2001.

He also worked closely with Janice Palmer at the Duke Medical Center to bring about the weekly Poetry Discussion Program. Every Friday at the lunch hour, members of the hospital community of all professions come together to read and discuss poetry—often their own. Poetry on Friday, but music every day; as he made his rounds, Pat brightened his patients' spirits by singing to and with them in their rooms.

This book was the natural consequence of Pat's long-time enthusiasm for the excitement of the arts community in Durham and his pride in observing and participating in many aspects of its impressive growth. Specifically, the book was born of Pat's willing acceptance of two requests by Marion Salinger to give a paper on the arts in Durham. He spoke first at a meeting of Marion's philanthropic and educational group, the P.E.O. Sisterhood, and again at the Duke University Campus Club. For this second assignment he prepared an extensive report. The response to these papers was so enthusiastic that the auditors at both meetings suggested that he expand his study into a book. At ten in the morning after the Campus Club session, he called Marion Salinger—his chief supporter—and said he would do it. He immediately set about inviting friends representing the various artistic activities in Durham to sit with him as a committee to plan and oversee the preparation of such a book.

Pat's dedication to the arts in Durham made him think broadly about the entire city, and he sought always to impress upon the members of the committee that they too should consider it broadly. His example and his influence maintain those friends still, as they seek to present the volume that Pat Kenan would have wanted.

Pat Kenan, 1969 *(Courtesy of Daniel Kenan and John Kenan)*

1. Beginnings

JEAN B. ANDERSON

The village that became the city of Durham, North Carolina, sprang up in the flat, unpromising landscape of the Triassic Basin. Equally remote from mountains and sea, it lacked even gentle riparian meadows to commend it. The land nevertheless had one inexpendable utilitarian advantage—a railroad running through it. Within a short time after the railroad was completed in 1854, the hamlet also attracted a tobacco factory, which, at the end of the Civil War, rose by a fluke of fortune from its devastation by marauding troops to become so profitable that one small group of entrepreneurs after another was drawn to the little town to try their luck in the booming tobacco industry.

A similar proliferation of small factories was soon occurring in a number of other North Carolina towns in the post–Civil War period. A newly united nation became a huge market for the burgeoning industry. Within only a few years, the industry's ancillary requirements—boxes, barrels, and cloth for bagging, all locally manufactured—and its ancillary businesses—auctioning, inspection, storage, and transportation—created dizzying growth and myriad jobs in Durham.

Not far from the village, to the north and northeast, the soil was particularly good for tobacco, giving small farmers there a product for the market and ready access to it. An accidental discovery of the substitution of charcoal for wood and later of flues for air in the tobacco curing process produced a bright orange color in the leaves. Soon this brightleaf tobacco, as it was known, became highly desirable and differentiated the region's product from that of other tobacco-growing areas. Ever larger amounts of brightleaf tobacco were grown, processed, auctioned, and marketed to the world until almost unimaginable wealth was produced in the unlikely town of Durham.

Durham's history diverges from that of other brightleaf tobacco towns of the region, however, in the character of its main players. Without the peculiar combination of business genius and philanthropic disposition of its leaders, Durham might have become just another tobacco town. In

Durham, the Duke family, father and sons—while not the first or only exemplars of this mix, they were its most famous—combined natural canniness and business acumen with considerable social conscience. Over time, while with one hand they ruthlessly mowed down business competition, resulting in a large tobacco monopoly, with the other they wooed and increasingly supported an educational institution that would crucially influence the quality of life in the region.

Equally possessed of raw ambition and genuine concern for his fellow Durhamites, though a native of Person County, was William T. Blackwell. In 1869 he had bought the factory and brand name, Bull Durham, of a pioneer manufacturer who had recently died, and took new partners to pay for the purchase. One of these men was another Methodist enthusiast, Julian Shakespeare Carr of Chapel Hill, whose imaginative and aggressive use of advertising set the business on a course that outdistanced all its competitors. Both Blackwell and Carr displayed generous, lifelong efforts in the building up of their town and its people. The phenomenal success of the Bull Durham Company challenged the Dukes to their utmost exertions. Two Duke partners, George W. Watts, originally from Baltimore, and Richard A. Wright, of Franklin County, North Carolina, added their own contributions to Durham's mix of moral fiber and money making.

Beginning in the mid-1880s, surplus money to invest led first Carr and then the Dukes, along with lesser players, into the cotton industry. This in turn attracted another group of contributing industries and businesses, and a workforce to run them and work in them.

Population and buildings continued to proliferate. The overwhelming image that this growth and bustle created was one of raw ambition and energy. Durham was an unapologetic factory and mill town, a fact that embarrassed some of its small, better-educated, well-to-do, and ambitious middle class. With their respect for the arts, they were responsible for the first stirrings of interest in literature and music in the 1880s. Before the days of radio, and with only limited phonographic music available, people depended on the exertions of local talent or infrequent visiting professionals for their musical entertainment. Music in church and factory and those who performed it were only as good as untutored talent could make them.

For the next twenty years only sporadic efforts in the arts are traceable, but by 1900 one prominent citizen felt more optimistic about the arts in Durham. The lawyer Robert Winston wrote of the city: "It must be admitted, Durham's industrial enterprises far surpassed her aesthetic equipment. It was several years before we Durhamites turned our attention to the finer things of life . . . . When we did get down to culture . . . we made her hum." About the same time, a parallel African-American society was forming, centered across the tracks in Hayti and made up of freedmen and a few African Americans whose ancestors had long been free. They were drawn to the multitude of jobs the industries produced, not only in factories but also in the service, crafts, and transportation sectors of the growing economy. Around the turn of the century, a middle class also began to grow in this separate culture with the establishment of the North Carolina Mutual Insurance Company. The success of this business within a short time led to many other enterprises—a bank, barber shops, drugstores, wood and coal supply stores, food and clothing stores, hardware, building, and carpentry trades, and brick manufacturing. The bank and insurance company and a few other businesses were located on Parrish Street, "the black Wall Street," in the heart of "white" Durham. Their owners, along with an influx of professional men like those in the white community, comprised a potential group of supporters of the arts.

The next fifty years saw slowly evolving efforts, in fits and starts, to cultivate native art and artists. A number of individuals and institutions contributed to the process, but especially vital to its initiation and ultimate success were Duke University, beginning as Trinity College, and North Carolina Central University, beginning as the National Training School and Chautauqua (later North Carolina College for Negroes). Only as late as the 1950s came Allied Arts, now the Arts Council, and most recently St. Joseph's Historic Foundation, to join the artistic impetus of the earlier institutions.

The city government too was a partner in the endeavor to nurture the arts. By erecting in 1902 a handsome Academy of Music, from plans drawn by the Charlotte architectural firm of Sawyer and Hook, the city provided the critical space needed for the performing arts as well as for other public gatherings and cultural events. When the academy burned in 1909, the city replaced it with an even finer structure that had increased space for dramatic and musical performances. Hook said of his new building, "It so far eclipses anything in this state, that I have no place in mind which gives you an idea of how fine it will be. . . . It will be a gem."

After the academy's demolition in 1924, the city again made a major contribution to the performing arts by building a fine Beaux Arts theater in 1926 from plans of the architectural firm of Milburn and Heister. The building, called the Durham Auditorium (later the Carolina Theatre), supplied a place for lectures and recitals as well as for plays and other performances. In its early decades it was host to a glittering array of artists, musical and dramatic. The importance of this series of municipally financed buildings to the support of the arts cannot be overemphasized.

The early struggles for the arts did not take place in a vacuum. Always closely tied to them and their success wherever they have emerged has been the local economy with its booms and busts. An organic part of the

New Academy of Music, N. C.

53-66

New Academy of Music, ca. 1910 *(Courtesy of North Carolina Collection, Durham County Library)*

community, the arts are affected by social forces and internal and external influences. The two world wars, the Great Depression, the decline of industry and the rise of technology, the growth of suburbs and decay of the city center, and the emergence of the huge Research Triangle complex—these have been the particular events of Durham's history that have affected the economy, demography, built environment, and development of the arts in Durham.

Artistic Stirrings

Although Durham was still a relatively new place in the 1880s, a few inhabitants stand out, either alone or together, as pioneers in the arts in their long, uneven development. Durham's earliest arts—music and architecture—had always been present in folk forms executed by amateurs as aspects of a culture, but professional musicians and architects first made their appearance in Durham in the 1880s. In 1882 two short-lived musical organizations were born: the Mozart Musicale and the Durham Glee Club. These were both made up of amateur musicians with a common desire to perform. The same decade saw the emergence of Durham's first professional musician—Celestia Southgate, the daughter of the town's early settler and insurance agent, James Southgate.

Celestia Southgate was trained in voice in New York City as part of her general musical education there. After returning to Durham and a stint teaching music in the Methodist Female Seminary, she founded the Durham Music School in 1886. She hired additional teachers for piano, violin, and other instruments, and taught voice herself. Unfortunately, her marriage in 1891 removed her from the scene and her school closed. Vernon Darnell, a teacher of violin and organ in the school, continued to teach with a few others. Darnell was perhaps a founder of the St. Cecilia Musical Society, of which little is known. Perhaps modeled on Charleston's famous social organization, in 1891 it had Darnell as its president, with Mrs. A. G. Carr, Miss Nola Woodward, and Mrs. L. A. Carr as vice presidents.

Concerts by students and teachers and a few traveling professionals provided the only musical fare through most of the 1890s, and Mrs. E. L. Bryan operated her

Lessie Southgate Simmons, ca. 1910 *(Courtesy of North Carolina Collection, Durham County Library)*

School of Art. Throughout the decade Stokes Hall, often called the Opera House, was the performance site and "only place of amusement in Durham." It was on the upper floor of a building at the northeast corner of Main and Corcoran streets. There the Durham orchestra played, a group acclaimed in 1900 as long the best orchestra in the state. At that time a new orchestra was being formed under the direction of Donovan Richardson, a violinist, who recruited many of the older orchestra's players. The Durham Choral Society, probably another short-lived organization, also performed in Stokes Hall, as did touring theatrical companies, playing old favorites, among them *Uncle Tom's Cabin*, *Kathleen Mavourneen*, and *East Lynn*.

Along with music, professional architecture made its appearance in the 1880s. Although a few stylish and expensive houses, reflecting current

trends, had been built in the 1870s with the first flush of tobacco money
by the Dukes, Carr, William T. Blackwell, Edward J. Parrish (Carr's brother-
in-law), and a few others, no known architect was behind their design. Not
until the later 1880s did one of the profession appear who made a mark
on Durham's built environment. Carrying a famous surname, Byron A.
Pugin, of mysterious antecedents and credentials, attracted the attention of
the town's leaders. His most notable buildings, strongly reminiscent of the
Richardsonian Romanesque style then fashionable, were Durham's first
courthouse (1887), E. J. Parrish's building on Mangum Street, Parrish's furniture "emporium," stores for John C. Angier and Rufus Massey, a house
for J. E. Lyon, and a mansion for Benjamin N. Duke. This last, called The
Terrace, stood on the site where Duke later built Four Acres (1908) and
where the landmark North Carolina Mutual Insurance Company building
now stands. At that time, The Terrace was probably the grandest house in
Durham except for Somerset Villa, built at the same time by an architect
from Albany, New York, John B. Halcott; Julian Shakespeare Carr was not
about to be trumped by anyone else's architectural pretensions.

In 1880 the Virginia architects and builders W. H. Linthicum (–1886)
and his son Hill Carter Linthicum (1859–1919) settled in Durham and proceeded to leave their mark on the town and state. The elder Linthicum
built, among other projects, a new factory for Z. I. Lyon and Company at
the corner of Main and Roxboro streets, an office building with a mansard
roof and ornamental glass at the corner of Main and Depot (later Church)

Durham County Court House, Durham, N. C.   Milburn, Heister & Co., Architects.

The Terrace, house
of B. N. Duke, 1895
*(Courtesy of North Caro-
lina Collection, Durham
County Library)*

streets, and a handsome brick smokestack for the Blackwell (later American) Tobacco Company. Hill Carter Linthicum wrote the first building code
for Durham, an undertaking precipitated by a disastrous fire in 1914, and
he organized the first North Carolina chapter of the American Institute of
Architects and Builders. Erwin Auditorium was a classic example of his
work.

The most significant event of the 1890s in all ways cultural was the re-
location of Trinity College, an achievement of cooperation between the
Dukes and Julian Carr. Both strongly held the belief articulated by Carr
that "nothing elevates and refines a community like schools." With the
college came another, always increasing, educated group—the faculty. It
supplied leaders with progressive ideas and a commitment to raising the
town's quality of life. From 1892, when the college opened, it became a beacon for the finer things of life and in time a major supporter of the arts. The
faculty brought the stimulus to intellectual recreation that found an outlet in clubs, which were being formed all over America in the 1890s. It was
not a coincidence that Durham's Shakespeare and Canterbury clubs were
formed in 1895 and 1896, with a scattering of professors as members. While

Harwood Hall *(Courtesy of Historic Preservation Society of Durham)*

the arts at that time had no formal place in the Trinity College curriculum, they enhanced the leisure of many students, faculty, and townspeople.

Fine residences as well as industrial, commercial, and public buildings were erected throughout the 1890s. C. H. Norton, who also called himself an architect, was the builder for Harwood Hall (1890s), Watts's second house in Durham and the most impressive of the Morehead Hill mansions, but the architect is unknown. Another architect to leave an indelible mark in Durham was Samuel L. Leary of Philadelphia, who moved to the city at Washington Duke's invitation to design the main building for Trinity College, which was supposed to open in 1891. Unfortunately for the college and Leary, the tower of the building collapsed (through the engineer's errors) and with it, unfairly, Leary's reputation. The same year he was also the architect for the successful St. Joseph's A.M.E. Church that still stands, a relic of the once thriving Hayti section of the city. Leary's own house, an example of the Shingle style, also survives from this decade.

The architect for the highly decorative brick tobacco storage buildings, dating from the end of the 1890s through the early years of the new cen-

Leary House, 809 Cleveland Street *(Courtesy of Amanda van Scoyoc and Eli Van Zoeren)*

tury, is unfortunately unknown. Built by the American Tobacco Company before the federal government won its antitrust suit against the monopoly and broke it up into four competing companies, these some dozen storage facilities with corbelled chimneys, stepped parapets, and ornamental brickwork have become signature buildings for Durham's raison d'être.

Another Duke initiative was the support given to Gilmore Ward Bryant's music school. The Southern Conservatory of Music, begun in 1898 and handsomely housed in a new building supplied by the Dukes in 1900, became a stimulus to musical learning and performance for the next twenty years. With fine professional qualifications, the Bryants and the teachers they hired taught aspiring local musicians, who always looked back on their experience with gratitude and praise for the school's excellence. Faculty and student concerts provided a steady diet of classical music to new and receptive audiences.

The influence of the conservatory was responsible for other musical organizations and schools. As already mentioned, a choral society and an orchestra were formed around 1900. Alex Findlay and his wife started the Findlay Piano Quintet and the String Quartet Club. Miss Mary R. Holeman and her sister established Miss Holeman's Private Music School in 1905, which seems to have catered to children of the Morehead Hill elite. In 1912 some of its students were Valinda Hill, Matilda Bryant, Mary Toms, Mary Stagg, Margaret L. Carr, and Clara Lyon. The Robbins sisters, Daisy and Alberta, established the Durham School of Music (chartered 1909).

One remarkable graduate of the conservatory (and recipient of its first

(Left) Mrs. Gilmore Ward Bryant *(Courtesy of North Carolina Collection, Durham County Library)*

(Right) Gilmore Ward Bryant *(Courtesy of North Carolina Collection, Durham County Library)*

Southern Conservatory of Music, ca. 1914? *(Courtesy of North Carolina Collection, Durham County Library)*

master's degree in 1904) and of Trinity College (1905) was Alice Hundley. A native of Virginia, she moved with her parents to Durham so that she could receive the kind of musical training her talents deserved. She became a musical force in Durham through a very long life. As long as it existed she taught at the conservatory, meanwhile extending her musical studies to voice, which she studied at Juilliard in New York. After the conservatory's demise, she taught privately—organ as well as piano, harp, and voice—and directed the music at several churches. A prize established in her memory encourages teenage competitors in their piano studies.

Although professional painters did not appear in Durham until much later, photographers were already on the scene in the 1880s: men such as William Shelburn and Charles Rochelle. Other photographers now unknown were responsible for many pictures of the fine, first generation of buildings in the town. The Duke company super-salesman Edward F. Small took a number of shots of the town in the 1880s in addition to his more famous use of photography in provocative and innovative advertising schemes. By the end of the century, commercial photography had become a livelihood for Waller Holladay, Oliver W. Cole, and M. H. Lockwood. Hugh

Mangum made it his living too, but primarily on the road and in other places. He left an archive of glass plates (now housed at West Point on the Eno), some of which capture Durham people and places. In the early years of the new century, Kate L. Johnson became the first woman photographer in Durham. Photography was a new profession and thus unrestricted by any tradition of gender. Johnson was still active in the 1930s.

In the New Century

After the turn of the century the town's leaders continued to evince civic pride by constructing the best and most pleasing buildings they could afford. The tobacco elite built new, high-style residential as well as industrial and commercial structures. Congregations built handsome churches. Bankers built imposing banks in classical styles. The federal government supplied a post office in its favorite Greek Revival mode. Even so famous

Trinity United Methodist Church *(Courtesy of Duke University Rare Book, Manuscript, and Special Collections Library)*

an architect as Ralph Adams Cram was called on to design two churches for Durham: St. Philip's Episcopal Church (1907) and, much later, Trinity United Methodist (1924), while the Boston firm of Kendall and Taylor, which in an earlier partnership as Rand and Taylor had designed the first Watts Hospital in 1895, was hired to build a new Watts Hospital (1909) and a house (1912) for Watts's son-in-law, John Sprunt Hill. The Benjamin Dukes and J. E. Staggs took their cue from the Watts "chateauesque" stone mansion and employed Charles C. Hook of Charlotte for their new stone houses, Four Acres (1908–9) and Greystone (1909–10), heavy, imposing, conservative piles, only the latter of which still endures.

Churches that added dignity to the landscape, and are still in use, were Duke Memorial Methodist (1907), St Joseph's Episcopal (1908), and First

Residence of Mr. Jno. Sprunt Hill, Durham, N. C.

Presbyterian (1916), gifts of the Dukes and their business partners, William A. Erwin and George W. Watts. The last much later First Baptist Church (1927), designed by Reuben H. Hunt of Chattanooga, took its place as a majestic and arrestingly sited landmark, looming at the head of Chapel Hill Street. New commercial structures were also architecturally noteworthy; the tobacco storehouses already referred to were replicated with elaborate variations. Durham still possesses a host of stylish, early buildings, in a variety of traditions, by nationally known architects.

Further experience in Durham of legitimate theater came about shortly after the turn of the century when the commercial venture Lakewood Park was established at the end of a trolley line. Besides a swimming pool and the usual merry-go-round, roller coaster, roller skating rink, live music for dancing, and other amusements, there was a rustic hall that could hold eight hundred people for summer stock performances. The Runkel Stock Company, a traveling troupe, played to enthusiastic audiences for a number of summers.

By 1910 the frenetic pace and energy of Durham's initial development were flagging. The Civic League, the creation of another Southgate daughter, Mattie, in 1911, challenged the city fathers with a long list of improvements that were desperately needed. Among the items were city parks, an architectural plan for the city's growth, and circulating art galleries

Memorial M. E. Church, Durham, N. C.

Duke Memorial Methodist Church, ca. 1910 *(Courtesy of North Carolina Collection, Durham County Library)*

and museums. These challenges have remained for the most part unmet, though Trinity College and later Duke University and North Carolina College soon initiated efforts toward picture galleries and museums.

In 1911 a group of town and campus music lovers formed the Durham Festival Association to bring nationally famous musicians to Durham. They enlisted subscribers for a series of concerts, the first of which presented Walter Damrosch and the New York Symphony Orchestra. This kind of high culture was being seriously challenged in the teens, however, by easy access to new, inexpensive popular culture that competed for audiences. Movies, although still silent, were garnering huge new audiences, and vaudeville, still very popular, usually accompanied movie shows. White patrons could enjoy the fare of half a dozen movie-cum-vaudeville houses, while a series of theaters owned and operated by black entrepreneurs, the Wonderland, Regal, and Rex, provided similar entertainment in Hayti. Many families could afford new player pianos, which were supplanting amateur musical efforts. The same was true of phonographs. Understandably, the average amateur musician preferred to listen to professionals performing on rolls and records than to exert himself with less satisfactory results. Musical entertainment thus became more and more passive as technology improved.

In general the period from 1910 to 1930 was not auspicious for the arts in Durham; efforts to cultivate them were all uphill. An editorial in the *Herald* in 1922 was harshly critical of Durham: "In material things it is a leader. Industry flourishes here as in few other places . . . But Durham has developed in a lop-sided fashion and is not making any progress in rounding up its life. There is too strong a spirit of commercialism, while the intellectual and esthetic side has been neglected, except by a few." The article stated that only 2 percent of the population took all the responsibility for making Durham a better place to live. It cited poor attendance records at musical and theatrical performances. It indicted the town leadership with fatigue and malaise, and the inhabitants with poor taste and a fear of the words "classical" and "classic." Instead, the city and the people looked almost entirely to the colleges for artistic direction and entertainment.

Perhaps as a consequence the colleges began to play larger roles in contributing to the arts in Durham. At Trinity, glee clubs and instrumental music clubs for the students became incubators of serious performers and performances both on and off campus. Music was for several decades the only art pursued at Trinity. A men's glee club, organized before the col-

Regal Theatre, Pettigrew Street, ca. 1940 *(Courtesy of North Carolina Collection, Durham County Library)*

lege's move to Durham, continued to attract a large number of students. From the glee club, quartets were formed of the best voices. In 1903 the glee club began making annual tours within the region and afield to other colleges. Edgar M. Howerton, a local professional musician, was hired to direct the singers. Trinity had a mandolin club as early as 1903 and a band by 1906, also dependent on Durham for its audiences when they performed. A large step forward for the public enjoyment of good music occurred in 1920 when Trinity supported a weekly, hour-long radio broadcast over Raleigh's station WPTF, which featured the glee club.

In 1910 Dr. James E. Shepard saw the materialization of a dream when he succeeded in founding the North Carolina Training School and Chautauqua for African Americans. Over the years this school evolved into North Carolina College for Negroes (NCC) to its present incarnation as North Carolina Central University (NCCU), one of the sixteen institutions making up the state system of higher education. Although his school was small and privately funded, and course offerings were limited, Dr. Shepard knew the value of the arts. From the start he arranged for visiting professional musicians to give recitals and concerts, if only a few a year, to expose the students to good music. Within a year of its founding, Dr. Shepard had succeeded in bringing to his school such nationally known African-American artists as the singer E. Azalia Heckley and the composer and pianist Clar-

James E. Shepard
(Courtesy of North Carolina Collection, Durham County Library)

ence Cameron White, as well as many others. In time a regular annual program of lectures and concerts attracted, besides the students, subscribers in the African-American and white communities.

Because Dr. Shepard was a friend of many of the star performers, he could persuade such artists as the singers Roland Hayes and Marian Anderson to come to Durham, a place not usually on their concert itineraries. Anderson sang at NCC in the 1920s, 1930s, and 1940s. For lesser-known performers Avery Auditorium on campus was commonly used. If the artist were Paul Robeson, however, the concert was moved to Hillside Park High School auditorium, or, after its construction in 1937, to the Benjamin N. Duke Auditorium on campus, which could accommodate larger audiences.

In time, music became part of the curriculum at NCC, with faculty that included experts on theory, voice, and composition as well as pianists and instrumentalists—a full-blown music department. Vocal music, particularly choral, was emphasized. Samuel Hill was hired in 1941 to train the choir and teach music. After a few years he left, but he returned in 1949 and remained until 1966 as director of the choir and its activities. He presented Christmas and spring concerts to the community at which the choir previewed the programs it would perform on tour, year after year, as far away as Massachusetts. As at Duke, this tradition was viewed as a recruiting tool in addition to providing experience and training for the students. At this time too, the college and community were also treated to a cappella choirs of other colleges invited to sing at NCC.

Although theaters and theatrical productions had not been viewed kindly by Methodists in the nineteenth century, by 1915, on the initiative of Frank C. Brown of the English Department, Trinity College was engaging touring repertory companies twice a year to perform primarily Shakespeare for town and gown. The college had erected a woodland stage behind the East Duke building on an earth platform four feet high in front of a backdrop of trees.

The first recorded Trinity student dramatic production was given in 1921 by the Athena Literary Society, a women's student organization formed the year before. The women asked Mrs. Gladys Estelle Peterson ("Peter") Gross (1893–1985) to direct a play that they wished to perform as part of their May Day celebration. She directed *Monsieur Beaucaire* for them again the following year, with men students invited to take the male roles. In 1923 the society's name was changed to the Taurians and included men as members. Working with J. Foster Barnes, Mrs. Gross helped them produce a few Gilbert and Sullivan operettas as well. Mrs. Gross continued to direct their performances until 1930.

In 1932 Duke University hired A. T. West to teach English drama and theater in the English Department and to direct plays. That same year the Taurians became the Duke Players and were able to use the new Page Auditorium for their performances. (Before that, Craven Hall and then Duke Auditorium on East Campus had been their venues.) This arrangement lasted until West's death in 1947, when Professor Kenneth Reardon replaced him in the dual capacity. Woman's College students additionally contributed to the dramatic scene by producing French plays under Professor Terry Dow's direction.

A slightly different kind of theatrical production was the annual Christmas pageant, begun in 1923 under the auspices of Hersey Spence of the Department of Religion. After A. T. West's arrival on campus, he helped with the staging of this popular event.

In the 1930s drama was being taught at NCC as well; the English Department hired a dramatic arts instructor in 1935. Only a few years later drama courses stood alone, no longer a part of the English Department, and a student dramatic society, directed by various faculty members, presented a roster of plays each year.

In the meantime some town professionals continued to cultivate music. Miss Felicia Kueffner began her vocal and piano school in 1917. In the early 1920s the Bryants' lease on the conservatory ran out. While the school still had 315 students, 40 of them boarders, the building was old and its facilities inadequate. Bryant built an entirely new brick building in the suburbs along Alston Avenue and moved the school there in 1923. The beautiful old building downtown was razed. Despite the new school's large acreage for sports and a bus to convey town students to and from the campus, the new conservatory did not thrive. The Depression finally extinguished its long-flickering spark.

The First World War permanently altered a long-settled life-style. The Jazz Age that followed it, occurring in an expanding, exuberant economy (though it should be noted that agriculture was already falling into a serious depression), infected even so remote a place as Durham with a new restlessness, new mores, new interests, and a new kind of popular culture by a pleasure-seeking generation with not much interest in serious art. Music began to assimilate, in more sophisticated form, folk idioms such as gospel, jazz, and blues, and professional musicians incorporated them into their work. At the same time, folk artists became quasi-professional and practiced their "arts" in more public ways. The blues musicians in Durham, with their characteristic Piedmont variety, were an integral part of the tobacco markets. They eked out an existence through handouts on market days by entertaining the crowds in the tobacco auction houses or by supplying music at "house parties," spontaneous gatherings in private spaces in Hayti where people were attracted by the music and illegal booze.

The largest and most important event in the town's history, after the coming of the railroad and the tobacco industry bonanza, occurred in 1924, when Trinity College became Duke University. Great expectations for the future of the college and the prestige and increased quality of life it would bring to the town made both town and campus rejoice. Ambitious plans began to unfold. With James B. Duke's death less than a year later, funding for the Duke Endowment unexpectedly increased. Already accepted plans for an entirely new Gothic campus with handsome stone buildings, as well as a Georgian reconstruction and expansion of the old campus, promised construction jobs for years to come. Stone masons from Scotland and stone carvers from Italy had to be imported, especially for the imposing chapel and its 210-foot tower. The remarkable architecture of the new university, while undertaken by the Philadelphia firm of Horace Trumbauer, which had built James B. Duke's mansion in New York City, was actually the work of the firm's principal designer, Julian Abele. Because he was African-American and the color bar at the time normally precluded members of his race from participation in white professional circles, his enormous contribution to Durham's architectural heritage was long unknown to the general public.

A whole new echelon of faculty members was hired to match the university's greatly enlarged educational undertakings. Among the new programs was a medical school and hospital. When it opened in 1930, it brought to Durham the brightest and best-trained young doctors in the profession. The hospital alone supplied a host of new jobs for nurses, orderlies, clerks, administrative assistants, cleaning crews, and service suppliers of many kinds. Despite a crushing national depression all through the 1930s, expectations, although diminished, were not disappointed. The university, with expanded law and graduate schools and new divinity, medical, nursing, and forestry programs, and an undergraduate Woman's College as well as Trinity College for men, changed the town incalculably.

Women at Trinity had not been very numerous until Southgate dormitory was built for them in 1920. With the expansion to a university in 1924 and the establishment of the new Woman's College, cultural activities for women increased substantially. While they already had had a glee club in 1919, directed by Mrs. K. B. Patterson, in 1928 a women's orchestra was formed, led by Miss Evelyn Barnes from 1931 to 1939 and afterwards by a faculty member, Julia Wilkinson Mueller.

The 1920s also saw the emergence of the architectural firm of Atwood and Nash, which in its permutations of partners continued in Durham over seventy years. It was responsible for a host of buildings in Durham and elsewhere. Thomas Atwood and Arthur C. Nash were the engineer and architect at its start. Nash had been trained at Harvard, MIT, and the

Beaux-Arts Institute in Paris. He was the architect from 1922 to 1930 for UNC-Chapel Hill, where he designed Kenan Stadium, Wilson Library, and Gerard Hall, among other campus buildings. From 1932 to 1942 Atwood's next partner was H. Raymond Weeks, who then continued the firm under his own name from 1942 to 1960, after which it became Harris and Pyne, for George C. Pyne and Wilton E. Harris, who had been working with Weeks. Atwood and Weeks designed many buildings in Durham, including the handsome, Classical-Revival United States Post Office (1934).

The 1920s and 1930s were rich in other new artistic influences. Perhaps the newspaper's criticism had had some effect. The presence of a few influential teachers must have made a difference. They were the match to the dry tinder waiting to catch fire. With William P. Twaddell's arrival in Durham, the schools and churches began to display a new impetus toward good music. Twaddell was a musician of excellence and taste with enormous energy and vision. He took charge of music classes in the high school and introduced choruses, glee clubs, bands, and orchestras. He played the organ and directed choirs of several city churches, incorporating into their services ambitious music, more technically demanding than they had been used to tackling and with more exacting standards of performance. He was also responsible for identifying in a local girl the talent that would carry

Durham Post Office, corner of Main and Corcoran *(Courtesy of Frank DePasquale)*

her on to the national stage. Twaddell recognized that Lucille Brown had a potentially fine voice and saw to it that she was sent to New York to study at the Juilliard School. She eventually became a Metropolitan Opera star, making her début in 1936 under her stage name, Lucille Browning.

In this era too, NCC and Duke University continued to bring to Durham a variety of star performers in drama and music, as well as encouraging their students to develop their own talents. In 1930 Duke hired J. Foster Barnes as musical and social director. He directed the glee club and took it to new heights, frequently winning competitions with other colleges. In 1932 Barnes established the University Chapel Choir, which still remains a vital musical force in campus and community life. By that time he had also instituted an annual series of visiting artists, world-famous professionals such as Mary Garden, John McCormack, Ezio Pinza, Kirsten

William Powell Twadell, 1940s? *(Courtesy of Warren Pope)*

Flagstad, Sergei Rachmaninoff, and Arthur Rubinstein, who performed in the newly opened Page Auditorium. In the same decade with the rise of college orchestras coming out of student musical clubs, popular and dance music began to dominate all other kinds, reflecting a national trend; and the glee club lost its popularity. Barnes was responsible as well for initiating the annual performances of Handel's *Messiah* at Christmas and productions of Gilbert and Sullivan operettas during the later 1930s. The 1930s saw as well regularly scheduled organ and carillon concerts by Anton Brees, the renowned carillonneur of the famous Bok "singing tower" in Florida.

Duke's carillon was a gift of George G. Allen and William R. Perkins, chairman and vice chairman of the Duke Endowment. At the time, carillons were rare in the United States, and the Duke collection of fifty bells was impressive, ranging over four chromatic octaves and varying in weight from ten to 11,200 pounds and in diameter from eight inches to six feet nine inches.

With so much musical talent on campus, both instrumental and vocal, it was not surprising that another group of Duke students should have wanted to produce musical comedy. Hoof 'n' Horn, as this group came to be called, gave its first performance in 1936. After an interim the group resumed productions in 1941, and it continues to the present, billing itself "the South's oldest student-run musical theater group." It now usually produces two or more shows a year. At first the shows were original musical revues with faint plot lines to carry the songs, in the tradition of Penn's Mask and Wig, or Princeton's Triangle productions. In 1952, however, the group produced Cole Porter's *Anything Goes*, and since 1961 they have adhered to reprising Broadway musicals.

In the mid-1980s Hoof 'n' Horn began to produce shows for children, such as *Winnie the Pooh*, which it performed at local schools and hospitals. Some of these were student-written, such as *Trust Me* (1989–90) and *The Last Bedtime Story* (1990–91), but others were professional scripts: *The Thirteen Clocks* (1995–96) and *Thumbelina* (2000–2001).

The 1930s and 1940s were best remembered, however, as the era of the big bands, and Duke University produced its share. The university hired George "Jelly" Leftwich as its first director of instrumental music and conductor of student orchestras in 1926. In the same year Bill Lassiter's was the first of many student orchestras calling themselves the Blue Devils. Leftwich and his University Club Orchestra garnered national fame during

George Leftwich & the Blue Devils *(Courtesy of North Carolina Collection, Durham County Library)*

their student years and then went professional in 1934. Following Leftwich, Les Brown emerged as a student leader, and like Leftwich, after graduation went professional, making a long and successful career with his "band of renown." The third of their colleagues to share the limelight was Johnny Long, leader of the Collegians (1931–35). Among the many student bands was one called the Duke Ambassadors; this name was carried on by successive groups of players over the years with considerable success.

The student bands were so popular that the Washington Duke Hotel hired one student orchestra led by Al Preyer to play during dinner three evenings a week. The Durham radio station WDNC, initiated in 1934, broadcast these performances. Preyer and his orchestra went to Europe to perform in the following summer (1935), earning their passage by daily performances on shipboard over and back.

The famous big band leaders such as Duke Ellington, Tommy Dorsey, and Benny Goodman and their orchestras were also heard in Durham when they came to play for dances on campus and in the tobacco warehouses. Jimmie Lunceford, a black orchestra leader, was invited to play for a Duke dance audience.

An entirely new artistic development of the 1930s was the emergence of a group of native painters. Another influential teacher, Mrs. Clement (Lucille) Strudwick, was the inspiration for some of them, whom she taught at Durham High School during 1931 to 1933. The group that emerged, determined to make art their livelihood, included Ralph Fuller Jr., Eugene

Les Brown, 1939 (Courtesy of Duke University Archives)

Erwin, Nelson Rosenberg, Murray Jones Jr., and Nathan Ornoff. Hardly a worse time for so radical an experiment could have been found—the Great Depression. The federal government initiated programs as safety nets for all kinds of talented citizens, from bookbinders to legitimate actors. These young men, each at different times, took advantage of the program that financed murals for public buildings, notably new post offices. Each discovered as well that Durham could not yet support artists; they had to move elsewhere to pursue their careers. They did not give up easily. Erwin, like Ornoff, tried to run an art school in Durham before better opportunities took him elsewhere. He also worked for a few years with the North Carolina Federal Art Project, of which he became director in 1937 before moving to New York.

Influence of the visual arts on the Duke campus arose out of efforts of the Woman's College Library. In 1930, under Professor William K. Boyd's prodding, the Art Association of Duke University was formed. He was director of libraries in addition to his English Department duties, and negotiated for the library the acquisition of the Margaret L. Barber collection as a long-term loan. Besides paintings it consisted of furniture, glass, china, and other decorative art objects, which were displayed in the library. The purpose of the association, which collected membership fees from town and gown, was to educate and delight and to provide exhibition space for old and new works of art. It also encouraged additional acquisitions. Art history courses could also profit from it. In effect it was Duke's first effort toward creating a museum. From 1939 to 1951 Duke's Department of Aesthetics, Art, and Music was responsible for the galleries. Duke returned to its owner all but a few pieces of the initial Margaret L. Barber Collection. Meanwhile Duke acquired and began collecting significant Chinese art through the assistance of James A. Thomas, J. B. Duke's business colleague in China and Asia. Only in 1962 did Duke finally embark on a separate museum facility with the renovation of a building on East Campus.

Wealthy residents had already long made use of professional landscape architects to design gardens for their private enjoyment; for example, John Sprunt Hill employed the services of Thomas Meehan and Sons of Philadelphia for his Spanish Revival mansion in 1912. Duke University initiated public landscaped gardens with the creation of the Sarah P. Duke Gardens in the 1930s. The impetus was from Dr. Frederic M. Hanes of the medical school, but the funding was Mrs. Duke's. Their initial collaboration failed when a nearby creek flooded and torrential rains wiped out the newly planted thousands of flowers. After her death in 1936, Dr. Hanes persuaded her daughter, Mary Duke Biddle, to establish gardens as a memorial to her mother. Ellen Shipman, an early nationally respected landscape designer, was engaged for the project. One element of her concept for the gardens was a magnificent bank of terraces with a wisteria-covered gazebo at their summit. While the gardens have expanded far beyond Shipman's plans, they preserve the only extant example of her work. Building upon the success of her vision for the site, the gardens have become nationally famous for their exceptional beauty.

The Second World War made huge demands on American industry and production, boosting the already recovering economy. The long war interrupted Durham's artistic progression. Thousands of men were in the armed forces or recruited for other kinds of service. Women were taking jobs where they had never been permitted to work before. Leisure had gone to war along with "Lucky Strike green." Compared to what had been taking place in the arts in many other parts of the country, the pace in Durham had been discouragingly slow. In 1940 another harsh critic vented his disgust in a national magazine: "In Durham as nearly everywhere else in the United States, the propagation of the arts, like the duties of spring-cleaning and putting up pickles, is left to the ladies. In general Durham's men let their ladies absorb Duke's 'advantages' while they root for its football teams. . . . In short, Durham's men—conscious of the fact that the South, with fifty percent of the nation's resources within its borders and a rapidly growing population is nonetheless the most poverty-stricken area in America—are out to get the business, and let him who will have the 'culture.'"

An early view of the terrace at the Sarah P. Duke Gardens (Courtesy of Duke Gardens)

When peace finally allowed a return to a more normal existence, and the economy continued to flourish as everything that had been put on hold during the war geared up and accelerated anew—manufacturing, construction, business, commerce, and education—pursuit of the arts was again possible. Many new opportunities arose in Durham for studying and practicing a variety of arts and crafts.

The Creative Arts Group was formed in 1947 with the ultimate goal of establishing a museum. The women behind this effort were Vivian Dai, Elizabeth Lyon, Rhea Wilson, Ruth Latty, Jeanne Whiteside, and Ola Mae Foushee. They met once a week to paint and benefit from the instruction of local university teachers. Another group at the same time made up of A. M. Tidd, James W. Hamm, and Randy Jones was trying to form an art guild. The two groups working together established the Durham Art Guild in 1949. Membership was open to any interested person as well as to amateur and professional artists. They met every month to hear lectures on art and art history, promoted art classes, competitions, and exhibits in the schools, and began to supply additional art classes and exhibits for local artists. This was the nucleus from which Allied Arts and finally the Arts Council developed.

All Things in Place

Much ferment for change began to occur in the 1950s and 1960s that would alter forever the face of American society and culture. Among the forces were the Civil Rights movement, and the decline of city centers as residents fled to the suburbs with the businesses that served them. These factors, along with the war on tobacco to combat alarming rates of illness and death and the establishment of the Research Triangle Park, had profound effects on Durham, a southern city with a large African-American population and an economy heavily based in tobacco manufacturing, and the home of one of the three universities participating in the new enterprise in the park. The next decades saw a continual influx of a well-paid and well-educated population from other parts of this country and other countries, an explosion of new technologies arising in research facilities that would replace the declining tobacco and cotton industries, and the creation of new wealth and disposable income. Concurrent with increasing national and local wealth was the expansion of NCCU and Duke University, particularly the latter's medical and research facilities. The town's character began to change, shedding its reputation as a mill town for the more aspiring one of "city of medicine." The growing diversity of the local population mirrored the change. A hundred years after its village beginnings, the town of Durham and its hinterland had at last reached a critical mass of population with sufficient money and desire to support and sustain the arts. During the long decades from the 1880s on, educational institutions, arts organizations, and local government supplied money, vision, energy, instruction, or simply space—each critical to the foundation and climate of appreciation of the arts. Within and beyond these incorporated groups must also be credited the many individuals, known and unknown, whose private philanthropy, determination, hard work, talent, and leadership were equally responsible for making Durham increasingly home to the arts.

2. Arts Institutionalized

The Interwoven Careers of the Durham Arts Council, Carolina Theatre, St. Joseph's, and the Community They Help to Shape

JIM WISE

In 1983 a Sunday feature of the *Charlotte Observer* proclaimed, "Durham: The Arts Giving City a New Image," and quoted the Durham Arts Council president, K.v.R. Dey—who was also president of Liggett & Myers Tobacco— that in Durham's art scene, "There's broad community involvement." During its annual "Art Fund" money-raising campaign that same year, the Arts Council published a brochure titled "The Durham Arts Council Means Business," which claimed that its member groups were pumping $1.17 million a year into the local economy. Also in 1983, the Chamber of Commerce booster film *Durham: We Want to Share It with You* opened with footage not of smoking factory stacks nor clean-room assembly lines, but of a string band playing old-time tunes beside the reconstructed West Point gristmill.

That fiddle and banjo music was just one sign of how much this "New Southern" outpost had changed. While economics has snuffed out cigarette commerce in the town Bull Durham built, culture—concerts, festivals, art movies, Broadway-bound plays—brings thousands of visitors to Durham and leaves millions of dollars in the county economy; besides, according to the Convention and Visitors Bureau director Reyn Bowman, it "adds panache" to all other efforts at promoting the city as a place in which to live and invest.

In Durham since the Second World War, arts and culture have been not just appreciated but institutionalized. Their development and promotion weave through the county's social, economic, and political history along with such other themes as racial integration, eco-consciousness, the health business, and sheer growth. The history of three cultural institutions—Durham Arts Council, Carolina Theatre / Durham Auditorium, and St. Joseph's Historic Foundation / Hayti Heritage Center—is a network of interplaying threads.

As far back as October 4, 1944, an editorial in the *Herald* lamented Durham's lack of an art museum. Durham would still lack a museum until Duke University's opened in 1969, but the exhibition of local artwork had long since become common practice. Indeed, the late 1940s saw an explosion of resident activism on a number of fronts. New political alliances appeared that challenged the old-business status quo and soon brought labor unions, women, and blacks into power positions; a war-postponed drive to improve housing conditions resumed with vigor; and residents organized to promote and practice the fine arts.

In 1945 the Junior League of Durham sponsored its first art contest and exhibit for school children, following by two years its creation of a children's theater. In 1946 a Durham Theatre Guild was formed, followed in 1947 by a "Creative Arts Group" meant "to further the art education and experiences of its members . . . by means of instruction, lectures and criticism of work done." The Durham Civic Choral Society began in 1948, and, in 1949, the Durham Art Guild—itself, significantly enough, created by the merger of separate men's and women's art clubs formed two years earlier. As if to give the lie to a comment by the *Atlantic Monthly in* 1940 that Durham's men left culture to the ladies, the Art Guild's founding officers were all male, and its constitutional committee was composed of four men—T. W. Gore, James W. Hamm, George C. Pyne, and Charles Sibley—and a lone woman, Mrs. Smith Whiteside.

According to a feature story, "In Durham Art Is for the People," by the *Morning Herald* writer Jon Phelps in 1961, these organizations soon found themselves in conflict. "Too many supporters of the groups were dividing their contributions of time and money. . . . Each was maintaining different quarters, different schedules, different efforts at public relations and public performance, and different methods of subscribing support. The cultural influence . . . cast over the city was weakened in its diffusion."

The Arts Organize

In 1953 the Theater Guild, the Art Guild, the North Carolina Symphony Durham Chapter, and the Duke-Durham Camera Club, prodded along by the Theater Guild president, Floyd Roberts, formed an umbrella organization, United Arts. After drawing interest from other cultural and civic clubs, United Arts was formally chartered as Allied Arts of Durham in May 1954. The Theater Guild, Art Guild, Choral Society, and Camera Club (renamed the Photographic Arts Society) became "participating organizations," with nine "associate members": Children's Museum, Debutante Ball Society, Duke University, Symphony chapter, Council of Garden Clubs, Woman's Club, Golden Age Society, Junior League, and North Carolina State Ballet Company. Allied Arts bylaws enumerated four purposes: promoting and coordinating what the various member groups did, holding a joint annual money-raising campaign, promoting public interest in arts, and creating a "civic cultural center."

A cultural center soon materialized as Watts Hospital loaned Allied Arts Harwood Hall at 806 South Duke Street. On October 8, 1954, in what the *Durham Morning Herald* declared "should be a milestone in the history of the cultural life of Durham," the Allied Arts Center opened with a members' gala, followed by a Saturday afternoon festival of flower arranging, talent tests, a piano recital, a puppet show, art movies, exhibits, and children's art. Lieutenant Governor Luther Hodges presided at the gala, praising "a new spirit of the finer attributions of life" while admitting, "I won't sail under false pretenses by saying I understood all I've heard and seen here." Things went so well that the center held a second open house the following weekend.

By the spring of 1955 Allied Arts had received an $8,000 pledge from the Junior League, which used the center to exhibit part of its annual show of art by city and county schoolchildren. White pupils' art went up on Duke Street; black pupils' was shown at Pearson and Little River schools. By early 1957 Allied Arts had a membership of two thousand and its affiliate groups were offering art and theater classes for children and grownups, photography field trips, art shows, plays, a children's classical concert, and advice to Durham citizens, schools, and churches.

At Allied Arts, Mrs. Paul (Gertrude) Young became the full-time executive director in 1957, and the organization adopted a slogan of "Art Is for Everyone." In that year, Allied Arts hosted the first Durham Craft Fair, which proved so popular that it was made an annual fund-raising affair and in two years grew so much that it had to be moved to the City Armory downtown. Another moving experience came when Watts Hospital sold the Allied Arts building to the Hospital Care Association (later Blue Cross). In 1960 the insurer told Allied Arts that it would have to give way to a new office building on the site.

Allied Arts bought an overgrown and long-vacant residence, the old Foushee Home on Proctor Street. With the attorney Kenneth Royall leading a drive for $69,310 to pay off the mortgage and equip the house for its new functions, Allied Arts held its second housewarming party on March 1, 1961. A crowd of five hundred attended, and later that year—a sign of things to come—the thriving Durham Craft Fair and Bazaar had among its sponsors the Durham Merchants Association and Chamber of Commerce.

Perhaps flexing new-found muscles, in 1962 Allied Arts diversified from "Art Is for Everyone" and introduced "Art in Business." The campaign promoted original art as a valuable complement to up-to-date living, and it succeeded in getting architectural firms to engage art consultants and in inspiring the Realtor Fred Herndon to use nine paintings by two Durham artists, Anne Basile and Betty Bell, and one artist from Chapel Hill, Irene Reichert, in a model "Horizon Home" for the 1963 Parade of Homes.

The Craft Fair was a growing enterprise, by now needing a printed guide for the three thousand patrons who attended each year and sponsoring an annual

North Carolina handicraft tour. In 1963 a Twelfth Night party marked the beginning of the Durham Savoyards, a Gilbert and Sullivan group that produced its first show, *The Pirates of Penzance*, in 1964 and became a fifth full affiliate of Allied Arts in 1965.

In the fall of 1963 Allied Arts initiated a music appreciation course, noting that the Philadelphia Orchestra had sold five thousand tickets for a concert in Durham. Nevertheless, Allied Arts' weekly calendar of events was still relegated to the society pages of the newspaper.

In 1965 Mayor Wense Grabarek, hoping to end what he called Durham's "cultural poverty" and having enlisted the interest of existing organizations and Duke University, proposed the creation of a "cultural steering committee" to plan "a vital, community-wide cultural emphasis." "There is a high level of artistic and cultural activity here," Grabarek told the *Durham Morning Herald* on April 22. "The problem is that a great majority of the people in the city are either unaware of it, or costs are prohibitive. Hopefully, we would be able to instigate and carry out a program that would gain wide participation—not just by the creative community, but by the general public."

In the long term, Grabarek's plan envisioned a community arts center, grander than the cultural "milestone" opened in 1954. In the short term, he had already begun an "audit" that produced a fifty-eight-page reference book called "Durham's Assets in the Arts," describing fifty-four organizations deemed culturally contributory and numerous others doing their helpful bits. More than half of the organizations were collegiate, operated by Duke or North Carolina College (NCC). The others ranged from the seriously arty Art Guild to the facetiously named "Bozart Arts Ball" and from the City Recreation Department to the Debutante Society and Durham Woman's Club. In short, it was just the sort of report that one would expect from a college town where, as the *Atlantic Monthly* put it, "propagation of the arts" was "left to the ladies."

The Arts Scene Widens

Still, it was the 1960s. Definitions were changing, and so was Durham's cultural geography. In 1966 the Art Guild relocated its annual Outdoor Art Show from Lakewood Shopping Center to the Market Street Mall, with support from the Merchants Association and from nearby stores, which displayed art in their windows.

The next year, the pottery teacher Vivian Dai and the weaver Sylvia Heyden shook up the Allied Arts establishment. Reflecting a new regard for crafts as art, they demanded that work in the Bazaar must be original designs made from raw materials. "That started an uproar," according to another potter, Pepper Fluke, but the first juried Triangle Festival of Crafts in 1967 raised a grand total of $500—"which in those days was a gold mine." By the time of the sec-

ond Triangle Festival of Crafts, in 1969, "All over the Triangle craftsmen were emerging because suddenly they were regarded as artists," Fluke said. Meantime a sprout was appearing from another artistic seed.

One weekend in early 1961, for example, five downtown movie houses offered audiences such similarly mainstream pictures as Bob Hope and Lucille Ball in *The Facts of Life* (at the Carolina), Susan Hayward and James Mason in *The Marriage Go-Round* (Center), Walt Disney's *Sleeping Beauty* (Uptown), the epic *Ben-Hur* (Criterion), and Disney's *Swiss Family Robinson* (Rialto). A year later, the Center, Carolina, and Uptown carried on similar trade, but the Criterion had begun to show "skin flicks" and occasional science fiction while the Rialto was out of business.

Then on November 14, 1962, the Rialto, across Main Street from the County Courthouse, reopened as "the South's first legitimate art movie theater"—according to its new manager Maggie Dent. The theater itself underwent a thorough scrubbing, including restoration of its engraved, bronze-finished ceiling. Dent stocked a lounge with motion-picture magazines, compiled a mailing list of art-movie aficionados, and used the lobby and stairwells to exhibit local artists' work. She planned occasional live performances, visits by critics and directors, and weekend matinees for children—with such art fare for children as the French film *Red Balloon*.

Beginning with Truffaut's *Jules and Jim*, Dent nurtured an audience for art and foreign movies, continuing for ten years with *The L-Shaped Room*, *Murder at the Gallop*, *Alfie*, *Blow-Up*, *The Shop on Main Street*, and *I Am Curious (Yellow)*—until her theater was urban renewed out of existence in 1970. The X-rated Criterion, just around the corner on Church Street, met the same fate; but by that time the Uptown—oldest movie house in town—had been long out of business and the Center had relocated to Lakewood Shopping Center, even as new cinemas had opened at Northgate Shopping Center and on Chapel Hill Boulevard. Only the Carolina, which occupied the city-owned Durham Auditorium, remained downtown; with its lease up for renewal in 1978, it was a losing proposition and ripe for the urban renewal wrecking ball. Luckily, there were new players in the downtown-revitalization picture.

Rocked, rolled, and reeling, Durham survived the 1960s with its downtown gutted by urban renewal, a freeway to nowhere (literally, Chapel Hill Street to Alston Avenue) giving visual form to an aggravated divide between white and black citizens, and a culture of mingled activism and flower power spilling off its campuses and into the community at large.

A turning point might be identified as the ascension of Harry Van Straaten in 1969 to the first of three terms as the president of Allied Arts. Van Straaten, a long-established downtown merchant, had led Allied Arts through a financial crisis that threatened the organization's continued existence. With the red ink in the past and a $1,500 grant from the North Carolina Arts Council in hand, Allied Arts felt secure enough in the summer of 1970 to hire a full-time director, Gay H. Baynes, a Greensboro native with extensive theatrical experience who had just completed a master's program in drama at Chapel Hill.

Allied Arts, she said, was "just buzzing, there's so much to be done." At the top of her agenda, after a painting party to spruce up the Allied Arts building, was dispelling the perception that her organization was strictly for "longhairs." Baynes's plans included a children's theater trouping by van from neighborhood to neighborhood, art diversions for children whose mothers were working, and a new theater adjacent to the Proctor Street headquarters—adding up, in the words of the *Durham Morning Herald* women's editor Lee Ridenour, to "an arts council that reaches everybody."

Baynes's regime lasted less than eight months; in the spring of 1971 she quit to work for a traveling children's theater. James McIntyre, a protégé of the Duke culture maven Ella Fountain Pratt, was still two weeks from graduation when his appointment to succeed Baynes was announced on May 17, 1971. McIntyre brought to his job a business-populist perspective much like Baynes's, perhaps reflecting in part his experience in the late 1960s with the college (counter-)culture and its mantras of "power to the people" and "grassroots participation."

Allied Arts in 1971 had a curriculum that offered thirty-four classes in dance, crafts, drama, art, music, photography, and something called "eurhythmics"—and accepted its first black pupil, after a great deal of internal dissension and a board discussion of how such a move would affect fundraising.

James McIntyre arrived for his first day of work to find janitor Charles Hardin dancing with a broom. It was a symbolic moment if nothing else, representing a spirit of the times that would characterize McIntyre's ten-year regime as the Allied Arts head. In 1972 McIntyre told the *Duke Alumni Register* that Allied Arts "should be serving as a cultural agency that looks at the whole situation of the arts in the community. . . . Allied Arts has to go out into the community and work." He further invoked creative activity as a spiritual uplift for those estranged from their complicated society. At this point, class registration had risen from 150 in 1970 to 325, and apparently McIntyre was finding managerial creativity uplifting as well. "I've discovered you can get things done. You *can* make things happen."

In April 1972 a citywide arts festival attracted a reported twenty thousand participants. The festival involved Duke and NCCU as well as the YMCA and the city Recreation Department, whose staffer Carl Washington proved a catalyst for Allied Arts' engagement with Durham's underserved black community. Along the same lines, later in 1972 Allied Arts took under its wing a public school Creative Arts Program founded in 1969 by the First Presbyterian Church, and linked its program with the anti-poverty agency Operation Breakthrough. Already McIntyre had publicly claimed a stake for Allied Arts in a proposed downtown convention center—a building envisioned even as the downtown "renewal" process was claiming the Rialto Theater and encouraging the area's former patrons to take their business elsewhere.

The Arts and the City

The year 1974 brought three seminal developments to Durham's cultural scene. In April a North Carolina Folklife Festival replaced Duke University's expired Joe College spring weekend. Two years later the festival evolved into the city's National Bicentennial celebration at the new West Point on the Eno Park; that event provided inspiration and a format for the Festival for the Eno, begun in 1979 by the Association for the Preservation of the Eno River Valley and held each Independence Day weekend since.

Allied Arts would get a boost from the Bicentennial Folklife Festival, which attracted 100,000 people over three days and exposed Durham residents to elements of their town most knew little about: Durham's blues heritage and its Greek community, for example. Further, the Bicentennial observance would awaken interest in local history and folkways, which had been long dismissed as "old-timey," bringing into the mainstream the impulse toward preservation, conservation, and cultural diversity.

The second development was the Allied Arts' first downtown Street Arts Festival in September 1974. It linked Allied Arts as an institution with the city center's envisioned future. It turned Main Street into what McIntyre called "a Renaissance Fair." There were arts and crafts by about 150 exhibitors, some from as far away as Fayetteville. There was a stage at Main and

Front page of the *Arterie,* the Official News Publication of the Durham Arts Council, Inc., vol. 1: no 6, December 1975. *Left to right, bottom row:* Sally Tompa, Roz Baldassare, Wanda Garrett, Brantley Watson, Jim McIntyre, St. Clair Williams, Melinda Hinners, Jacqueline Erickson, Charles Hardin. *Second row:* Joan Schempp, Ella Fountain Pratt, Candy Peete, Jeannie Everett, Rev. Albert Nelius, Dot Loftis, Judi Bradford. *Third row:* Frank Holyfield, Joanne Sharpe, Tim Sublette, Bea Palethorpe, Janice Palmer, David Bradley, Vicki Bachman, Scott Schuett. *Last row:* Steve Janesick, Paul Hodges, Hassie Warren, Joelle Logue, Susan Robell, Henry Minor. Missing from the photograph are Hale Sweeny, Alex Rivera, Harry van Straaten, Thayer Smith, Scott Gwynne. *(Courtesy of Jacqueline Erickson Morgan and the Durham Arts Council)*

Market, where eight acts performed and disc jockeys from WTIK were emcees. Kids got their faces painted and drew on the sidewalk with chalk. It was all quite a novelty, and attracted about twenty thousand people during its seven-hour run—and they did it again the next year.

Capping the effort to move the arts into Durham's mainstream of concern came the announcement that Allied Arts had engaged the consultant Alvin H. Reiss of New York "to begin charting new directions for the Durham art council," as the *Morning Herald* arts reporter Willis Mason wrote. "Allied Arts is growing up," McIntyre told Mason. "The community is saying every day, 'We want more.' . . . We are going to have to make some major progressive steps to keep up with the demand." McIntyre envisioned the transformation of Allied Arts into "a vital force in urban development," and an alliance between the arts and city government.

By changing its name in 1975 to the Durham Arts Council, and by its move in 1978 to the Old City Hall Building (1904, originally the High School), Allied Arts linked itself with the preservation movement and downtown revitalization. With the newly formed Historic Preservation Society of Durham (HPSD) and the city, it also shared concern for the newly formed Carolina Theatre / Durham Auditorium and St. Joseph's Historic Foundation / Hayti Heritage Center as two more cultural institutions for the twenty-first-century Bull City.

St. Joseph's Historic Foundation

In the meantime, urban renewal was having just the opposite effect. Not only were businesses relocating where parking was plentiful and free, but the inconvenience of getting to downtown through its reconstruction encouraged shoppers to change their habits. Court-enforced integration of public schools in 1970 had prompted a critical mass of consumers to depart from the inner city and what was left of its commercial district. The out-migration was not a strictly white phenomenon; Durham's black middle class was also moving out, and taking its institutions with it.

One of those was St. Joseph's African Methodist Episcopal Church. In February 1976 the congregation—with that of White Rock Baptist Church, the most socially prestigious and politically powerful in African-American Durham—abandoned its 1892 sanctuary on the Fayetteville Street ridge for a new, modern building twenty blocks south. While the old church had been expressly protected in the 1961 plan for revitalizing its neighborhood, its departure left the building untended, running down, and slated for the wrecking ball.

Old St. Joseph's was already a recognized architectural and historic landmark. Home to Durham's second-oldest black congregation, established in

1869 by the evangelist Edian Markum, the church counted among its luminary communicants John Merrick, founder of the North Carolina Mutual Life Insurance Company; the pioneer educator W. G. Pearson; the physician Stanford L. Warren; and the entrepreneur Richard Fitzgerald. The
building is made of Fitzgerald's brick, in Gothic Revival style, and boasts
ornate chandeliers, pipe organ, and twenty-four stained-glass windows.

Within a month of the congregation's departure, an ad hoc group had incorporated itself as the St. Joseph's Historic Foundation, aiming to save the
sanctuary and the education building (dating from 1951) and to restore them
for office space and public functions. Even before it was officially organized,
the group had nominated the church for the National Register of Historic
Places and secured $20,000 from the Durham Redevelopment Commission

First White Rock Baptist Church *(Courtesy of White Rock Baptist Church)*

and a promise of $35,000 from the city if they received a matching amount from federal sources.

First movers in St. Joseph's salvation were J. J. Henderson, a retired North Carolina Mutual executive, and Aylene Cooke of HPSD. Joining them on the board were others prominent in Durham's arts and preservation communities—including the HPSD founder Margaret Haywood, who became a St. Joseph's vice president; the historian John L. Flowers III; the potter and Savoyard Pepper Fluke; and the singer and art-film fan Connie Moses. Bob Chapman, coordinator of the county Bicentennial celebration, was a member and the foundation's first spokesman. By December the Redevelopment Commission had agreed to sell the St. Joseph's property to the foundation for $1, and Chapman asked the City Council for $28,300 more.

Plans had changed, he said. In the intervening months a drama company, the Pocket Theatre, had begun using the deconsecrated sanctuary for performances. Instead of restoring the church to its original condition, the foundation now intended to rehabilitate it as a community center, which required more refitting to suit a more stringent building code.

One councilman balked at the second request, but St. Joseph's was the beneficiary of groundwork done earlier by the Durham Arts Council and a new willingness of local government to use tax money to support the arts. In 1975 and 1976 the city and county had each given the Arts Council $5,000 to help match a grant from the National Endowment for the Arts (NEA). The money had gone for various community outreach projects, including a dance class at the John Avery Boys Club and a Black Cultural Arts program; for the Street Arts Festival; and for hiring the Arts Council's first associate director, Henry H. Minor. In February 1977 the county gave the Arts Council $20,000 for a feasibility study on turning the Old Courthouse into an arts center; days later the city gave the council $5,000 to cover salaries and match $15,000 from the state; invoking an "expanding role in the community" (which had been financed with public money), the Arts Council asked the county to double its subsidy to $10,000 for fiscal 1977–78.

Years of maneuvering to align and entwine Durham's cultural interests with those of its image-conscious business and political sectors were now paying off. With the creation of the National Endowment for the Arts under Lyndon Johnson's Great Society, arts won access to taxpayers' money, and arts boosters in Durham and elsewhere were quick to take advantage of that precedent and new dispensations from on high.

With prospects bullish—its annual budget rising from $17,000 to $140,000 in the first seven years of McIntyre's administration—the Arts Council in 1976 engaged a consultant, Ralph Burgard of Associated Councils of the Arts, to create for Durham a "cultural action plan." According to McIntyre, the need for such a plan had become apparent during the feasibility study for conversion of the Old Courthouse. That project was put on hold until Burgard's report was received on July 1, 1977.

Burgard's report recommended a new arts center as "a vital element in revitalizing the central area of Durham." He analyzed the seventeen cultural institutions and their finances: $407,700 went into their accounts in fiscal 1976–77 and out again into the local economy, but that was less than half their operating costs. They needed more money.

Carolina Theatre Reborn

In the meantime, yet another cultural institution was emerging in Durham, on a somewhat less ethereal plane. Constance (Connie) Roy Moses moved to Durham from New York City in 1959, when her husband, Monte (Montrose J.), joined the Duke microbiology faculty. Connie had a professional background in radio and theater, and in New York the couple had enjoyed art-house cinema. They enthusiastically patronized Maggie Dent's Rialto theater enterprise when it started in 1962. "The art films were a relief and a delight," Moses recalled in 2003. The theater's demise left a gap that took several years to fill. In the meantime, Connie and Monte Moses became early members of HPSD, and in 1977 they learned that the Durham Auditorium / Carolina Theatre, an art deco structure directly behind City Hall erected in 1926, was probably coming down to make way for a parking deck.

"That I can't take," Connie Moses told the *Durham Sun*. In July 1977, the same month that Burgard's report appeared, the couple called a meeting of about twenty-five others interested in saving the Carolina. With mentoring by Margaret Haywood, the group first proposed to return the auditorium to its original function as a live-performance hall. However, after assessing the building's structural constraints, the group settled on advocacy for a new art house.

The project attracted widespread support, especially as the entire downtown business area was designated a National Historic District in November 1977. On May 16, 1978, the City Council approved a three-year lease to the group, now incorporated as the nonprofit Carolina Cinema Corp., to operate the Carolina as an art house. Carolina Cinema secured loans from the city and a bank, with twenty-two co-signatories for equipment, film rentals, and fixup, and on June 14 opened for business with a Charlie Chaplin festival, under the management of Maggie Dent. By this time the Arts Council had permission from the city to move into the old City Hall, which the municipal administration was preparing to leave for a new building several blocks to the east, in time to stage its fifth Street Arts Festival and begin planning its own twenty-fifth anniversary.

For the arts of Durham, the summer of 1978 could hardly have been more promising. Completing what McIntyre called its most exciting year ever, the Arts Council had quickly moved to implement Burgard's proposals. It had sent performers into nursing homes and hospitals, run a summer concert series in the city parks, started a monthly newsletter, opened art classes for senior citizens, held a seminar on the arts and religion, and begun Neighborhood Taproots to find and preserve local traditions such as the Durham blues. "Society may be moving us away from tradition too rapidly," McIntyre said, whose visions of arts for Everyman and arts as a participatory sport were reaching realization even as the arts staked a geographical claim at the heart of Durham and in the public's own buildings.

Far from the society pages, the arts—or at least their organizations—

Carolina Theatre *(Courtesy of Frank DePasquale)*

were getting front-page treatment in the Durham press. Both the *Morning Herald* and the afternoon *Sun* introduced weekend arts-and-entertainment sections. The arts were on the cutting edge of downtown renewal. And as if to put an exclamation point to this home-grown cultural activity, the American Dance Festival arrived from Connecticut for its first season at Duke University.

In October Carolina Cinema held a black-tie benefit party at the Carolina Theatre. George Watts Hill Jr., chairman of Central Carolina Bank, was the master of ceremonies. The evening's movie was *42nd Street*, recalling that show's performance at the Carolina in 1933. Almost as soon as the Carolina reopened, Connie Moses undertook reclamation of its once-ornate lounge (she called it a ballroom), which had been partitioned into offices with cinder blocks and where the tall windows still bore blackout paint from the Second World War. Other volunteers were set to work in dressing rooms that had served the likes of Marian Anderson, Will Rogers, Alfred Lunt and Lynn Fontanne (*There Shall Be No Night*), Tallulah Bankhead (*The Little Foxes*), Lillian Gish (*Life with Father*), and Katharine Hepburn (*The Philadelphia Story*), but that years of neglect had left with stained floors, cracked plaster, and peeling paint. Scrounging in dusty niches, the volunteers found a moth-eaten stuffed duck, a statue of Dracula, and a pop-corn machine from the 1920s, which was promptly restored and put back on the job in the lobby.

The spirit was somewhat dampened when in October 1978 the Arts Council announced that it was facing a budget deficit of $15,000, due largely to declining corporate contributions. "The Arts Council suffers tremendously from a lack of broad-based community support," said President James B. Maxwell, who with McIntyre raised doubts whether Durham was really as big on the arts as local boosters were claiming. The Arts Council's growth, its friends said, was outstripping the public's generosity; at the same time, the council was claiming a wider public role.

The Arts Council's first-ever published annual report claimed that 150,000 people had in one way or another taken part in its programs during 1978–79, and it set a money-raising goal for 1979 of $100,000. The remodeled building by now housed five art galleries, a 130-seat theater, dance and art studios, darkrooms, rehearsal and meeting rooms, and storage space. Despite an ongoing deficit, which had reached more than $18,000 by the time the report was printed, the Arts Council set a budget of $142,000 and hired a part-time development director. The following spring, for the first time, the Arts Fund drive exceeded its goal, and raised its sights for 1981 to $115,000.

(Far left)
Carolina Theatre, interior detail of proscenium arch *(Courtesy of Frank DePasquale)*

(Left)
Carolina Theatre, interior detail of Connie Moses ballroom before remodeling *(Courtesy of Frank DePasquale)*

Shoring Up Foundations

On the other side of town, St. Joseph's was progressing on its own. By early 1979 it had a director, William T. Cash, who had run the Triangle Coffee House on Broad Street in the early 1960s. Cash set up classes in jazz, poetry, dance, photography, and folklore; a dance company took up artistic residence; oral historians taught interview techniques; feminists were publishing a magazine; a video-production company had taken root; and the Pocket Theatre was renting the basement, which had been drained of several feet of water. Cash invited musicians of all kinds to make the former church "their hangout."

In January 1981 a delegation from St. Joseph's asked the City Council for money for its roof, which had fallen far short of code when an engineer inspected the structure more than a year before. The St. Joseph's Foundation had reduced its request from $77,000 to $15,000, but then heard from the city inspections chief, John Parham, that the building was in danger of being closed down. City officials said the money might be available; Rebecca Newton, who had replaced Bill Cash as St. Joseph's director, said that the foundation would get the building reinspected. A $3,000 patch job kept the roof up, and the foundation came up with money to cover Newton's pay when her job's federal funding ran out. With two crises survived, St. Joseph's went on to hold concerts, show films, and stage an art-and-jazz People's Day Celebration.

By 1983 things were rough, as management had split with the foundation. The building's condition had deteriorated to the point that the foundation was seeking a buyer who could afford its restoration—despite $150,000 that the city had already spent for that purpose. Sale plans were dropped after the North Carolina General Assembly approved a $50,000 donation and the city agreed to match it, if someone concerned came up with a detailed accounting of how the money would be spent.

By 1985 the St. Joseph's Historic Foundation director Bob Chapman lamented the building's condition, saying, "The building is practically worthless," but the foundation board stirred some optimism by securing the donation of a heating system and by rethinking the use of the historic church—switching it from an arts and performance facility to a black cultural heritage and education center. By March 1986 George and Mary Pyne and the architectural firm of O'Brien Atkins had helped the foundation develop a five-year renovation plan to show the City Council and contracted with the city to use the $100,000 in city and state grants to rebuild the roof, waterproof the foundation, and generally bring conditions up to modern standards. Besides a fix-up, the St. Joseph's Historic Foundation agreed to set up educational and cultural programs, engage a director of volunteers, and conduct a membership drive to raise money on its own.

The foundation had also changed its mission to reflect the expanded programming goals and objectives for the facility and to fill a niche in the community that encompassed more than cultural and performing arts. Benjamin Speller, newly elected vice president for programming, and Lionel Parker, vice president for development, had insisted that this mission change was necessary to take the foundation out of direct competition with other cultural and performing arts groups in Durham, especially the Durham Arts Council.

In the summer of 1986 the foundation selected the architectural firm of DePasquale, Thompson and Wilson (DTW) to prepare plans and specifications for restoring the church. Estimates had reached $3 million, and the foundation was hoping to get $2 million of that from a county bond issue. Plans included renovating the church's education building as a multipurpose center with galleries, meeting space, and office space, and connecting it to the sanctuary, which would be fitted up for performances and public forums. Work began in February 1987. The foundation hired Walter Norflett as its executive director and Al Stevens as project manager to oversee the restoration.

A New Vision for the Arts

Not only concerned with the theater, Monte Moses had a large vision of what Durham's downtown could become. In an op-ed piece for the *Morning Herald* in February 1980, Moses wrote of turning downtown into a "Rialto"—in the dictionary sense of "a center of commercial activity . . . frequented by plays and playgoers, hence the theater district." Invoking Durham's historic lack of "a true center of the community" (a notion with which many who had known downtown before urban renewal might have taken issue), Moses saw the new Rialto as centered on a restored Carolina Theatre and a new convention center with a hotel and new places to meet, shop, play, eat, drink, and be inspired in a physical mix of open space, historic buildings, and new construction. "New life, a new face, and a new heart," he wrote.

Moses's optimism was backed by experience. The Carolina was open every day, running in the black, and drawing an average of a thousand paying customers each week. Its success was unique between Washington and Atlanta. In 1979 the DTW architecture firm had completed a favorable feasibility study on the building's restoration to accommodate both live shows and cinema. Cleaning and restoring the old ballroom continued under Connie Moses's drive.

In the meantime, visions at the Arts Council and Carolina Cinema were coalescing, and those two groups, along with the American Dance Festival and HPSD, formed an ad hoc committee to plan for "making a gracious central home for the arts in downtown Durham." Its draft report, dated November 6, 1981, recommended remodeling the Arts Council Building and Carolina Theatre to better suit their present uses, and bringing in the nearby Civic Center/Armory (an Italianate structure built in 1937 under the auspices of the Works Progress Administration) as a performing hall capable of various configurations for various productions. Also nearby, the report envisioned studios for the Dance Festival in a former tobacco storage warehouse. The whole arts complex would be coordinated with the new civic center, their combination jump-starting other enterprises that would capitalize on the trade that art, entertainment, and conventions would bring.

On December 17, 1981, Jim McIntyre resigned to become director of the Carnegie Fund of New York. Under his leadership the Arts Council had grown from being an umbrella organization for four affiliate groups to sheltering more than thirty. What was hung in the Art Guild's galleries was as good as anything in the Southeast, he said. The council's budget had risen from less than $20,000 to more than $240,000. Its fund drive receipts had jumped 22 percent in his last full year on the job, from $117,000 to $143,000. At the same time, McIntyre said in a parting interview, Durham had gone from being "tobacco town" to the self-styled "City of Medicine."

The four groups that had formed the ad hoc committee quickly threw their weight behind a $10.5 million bond issue for the new civic center, which was going to the voters at the end of June 1982. Shortly before the referendum, the Arts Council held an off-season street festival, just to prove that people really would come downtown, and attracted five thousand on a sweltering afternoon. The bond issue passed, but visible progress on the civic center or the arts complex would be years in coming.

Earlier in June, the Arts Council named Michael Marsicano to succeed McIntyre. Soon dubbed "the boy boss" by some of his office staff—in part because of his boyish looks—Marsicano was twenty-six, four years older than McIntyre had been when he assumed the post, and held a Ph.D. in music from Duke; there, like McIntyre, he had been a protégé of the city's cultural affairs director, Ella Fountain Pratt. Marsicano's number one charge was getting the arts complex built. The Arts Council and Carolina Cinema announced that they would ask for $50,000 to $75,000 in "cash and in-kind support" from the city and county to initiate a planning process with a budget of $150,780 for the arts complex.

The Arts Council's New Face

For the next six years the Arts Council and DTW were in continual space planning and financial studies. It was also a phase remembered for pink hardhats—which supporters wore to City Council and County Commissioners' meetings to dramatize the crumbling state of the building they had so lately occupied.

"I remember the interesting and fun presentations we used to make for the City Council to request money to renovate the building," writes Meredythe Holmes, who became the first African-American president of the Arts Council during the 1980s. "We brought in performers, sang songs to them and once even served them birthday cake. . . . They were always fun and everyone enjoyed them."

By mid-1983 the Arts Council had a paid staff of twelve and a budget of $306,000, of which the city and county were supplying $30,000 each. It now had drawings for the arts complex, which called for adding wings to the Carolina Theatre for cinemas, rehearsal space, and dressing rooms, remodeling the existing theater with an enlarged stage, and adding an entrance "atrium" to the Arts Council building, as well as enlarging its theater and galleries. Cost estimates, when they were revealed later, ran to $8.5 million. That fall the council began a Sunday afternoon children's program, "Magic Tree: A Family Hour with the Arts," followed in February by "Durham Showcase," a Sunday night series to attract grownups downtown and give musicians, poets, and storytellers a place to show what they could do.

While planning, politicking, and looking for money went on in Marsicano's office, the rest of the Arts Council was busy as well—changing the name of its annual festival from "Street Arts" to "CenterFest" in 1984; introducing its Emerging Artists Program, which gave money to help up-and-comers establish themselves as professional artists; staging a "street opera" in the spring at Brightleaf Square; and, with the newspapers, sponsoring a holiday decorations contest. In January 1985 Marsicano announced that the Arts Council building was in such sorry condition that the council would move out until the place was fixed. A slide show prepared for the City Council revealed exposed wiring, falling plaster, water damage, and mushrooms growing on walls. The council passed Marsicano's hardhat, collecting only $41.25—but it assured Marsicano that he had the city's backing.

The Carolina Theatre was undergoing some changes of its own. Maggie Dent was succeeded in September 1982 by her assistant, Jim Steele, in turn succeeded by Darcy Paletz, a founder of Carolina Cinema. Paletz, sadly, was stricken with a terminal illness; management passed to Bill Cash, formerly of St. Joseph's, until Stephen Barefoot, singer and former nightclub owner, took over in August 1985.

Nevertheless, after six years' labor by untold numbers of volunteers, renovation was finished on what had been renamed the Connie Moses Ballroom—at the request of HPSD. It opened in June 1984, hosting chamber concerts, private parties, lectures, business meetings, and the realization of a Connie Moses dream—a performance in a Sunday Salon in which she sang her favorite songs, accompanied by the pianist Paul Montgomery and the bassist Rick Jones. That was March 31, 1985; less than a month later, she died.

The theater was having a rough go of it, quite aside from its managerial turnover. By now it had become "phase two" in the arts complex planning, and it had, for the first time, finished a fiscal year in the red. When Barefoot started his job the Carolina owed money to two hundred vendors. "They would not give him a kernel of popcorn," Monte Moses recalled. Still, Moses said, there was a "joy" about the Carolina and a "family" feeling among the Carolina Cinema set. "Everybody did everything," he said. "Even Stephen took his turn cleaning toilets."

Besides just staying in business, over the summer the theater received a new marquee, brought in new sound and projection equipment, ordered new theatrical lights for the ballroom, and contracted with a booking agent who could get cut rates on film rentals. The same week the Arts Council moved out of its building, Barefoot cut a ribbon at the Carolina's door to symbolize the theater's own new beginning.

Barefoot put his nightclub experience to use with a series of live shows, including a benefit by the jazz singers Mike Palter and Lynne Jackson that sold out to the tune of $5,500 for the new ballroom lights. In December 1985 the soap opera star Ruth Warrick performed her one-woman show *An Evening with Miss Phoebe* in the main theater.

In 1986 the theater began selling corporate sponsorships at $8,000 to $12,500 each, and the bond issue that benefited St. Joseph's also brought $7.8 million for the Carolina. A designer from New York was signed on for the renovation in May 1987. The theater was soon surrounded by construction sites and chain-link fences as work on the oft-delayed and much-anticipated Civic Center finally began in the fall of 1987. By then construction was also under way at the Arts Council, and on an office tower right across the Downtown Loop. With access and parking becoming more and more of a problem, the Carolina cut its schedule back to weekends only in the spring of 1988, and then closed completely on July 31. For a couple of last flings, Barefoot brought back Palter and Jackson for a benefit with an assortment of local talent, including the up-and-coming jazz singer Nnenna Freelon and the swing band Rebecca and The Hi-Tones, led by St. Joseph's former director Rebecca Newton—and hosted the world première of the movie *Bull Durham*.

Nnenna Freelon
(Courtesy of the Eno River Association)

Two months later, the Arts Council moved back into its renovated home before the grand reopening on CenterFest weekend. The main hall at the Carolina Theatre was named for the Raleigh philanthropist A. J. Fletcher, whose namesake foundation had just given the theater $750,000 for an endowment, and the Arts Council named its building for State Senator Kenneth Royall, leader of the drive to renovate the Proctor Street headquarters in 1960 and more recently a good friend with state appropriations. President Meredythe Holmes released a handful of helium balloons into the overcast morning.

The previous evening, the Arts Council's festivities had had a prelude—opening night of the Bull Durham Blues Festival, held at the Durham Athletic Park and sponsored by St. Joseph's Historic Foundation (as distinct from the sponsors that had staged a Bull City Blues Festival the year before in conjunction with the U.S. Olympic Festival). The festival invoked Durham's past association with the

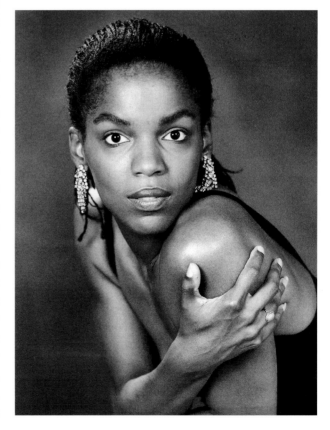

music, but a lot more as well. "Blues is not a single idiom, it's a mixture of a lot of things," said Walter Norflett, who was by now the St. Joseph's director. "We hear of the strength and the history of the blues in the piedmont and in Durham, and knew we had to deal with that . . . and with the incredible energy and enthusiasm in the blues nowadays. Blues is the root of so much—gospel fans, jazz fans, rock and roll fans, all are exposed to the blues." With the festival, St. Joseph's brought itself into the downtown visibility mix, and with the music it brought an earthier—and more electric—style and patron base into the downtown cultural mix, which had been rather self-consciously artsy. The blues festival would quickly gain a place of its own in the city's calendar.

In the meantime, the Carolina Cinema Corporation turned the theater renovation over to the Arts Council. Carolina Cinema had seats on an oversight committee created by City Manager Orville Powell, but it was one agency and one interest among others. The volunteers did what they could in preparation, stripping the theater of light fixtures, banisters, moldings, artifacts, and seats, and getting them all into safe storage for the duration.

The Arts Council was in a hiatus of its own. With the building done, Marsicano resigned in January 1989. The organization carried on, staging jazz on the new Civic Center Plaza in front of the shuttered Carolina Theatre, advocating a plan to turn the old Civic Center / Armory into an art museum, and commissioning sculpture. But trouble was brewing. Some of the affiliates, which had created the Arts Council in the first place, complained that the council was squeezing them out of the new building. Tom Link of the Durham Art Guild, which had one of its own exhibitions canceled to make way for another sponsored by the Arts Council, said, "I just don't think the taxpayers knew that the Durham Arts Council was going to turn into an arts bureaucracy and snuff the grassroots affiliates right out from under it." The conflict, he added, had been going on for years.

Such was the situation awaiting the new director, Skip Schreiber, in July. In November the Durham chapter of the American Civil Liberties Union rented gallery space for a show of "Banned Art," including Andres Serrano's notorious photograph of a crucifix submerged in urine, titled "Piss Christ." About seventy protesters showed up to sing hymns and read scripture outside the building, while a thousand stood in line to get in to see the show. The Arts Council was careful to distance itself from the exhibit—reminding everyone that it was not the sponsor, but neither was it a censor. More worrisome was the $400,000 operating deficit that Schreiber discovered that fall. Operating expenses for the renovated building had far outstripped expectations, and seven years' preoccupation with a physical symbol were about to force the Arts Council to rethink just what it was all about.

In that, the Durham Arts Council faced the same dilemma that had already confronted St. Joseph's and Carolina Cinema, only on a much larger scale: Was it a building or an agency? St. Joseph's had begun as an effort of historic preservation, Carolina Cinema in part as preservation and in part as movies. The Arts Council began as a coordinating service for four organizations with identities and purposes of their own, but its leaders' ambitions and purposes had long since exceeded any such limitation. Now, with civic prominence and credibility to uphold, programs of its own to run, responsibility for millions of dollars of mostly taxpayers' money, and almost half a million dollars' worth of red ink, some chickens had come home to roost.

In fairness, money problems were hitting the arts across the board. The gusher of federal financing of the 1970s had long since dwindled in the face of fiscal realities and political priorities, and with a national recession in 1990–91 the arts were forced to account for themselves and rediscover their agendas, reasons for being, and bootstraps. The fable of entitlement was replaced, grudgingly in some cases, by an appreciation of endowment; the public was not a patron, after all, but a consumer.

Facing facts, Schreiber cut the Arts Council staff by 24 percent, as well as his own salary. In May 1990 a planning committee recommended a complete overhaul of the organization. While holding onto CenterFest and the Kwanzaa celebration it had started in the 1980s, the Arts Council would drop sponsorship and co-sponsorship of other programs including Magic Tree, the Blues Festival, and Jazz in the Parks. Most significantly, it cut loose the "funded affiliates," now twelve in number, including such founding groups as the Art Guild and the Theater Guild: in the future, those agencies would have to apply and compete for Arts Council money right along with more than 145 others that had appeared in Durham during the roaring 1980s, while the Arts Council would be an advisor and funding agent, with particular attention to individual artists on the way up.

Although the proposals were not well received by the former affiliates, the council's board adopted the restructuring plan, and the city followed with $50,000 to help the agency over the hump. A year later the Arts Council finished with a balanced budget of $1,170,000 for fiscal 1990–91—a far cry, even with inflation, from the $17,000 of just twenty years before. After another year, showing a $40,000 surplus, the Arts Council reorganized itself, delegating day-to-day responsibilities out of the director's office and into those of the staff while assigning to the director work on good relations with artists, arts organizations, and the community in general. Schreiber resigned in the summer of 1992, and E'Vonne Coleman was hired as director. She had started her career with the Durham Parks and Recreation

Department and was then assistant director of the Expansion Arts Program and special assistant to the Chairman of the National Endowment of the Arts.

While the Arts Council was wrestling with itself, and the Carolina Theatre waited through planning, replanning, and renovation estimates, which at one point reached more than $20 million, the Hayti Heritage Center at old St. Joseph's opened in September 1991 as Durham's first African-American cultural heritage institution. There was more work to do—it would be another decade, another bond issue, and more than $2 million before restoration was complete in the former sanctuary—but the center was in business with a diverse contextual programming agenda, an African-American archive managed by Benjamin Speller of the School of Library and Information Sciences at North Carolina Central University, and artwork and memorabilia from the old Hayti business district to show in its Lyda Merrick Art Gallery. The Hayti Center had a grant from the North Carolina Arts Council for a program director and a pledge of $126,000 from the city, with a mandate to produce at least four programs a year relevant to Durham's black history and community. One of those was the Blues Festival.

Speller, who had been president of the St. Joseph's Historic Foundation throughout the reconstruction phase, reminded the board members and audience at Hayti's opening of the promise made to city and county elected officials and managers—the County Commission chair Bill Bell, State Senator Wib Gulley, County Manager Jack Bond, and City Manager Orville Powell—"We are not going to operate in the red. We've taken public money and managed it appropriately, and we will continue to do that."

Walter Norflett, the St. Joseph's director who organized the first Blues Festival in conjunction with the Arts Council's reopening, had been a bridge between the two organizations. He was succeeded by Dianne Pledger, whom E'Vonne Coleman had met from her time with the NEA. On Coleman's arrival at the DAC she was asked how she would deal with the "black arts council." Instead of succumbing to considerable pressure to compete, she became a confidante of Pledger and even used her political savvy to direct money Hayti's way.

But Coleman, the DAC's first African-American boss, had her own ideas for the agency, which despite its years of outreach rhetoric still had an image as an in-group catering to the country-club set. "There's a perception that the DAC has not served half the city's population—the African-American communities," she told a newspaper interviewer soon after her arrival back in Durham.

At the same time that the Arts Council was bonding with Hayti, it was separating from the Carolina Theatre. The Carolina's construction cost was brought back to within the $7.8 million appropriated in 1986, and management was put in the hands of the board and hired staff of what was now the Carolina Theatre of Durham Inc. Reconstruction began in 1992, and on its sixty-eighth birthday, February 2, 1994, the theater reopened in all its 1920s splendor—three tiers of seating to accommodate 975 customers, box seats (to accommodate stage lights instead of social illuminati), and a color scheme of turquoise and glowing gold. Fletcher Hall was now devoted to living arts; a pair of new cinemas next door, seating 276 and 76, showed art movies. The popcorn was again the best in town.

Over the next ten years, the Arts Council achieved numerous milestones, in Coleman's reckoning. One of her first orders of business was a written policy on freedom of expression to cover just such eventualities as the "Banned Art" exhibition. No other arts organization in North Carolina had one. The policy affirmed "the right to create and the right to respond," she said, "and to be respectful in facilitating the dialog with sensitivity to both sides." And to recognize that controversial work may not be very good art.

Ella Fountain Pratt *(Courtesy of Ella Fountain Pratt)*

The Arts Council observed its fortieth anniversary and Emerging Artists its tenth in 1994, CenterFest its twenty-fifth in 1998. The Durham Public Schools approved teacher credit for taking part in residencies run by the now-longstanding Creative Arts in the Public / Private Schools program (CAPPS), and the city approved a one-cent allocation for the arts from each dollar received in property tax—later raised to a penny and a half. The Arts Council installed a digital art studio and satellite studios on Foster Street, began a youth program called "Arts as Part of the Solution," and ten years after reoccupying its building, gave it another refurbishing to counteract a decade of wear and tear. It established an endowment fund in honor of Ella Fountain Pratt, who had joined the Arts Council staff after retiring from Duke and managed the Emerging Artists program and the Brightleaf street operas. By 2001, when Coleman left for a continuing-education position at Duke, the Arts Council had an annual budget of more than $2 million, and its United Arts Fund was taking in close to $800,000 a year. Sherry

DeVries, a Lenoir native who had been directing an arts center in Chicago, succeeded Coleman. The Arts Council became the lead agency in a consortium charged with devising a cultural master plan for Durham.

The Arts Council, the Carolina Theatre, and the Hayti Heritage Center had become established institutions, with art movies, festivals, and touring shows absorbed into Durham's sense of itself. In sixty-plus years, the very nature of Durham, as well as the place of arts entertainment in the national psyche, had profoundly changed.

3. Architecture

Dur'm since the Second World War

JIM WISE

In 1952 Clyde Lloyd began building a house on Nelson Street, in southeast Durham near the North Carolina College for Negroes. It was an unusual house, and Lloyd did the work himself.

Lloyd was not a professional builder. By trade, he was a chauffeur employed by a well-to-do family, the Tomses. Years earlier, Lloyd had seen a stylish, Art Moderne house plan in a magazine and promised his wife, Eleanor, that one day he would build the house for her. He tore the plan out and kept it in his pocket.

After serving in the Second World War Lloyd taught himself to lay brick and spread plaster, but the house remained a dream until the Tomses saw him looking at the plan, heard his story, and gave him 39,000 bricks to get started. Construction took him four years' worth of spare time, but he kept his promise, and he and Eleanor lived in the house together until Lloyd died on March 25, 2002. In a quiet and tidy neighborhood of typical suburban red-brick ranch styles, the Lloyd house remains a two-story anomaly of white brick and glass block that rises prominently on the side of a ridge. The Lloyd house story illustrates two truths about the architectural art in general, and about its postwar career in Durham in particular: architecture may have its fashions, but what gets built is a matter of personalities; it helps to know somebody.

Lloyd House, 126 Nelson Street *(Courtesy of the Historic Preservation Society of Durham)*

Since 1945 the built landscape of Durham has changed in ways that are both dramatic and ironic, reflecting shifting tastes, materials, economics, and values. While architecture as an intellectual process is much like painting, music, or drama, its practical realization, far more than that of other arts, is the result of interplay among persons—architect, client, and builder—as well as

among physics, law, nature, material, whim, and money—not to mention factors as ethereal as the zeitgeist. No building is the product of an artist's inspiration in the way that a still life, symphony, or work of modern dance might be. Moreover, while the aspiring novelist or composer may work in isolation, hoping to catch the fancy of a publisher or recording artist, the architect's ability to realize his inspiration—that is, to actually build something—requires an "anointing," as one Durham architect put it, by the business and financial community that has the wherewithal and reason to build.

No matter how vernacular or trendy a building may be, its creation and existence help to shape what comes after. The directions of Durham's postwar architecture may be seen in designs from the decade before, the same 1930s that produced the plan in Clyde Lloyd's pocket.

Pre-war Influences

Arguably Durham's most distinctive buildings from before the Second World War are its red-brick tobacco warehouses, constructed around the end of the nineteenth century and suggesting, by their ornate brickwork, their owners' opulence, and by their fortress-like parapets and chimney stacks, something about the competitive business practices that went into creating that wealth. Like these Romanesque Revival warehouses, other notable structures allude to eras past, and thereby communicate authority, dependability, bulk, and class—for example, the Georgian Revival Old Hill Building from 1925, the

Neoclassical Post Office from 1934, and even the Art Deco Durham Auditorium of 1926.

As if proclaiming a new deal in Durham, though, in 1937 there soared from the heart of downtown the Modernistic tower of that most responsible, respectable, and weighty of institutions, the hometown bank. Still dominating the downtown skyline, the new Hill Building, headquarters of Durham Bank & Trust (later Central Carolina Bank and now SunTrust), rose seventeen floors with an ascendant design reminiscent of the Empire State Building. The similarity is hardly surprising, for the designers of the Empire State Building, the New York firm of Shreve, Lamb, and Harmon, were the principal architects engaged by the founder of Durham Bank & Trust, John Sprunt Hill.

Working drawings for the building were executed in the Durham offices of George Watts Carr Sr., the project's supervising architect and a member of one of the city's founding families. The Hill Building's shape was not its only hint of things to come, for Carr's firm, in its own right and as an incubator of architects, would play a huge role in Durham building into the next millennium.

According to Robert W. "Judge" Carr, who now heads the firm his father established in

Central Carolina Bank Building, 1940 *(Courtesy of North Carolina Collection, Durham County Library)*

1926, George Watts Carr came to architecture in a roundabout way. As a young husband and father, he owned a shoe store on Main Street—until his partner absconded with the store's money. Carr was left "in a bad way," but his wife encouraged him to take up the artistic talent he had abandoned. Having built model buildings out of shoeboxes as a hobby, he enrolled in an architecture course by correspondence; Judge Carr remembers his father sitting up late, studying in the family home.

Favored with social and business connections in the tobacco and textile industries that were Durham's foundation, Carr began getting residential commissions. In 1933 he oversaw completion of the landmark Art Deco Snow Building downtown, and as business languished during the Great Depression, he and his partner Roy Marvin occupied themselves by reading design magazines, clipping ideas they liked, and drawing plans on speculation for the future.

Streetcar suburbs such as Trinity Park and Lakewood appeared around 1900, followed in the 1920s by Durham's first residential sections planned around golf courses—Forest Hills and then, between Durham and Chapel Hill, Hope Valley. George Watts Carr was commissioned to plan Forest Hills and designed a number of early residences in Hope Valley.

Much of the population, though, was accommodated far more modestly. Mill villages spread around the booming cigarette plants and cotton mills, and black enterprise boosted itself in Durham as the supplier, developer, builder, and insurer to residents and businesses of color. An unusually high percentage of residential units in Durham have been and are renter- as opposed to owner-occupied. The figure was 71 percent, compared with 44 percent nationally and 42 percent in North Carolina in 1940, when a survey by the Works Progress Administration found that 62 percent of the town's living spaces were "substandard." That revelation spurred civic pride into a burst of energy and activity to improve housing conditions, which was only delayed by the United States' entry into the Second World War.

In the 1930s the cigarette economy continued to boom, and the James B. Duke bequest of 1924 fueled the construction industry and services for a growing civilian, student, and staff population. But Depression constraints that turned Art Deco into Art Moderne in most of the country largely bypassed Durham during this period of architectural expansion. The beginning of the war brought a challenge to Durham's housing stock, as the families of GIs training at nearby Camp Butner flocked into the city. The war also produced a reservoir of spendable wealth and pent-up demand for consumer amenities, including education under the GI Bill, medical care, and housing that would fuel an economic boom in the late 1940s and early 1950s.

During the war and the years following, many new architectural design projects acquired an appearance of nouveau austerity. This boost to no-nonsense Modernism was primarily due to the shortage of construction manpower and materials for civilian building needs. One may see a case in point by comparing the 1939 Fowler Building at the south end of the American Tobacco factory complex with a six-story factory built by the Liggett & Myers Tobacco Company in 1948. Both are big, Fowler's factory enclosing 125,000 square feet and L&M's 340,000. However, where the Fowler's bulk is relieved by eye-catching verticals of brick pilasters and wall-length courses of glass, the L&M factory is an exercise in mass, minimally relieved by alternating bands of red and magenta brick broken by casement windows so small that they afford little visual relief from the overall impression of solid walls.

Snow Building *(Courtesy of Frank DePasquale)*

Reflecting wartime modesty with a morale-boosting spirit, the Union Bus Station—opened in 1942 to serve, in large measure, traveling servicemen and now demolished—featured severe geometrics and dominating horizontal lines with expanses of yellow brick, but its pronounced entrance bay was decorated with vertical columns of recessed glass blocks and a curved metal awning to suggest speed, streamlining, and the Art Deco lurch toward the future.

Right across Main Street, the postwar boom in consumer spending led the Sears, Roebuck Company to construct its first full-service department store in

Durham bus station
(Courtesy of Wyatt Dixon papers, Duke University Rare Book, Manuscript, and Special Collections Library)

Durham. It opened to great fanfare on March 6, 1947, and looked like the bus station's larger companion piece. A vertical sign, jutting from the street front at right angles to the sidewalk, reflected a similar feature on the bus station, but Sears's other lines were strictly on the level—that is, horizontal. Flat awnings shaded sidewalk-level display windows, with the corner awning several feet above those on the street and parking lot sides. Facing the parking lot, the show windows and entrance were dominated by two stories of yellow brick wall where alternating recessed string courses set off a flat rectangle that proclaimed "Sears Roebuck and Co." While the broad windows filled with merchandise enticed passing pedestrians up close, motorists seeing the brave new store from a bit farther away must have found the view somewhat intimidating. That quality was magnified in the 1970s, when Sears moved to a new store in the Northgate shopping center and Durham County took over the building for social-service offices.

If the giant retailer retained some Art Deco elements, Durham's education establishment was heading in another direction. Duke University, epitomizing academic tradition with its Georgian East and neo-Gothic West campuses, began building in a style described as "stylized Georgian" and "20th-century post office." In 1948 the red-brick Physics and Engineering buildings went up to the west of the university's signature chapel, downhill from the main campus and screened from it by fifty yards of woods. While their plain façades are relieved

with stone courses and window headers, the two buildings are a utilitarian, if Georgian-inflected, departure from the university's medieval flamboyance of two decades before, and their style was continued with the Graduate Center and Hanes House dormitories, constructed just north of Duke Hospital in 1950 and 1951.

Meanwhile, back in town, the postponed drive to clean up Durham's slums revived in 1945, and its proponents found themselves in the vanguard of a nationwide movement. The *New York Times Magazine* called urban blight "our number one national disgrace" in hailing the Federal Housing Act of 1949, a measure establishing what came to be called "Urban Renewal." Along with devising building codes and bulldozing shanties, Durham latched onto the federal mandate to enter the public-housing business in 1953. The city's first projects, Few Gardens (white) and McDougald Terrace ("colored"), both opening in the depressed districts east of downtown, afforded tenants clean and safe accommodations with up-to-date amenities such as complete kitchens and indoor bathroom facilities.

Urban renewal was informed by the same can-do, quick-fix spirit that had led the recent war effort, and its architecture owed much to the prewar Bauhaus, or Internationalist, perspective that celebrated mass production and eschewed decoration.

New Forces

Buildings and how they look are not just functions of use and ideology. The overriding concerns are practical, and architects and builders have to live and work with what materials and funds are available. "Contemporary architecture is architecture for the time you live," says the architect Frank DePasquale, who first came to Durham as a GI at Camp Butner and returned after the war to stay. In the postwar period architects in North Carolina had access, at reasonable prices, to wood, brick, and tile, as well as steel and concrete. Fancier material, such as limestone and granite, was prohibitively expensive, and designs reflected that fact as well as the ideas being espoused in architecture schools—such as the one just established at North Carolina State College in Raleigh.

What is now the North Carolina State University (NCSU) School of Design was founded in 1948, and its first dean was the architect Henry Kamphoefner, a Midwesterner steeped in Internationalism and the Prairie Style of Frank Lloyd Wright. Wright became one of Kamphoefner's visiting professors, along with such luminaries of the field as Ludwig Mies van der Rohe, Walter Gropius, Buckminster Fuller, and Lewis Mumford, helping to train new generations of North Carolina architects, including DePasquale, John L. Atkins, Philip Freelon, John Thompson, Felix Markham, and Edgar Toms Carr (son of Robert Winston Carr and grandson of George Watts Carr Sr.).

The war had proved a boon to the Carr firm, which won the contract to design Camp Lejeune on the North Carolina coast for the Marines. Interviewing him for the job, an admiral asked Carr how many architects he had on staff. In fact, he had only one, his partner Roy Marvin, but he knew that the Depression had left architects all over the state out of work. So Carr told the brass that he could get the staff he needed, and got the job. By 1945 Carr had "a real fine architectural team" to bring back to Durham. With the addition of Joe Rivers, Vernon Harrison, Jack Pruden, and his son Robert W. Carr, the firm proceeded to design and build hospitals all over North Carolina. In 1951 the U.S. Army chose the firm for a new, $12 million Veterans Hospital in Durham. Opened April 10, 1953—the same month Durham celebrated its centennial—the hospital became the city's fifth (after Watts, Lincoln, Duke, and McPherson), strengthening the town's identity as a medical center and laying more groundwork for an economic transformation that no one could have foreseen at the time.

In truth, Durham in 1953 was a complacent city. There were acknowledged social needs—as detailed in a five-part newspaper series by the Duke sociologist Howard Jensen—and civic leaders fretted over traffic congestion downtown during a centennial-week radio panel, but with its factories churning out cigarettes, stockings, towels, and B.C. Headache Powders, things seemed to be

running just fine. Nevertheless, developments were going on in and around Durham that would radically affect the city even as its stature as an industrial power was slipping.

McPherson Hospital
(Courtesy of Mrs. Samuel McPherson)

Despite a rising population, between 1945 and 1959 Durham would fall from second to fourth place among central North Carolina's major manufacturing centers. (The others were Raleigh, Charlotte, Greensboro, and Winston-Salem.) In that time Durham fell from third to last as a wholesaler, and its average weekly wage ($64.41 in 1959, or $460.20 in 2007 dollars) from second to last; and industrial employment, while increasing elsewhere, decreased by 19 percent.

In architectural terms, "contemporary design" in the late 1940s to early 1950s meant simplicity of shape, such as the severe brick walls of Sears and L&M's New Factory. Architects avoided designs that required cuts in the brick, which were expensive and required extra structural support, such as stone headers over windows and doorways. As the 1950s went along, costs dropped and new materials and products came on the market, such as sheetrock, aluminum exterior siding, plastics, and prefabricated modules, which accelerated the pace of construction, especially for the booming home market.

The 1950s manifested the popularity of the Prairie Style. Low, long "ranch-style" homes replaced the Cape Cod and Bungalow styles favored before and just after the war in new subdivisions north and west of town. Some homeown-ers went truly avant-garde: the Benjamin Boyce home (1952) on Dwire Place in Duke Forest, designed by Lawrence A. Enersen, a student of Walter Gropius at Harvard, was judged by many Durham folk as "daring" and "severe"—as Boyce put it in a written history of his home in the 1980s. The house plans won praise from the American urban critic Lewis Mumford, as did the finished product from the British art critic Herbert Read. The Boyce home is faced with platinum gray vertical siding and dark gray horizontal panels over the front door and windows. Outside, a pink-brick terrace leads under the windows, through the entrance, and for several inches inside; the color is repeated in the chimney and fireplace. The home's east and west sides are continuous windows upstairs and down, shaded by roof and wall extensions; interior and exterior are further related by color, the exterior gray continuing on interior plaster and echoed by gray slate mantel and window ledges, and a dark blue-green on inside and outside doors. Boyce was particularly charmed by an inte-rior newel post, designed by Roy Gussow, a design professor at North Carolina State who called it a "hyperbolic parabola." Constructed of small steel rods, the post has curves that make an intriguing counterpoint with the vertical lines of an interior screen that separates living and dining rooms.

Such "daring" also applied to Durham's religious institutions, which went International in the 1950s and would stay with that style for quite some time. For those used to getting their religion in traditional forms, the decade brought

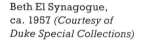
Beth El Synagogue, ca. 1957 *(Courtesy of Duke Special Collections)*

architectural departures that were dramatic if not downright radical. While the red-brick building of Northgate Presbyterian on Roxboro Street (1953) stuck with a Classical Revival thrust toward heaven, the city's Hebrew and Roman Catholic congregations were in the vanguard with low, visually grounded sanctuaries emphasizing the new looks of brick, glass, and dominating horizontals. While the new Church of the Immaculate Conception, designed by John D. Latimer of Durham, replaced an older building on the Chapel Hill Street lot that the congregation had occupied since 1906, the move of Beth El Congregation was architectural, geographic, and symbolic. Based in East Durham since 1905—first in a former Christian church on Liberty Street, and from 1921 in a new synagogue at Holloway and Queen—Beth El's new home was on Watts Street, in the Trinity Park neighborhood adjacent to the Duke East Campus. The changes represented growth for the congregation, dissolution of the old Jewish neighborhood as its members moved out to new subdivisions, and the increasing number of Duke and UNC-Chapel Hill families who not only became members but took leadership roles in the synagogue.

Faced with losing its home on Vickers Avenue to the Durham Expressway, St. Paul's Lutheran Church began planning a move of its own in 1964, and after securing a lot at the corner of Cornwallis and Pickett roads just south of the Duke Forest neighborhood, it chose Walter C. Burgess of Raleigh as its architect. When construction bids ran almost double the church's $350,000 building budget, Burgess and the congregation made cutbacks and compromises wherever possible, including eliminating (for the time being) two wings that were to extend from the nave and abandoning prestressed concrete in favor of brick

St. Paul's Lutheran Church (*Courtesy of Amanda van Scoyoc and Eli Van Zoeren*)

for the exterior. Burgess did not live to see the building finished, but it came in
on time and even a bit under budget, and was dedicated December 8, 1968.

St. Paul's is a rectangular box, its thirty-foot height accentuated by eleven
buttress-like protrusions spaced evenly along each side wall. To Cornwallis
Road, St. Paul's presents a wall of solid brick, relieved by recessed bays between the "buttresses" and a stair-step roofline leading to a central cross. At
the far end of the sanctuary, a glass-walled, breezeway-like room forms the
main entranceway, which opens to the side parking lots rather than the street.
This breezeway also connects the sanctuary with a low, flat-roofed education
wing, which forms the bar in the church's traditional cruciform configuration.
The education wing's low profile is offset by strong vertical windows, which
also replicate the sanctuary's upwardly thrusting lines.

By contrast, St. Luke's Episcopal Church at Hillandale Road and Interstate
85 has emphatic horizontals topped by a pyramidal roof that reaches thirty-five
feet above the sanctuary's central altar, and is topped in turn with a fifty-two-
foot steeple, whose erection was toasted with a bottle of Cold Duck on August
7, 1970. Designed by Frank DePasquale, also a parishioner, the building en-
closes 12,500 square feet in a Greek cross plan that puts no worshiper more
than seven rows from the altar. Seating flanks the altar on three sides, with
organ and choir on the fourth; the pulpit is set behind and to one side of the
altar, which is square itself and raised one step above floor level. Exposed steel
beams support the roof, resting on load-bearing brick walls relieved by floor-
to-ceiling windows with wooden framing and doors.

The 1950s and 1960s

Modernism made strong showings on other institutional fronts through the 1950s and 1960s. By 1960 the School of Design at NCSU had graduated eleven classes of architects, exceeding 150 in number. These architects would play a major role in shaping the new architecture of Durham.

Additions to the Walltown and Holloway Street elementary schools, completed in 1955, and to Watts Hospital in 1956, were characterized by strong horizontals, flat roofs, and lots of glass. Northern and Southern High Schools, opened in 1955 and 1956, combined International features with Prairie proportions, sprawling across their grounds rather than rearing high above them. While the buildings' size and broad surrounding grounds still suggested their function, their design was a far cry from the bulk and classicism exemplified by such landmarks as Milburn and Heister's Neoclassical Durham High (1923), George Watts Carr's Colonial Revival Carr Junior High (1926), and R. R. Markley's Fuller School (1937). Such designs were typical of school architecture in the early twentieth century, and elevated primary education from the rustic "little red" archetype to the same weight, tradition, and authority expressed by buildings of government, finance, and religion. In the late twentieth century those allusions were replaced by broad, ground-hugging, un-institutional school facilities. The new "Contemporary" architecture would house students in spacious, bright, colored classrooms and ancillary support areas with much

Allen Administration Building, Duke University *(Courtesy of Amanda van Scoyoc and Eli Van Zoeren)*

day-lighting, respecting the age and humanity of the student. These schools are compatible with the land and part of the natural environment, disturbing as little as possible of the surrounding flora and fauna. In addition to their educational program, the schools' environmental settings serve an educational purpose.

NCC built its Shepard Library in 1947 to 1951 from plans drawn in 1937–38 that followed the university's established Georgian Revival style; subsequent construction at NCCU has followed the principles of the Bauhaus. Duke University left the red brick on its fringe, and for its Allen administration building (1954) and Wannamaker Hall dormitory (1957) went back to the concept of Julian Abele, the African-American architect from Philadelphia who had designed the Gothic West Campus in the 1920s and 1930s. In 1959 the university trustees decreed a physical barrier between architectural styles: "A green belt of not less than 150 feet in width [shall] enclose the section of the campus which has been developed in stone Gothic Architecture. Within this belt there should be a stand of trees . . . and no building or parking facilities." However, on Duke's older East Campus, the V-shaped Gilbert-Addoms residence hall retained a Georgian symmetry but applied it to a tan-brick and stone exterior.

Height and lightness, on the other hand, were hallmarks of the Home Security Life Building on Chapel Hill Street, a T-shaped structure hailed as "a new symbol of progress" in a special twenty-page newspaper supplement published for its opening in January 1959. Enclosing 80,000 square feet of floor space with aluminum siding and 24,000 square feet of glass, the building used a steel and reinforced-concrete frame to support five floors of large, open work space organized by movable partitions and with a temperature kept between 70 and 78 degrees by a state-of-the-art heating and air-conditioning system. The design, by the Raleigh firm of Milton Small—a disciple of Mies—with consultation by the New York architect Aldo Rossi, was a victory for Home Security's younger generation. The company's founder, John Sprunt Hill, favored a traditional Southern look, but his son and grandson, George Watts Hill Sr. and Jr., the firm's chairman and president, liked modern architecture and managed to prevail in the family's clash of tastes. The building was also a victory for the new generation of architects produced by institutions such as NCSU, whose Modernist, Internationalist, and Contemporary thinking often "hit a brick wall" in the real world of paying clients.

Tastes and times were clashing downtown as well, as the "Camelot" era approached and industrial giants proclaimed "Better living through chemistry" and "Progress is our most important product." Wachovia Bank abandoned its long-time quarters in the Italianesque Geer Building, intending to build anew on the same site at the northeast corner of Main and Corcoran streets. However, when Thalheimer's department store deserted its still-new glass-and-steel building, just across the intersection of Main and Corcoran, in favor of Lakewood Shopping Center, Wachovia simply moved over—still making the implicit statement that the bank was keeping up with the times. Subsequently, the part of the Geer Building that Wachovia had occupied was demolished, leaving only a fragment of classical archway, a vacant lot, and the vault, swathed in Cosmoline and buried where it stood under ground. American Tobacco, located beside the city's point of origin at Blackwell and Pettigrew streets, hid its original Bull Durham building (1874) behind a screen of hip pink aluminum.

(Above)
Geer Building symbol—
Phoenix Rising from the
Ashes *(Courtesy of Frank
DePasquale)*

(Left)
Geer Building, ca. 1910
*(Courtesy of North Carolina Collection, Durham
County Library)*

Geer Building, Durham, N. C.

Residence of Mr. B. N. Duke, Durham, N. C.

About the same time, Duke University decided that the Four Acres mansion
of its patron Benjamin N. Duke (1910) had outlived its upkeep—specifically,
its wiring—as guest quarters. An antiquated Chateauesque Revival residence,
just across Duke Street from the new Home Security Building and across Chapel Hill Street from an A&P that had replaced Benjamin Duke's first mansion,
it was sold to the North Carolina Mutual Insurance Company, founded in Durham in 1898 and subsequently the largest black-owned insurance company in
the world. The Mutual tore down the mansion and in its place erected what
would become the city's most distinctive and architecturally distinguished
building of the late twentieth century. Vice President Hubert Humphrey was
on hand for the new Mutual's dedication on April 2, 1966. The Modernist,
fourteen-floor building, in pre-cast concrete and steel, was designed by Wel-
ton Becket and Associates of Los Angeles. It rose from the highest point in
Durham to, as Becket said, "face the city in all directions" from a lobby-floor
elevation of 419 feet.

The four identical faces were divided into vertical thirds by twin support
columns, which left the building's corners dramatically cantilevered thirty-
four feet from their supports (they were later reinforced with corner supports).
Following the Modernist aesthetic—and the architectural and engineering
collaboration required by new materials and mechanical systems—the Mutual's design displays its structure of large, open floors around a central core.
Floors alternate between recessed glass walls and projecting walls of concrete-
framed vertical windows that strikingly combine vertical and horizontal lines
while producing a visual play of light and shadow as well as providing a degree
of interior protection from direct sunlight. The ground floor is surrounded
by a pedestrian concourse, and the floors above are supported by a system of

twenty-eight pre-cast, post-tensioned concrete Vierendeel trusses. Interior amenities included four high-speed elevators, a vertical conveyor system for mail distribution (a first in the East), and a four-zone system for climate control. At 625 feet above sea level, the Mutual's penthouse afforded the highest vantage point in the city. The tallest pre-cast, post-tensioned building at that time in the United States (Beckett's taller Gulf-Life Building in Jacksonville, Florida, was not completed until 1967), the Mutual won top honors from the Prestressed Concrete Institute and recognition by *Forbes Magazine* as one of the ten outstanding buildings of 1966 and by *Fortune* as one of the top ten of the decade.

North Carolina Mutual, photograph by Charles Cooper *(Courtesy of the Herald-Sun)*

However, while Durham gained one architectural landmark downtown, it was losing others. America's postwar car culture manifested itself on several fronts in Durham. In 1952 a new boulevard opened between Durham and Chapel Hill, the university village eight miles to the southwest. Traffic congestion had already alarmed downtown merchants, and in 1956 Durham gained its first suburban shopping center, on University Drive between the white Forest Hills and the black St. Theresa neighborhoods. A second shopping center, Wellons Village on the eastern edge of town, followed in 1959. A third, Northgate, was built overlooking the U.S. 70 Bypass (future Interstate 85) in 1960.

To the southeast, in what had once been known as the "dark corner" of Durham County, the Research Triangle Park was just beginning. Inspired by the success of the technological corridor along Route 128 in Boston, Romeo Guest, a builder in Greensboro, convinced Governor Luther Hodges that something similar could be done in central North Carolina, taking advantage of the proximity of UNC-Chapel Hill, NCSU, and Duke. In 1955 Hodges created a commission to study creation of an industrial-research complex in the area. Frank Pierson, head of the Durham Chamber of Commerce, was cool to the idea, and support for the Research Triangle from Durham lagged behind that from Raleigh and Chapel Hill, reflecting longstanding jealousies among the three municipalities. Duke University and the banker Watts Hill Sr. were enthusiastic about the park, however, and brought Durham into the mix by the time ground was broken for the first buildings in late 1959. The next year the federal government announced that it would locate some laboratories in the park, and Durham County's first true suburb, Parkwood, went up on the park's perimeter.

On the other side of town, Duke University added a new red-brick Biological Sciences building in 1961 and a building for the Law School in 1962, the latter's plain exterior relieved by a stone entranceway featuring six squared Doric columns as a nod to precedent. With the Baby Boom generation due to reach college age in 1964 and the Sputnik-scared feds pouring money into higher education and scientific research, the university embarked on an audacious "Fifth Decade" program of building and expansion.

The Freeway and Downtown

Washington Duke Hotel, ca. 1925 *(Courtesy of North Carolina Collection, Durham County Library)*

In the meantime, even as the Mutual tower rose, inner Durham was in the throes of urban renewal and schemes to revitalize downtown. A bond issue in 1960 paved the way for work to begin on a through-town freeway, meant to both alleviate congestion and provide easy access from Durham to the Research Triangle Park. Work had begun by 1967, but its first leg, when opened in 1970, extended only from Chapel Hill Street to Alston Avenue. It would be three more years before the road extended to the park, and twenty-four years before it was complete to I-85. Just north of the Freeway, urban renewal was under way in Hayti, Durham's original black section; once a showplace for African-American enterprise, Hayti by 1960 had become the city's worst enclave of crime, disease, poverty, and general blight. The Jack Tar Hotel (originally the Washington Duke in 1925), a sixteen-story structure at the heart of downtown beside the Central Carolina Bank tower, gave in to the automotive age by adding a motel-style addition, complete with rooftop swimming pool and courtyard, connected with the main building by a glass-and-steel pedestrian bridge spanning Corcoran Street. One victim of downtown renewal was the Southgate Jones Sr. residence on Chapel Hill Street, a Victorian mansion that Jones had offered to the city for a local-history museum in the 1940s. The

Union Station, photo-
graph by John Flow-
ers (Courtesy of Frank
DePasquale)

house was replaced in 1967 by the concrete and functional Downtowner (later
Heart of Durham) Motel. Also in 1967, the Italian Renaissance Revival Union
Station, built in 1905 for joint use by the passenger railroads serving Durham,
was torn down in favor of a parking garage and the Downtown Loop.

For downtown proper, a warren of odd-angled and narrow streets, there was
a plan to create a pedestrian-friendly mall along Main Street from Five Points
to Church, with off-street parking facilities, restricted vehicular access, and
the Loop road to enclose the central downtown ridge. Conceived by the consultant Julian Tarrant of Richmond and presented to the City Council and
Downtown Development Association in October 1959, the plan had for its
centerpiece, besides the mall, a monumental municipal government center.
Tarrant located the center at the northeast corner of downtown, in the area
then defined by Chapel Hill, Holloway, Mangum, and Cleveland streets—the
former site of a tobacco warehouse that had burned in 1944. The Council referred the plan to a committee, but after discovering a $1 million surplus in the
city budget, it voted to go ahead and buy the property.

What ensued is a prime example of how conflicts and contradictions affect
architecture. By 1963 a new city government complex was indeed taking form
downtown. Designed by the Carr firm, the complex consisted of three build-

ings: a new fire station #1 on the east side of Morgan Street Extension at the intersection of Holloway Street, and the proposed police headquarters, City Council chambers, and seven-story office building on the west side of Morgan Street. Frank DePasquale, who had joined the Carr firm in February 1962, was the designing architect for the project and had purposely separated the fire station from the two other general public buildings for safety reasons. The police building, City Council chambers, and City Hall office building were placed on the west side of the Morgan Street Loop extension. The police building would be at the north side of the site and the City Hall office building on the south side, parallel to Holloway Street (City Hall Plaza). The two buildings would be connected by a continuous one-story structure which would become the main entrance to the two buildings from Mangum Street. In the center of the connection would be a council chamber capped by a dome. One level down, a large enclosed parking facility would be achieved from Mangum to Morgan Street.

For lack of funds, only two buildings were constructed: the fire station and the police building. At this point in the cold war, nuclear attack was regarded as a serious threat, and the city fathers, looking to the future, had added a civil defense command post and police communication center below the parking garage of the police building. The two buildings, finished in the mid-1960s, are International in style, with Federal and even Classical touches to suggest their official stature. Both have symmetrical rectangular façades with rectangular columns enclosing large porticoes at the entrances, flanked by vertical window recesses, and both are sheathed with light gray stone and buff-colored brick. Material and design tie the two government buildings to the Classical Revival First Baptist Church one block northeast of the fire station, and at the time within clear view of it.

By the time the city was ready to proceed with its City Hall, there were new

Firehouse *(Courtesy of Amanda van Scoyoc and Eli Van Zoeren)*

occupants in the Council seats and the mayor's chair. The job of designing City Hall went not to Carr's firm but to John D. Latimer and Associates of Durham. Originally from Massachusetts, John Latimer turned an early interest in drawing toward a career in architecture. Influenced by the textile industry he was exposed to by his father, the head of Mount Hope Finishing Company in Butner, Latimer got his start designing textile factories. Big and outgoing with a Boston accent, a colorful character whom one former colleague described as a "blond Adonis," Latimer readily made and nurtured business contacts that brought him a tremendous amount of industrial development work across North Carolina. Like Carr's firm, Latimer's became an incubator for rising young architects, and in the 1970s, with the national economy in decline and builders doing more of their own design work, Latimer turned to more modest projects. In Durham those included the Cedar Terrace office park in the late 1960s and Rogers-Herr Junior High School.

Latimer's firm tossed out the Carr plans and went with something wholly new. With John L. Atkins III—son of the longtime Democratic Party boss Les Atkins—as supervising architect, the new City Hall filled what had been a parking lot between Police Headquarters and Trinity Methodist Church. Faced with dark, purplish brick and stone panels, the design was influenced by some newly fashionable environmental concerns and incorporated materials and angles as part of the heating and cooling system. In another break with convention, the firm's associate Bill Kingsbury told the *Durham Sun*, rather than create wide-open interior spaces, the Latimer floor plan was "a conscious effort to break up the linear feeling."

Inside and out, the building is a mix of levels, angles, and shapes. Facing the Police Headquarters—the front of which it totally obscures—the City Hall presents a series of stepped floors above a connecting patio at the level of the Council chamber. Its rear face, opposite the church and the Tempest Building, suggests a department store. Pedestrian access to City Hall and the Police building (now housing the City-County Planning Department) is by a staircase from Mangum Street, set to replicate the angles of downtown's main street axes; by a sidewalk from the Loop; and by a street-level entrance off City Hall Plaza (formerly a section of Holloway Street).

The new City Hall opened for business in the summer of 1977. At the same time it was going up, another design by Latimer (done in conjunction with the Raleigh architect Roger Clark, a former Latimer associate), a regional headquarters for the Public Service

City Hall *(Courtesy of Amanda van Scoyoc and Eli Van Zoeren)*

Company of North Carolina, was under construction across the Loop, between the Fire Station and the Baptist Church. The Public Service Building is faced in the same dark brick as City Hall, and architecturally is a smaller companion to it. For the Public Service Building, the Latimer firm won highest honors for excellence in design from the North Carolina Chapter of the American Institute of Architects in 1979. The Durham public, however, was not so kind in its response to City Hall.

Even before city employees contended with leaky roofs and temperatures inside the building that dropped into the fifties, the attorney (and future mayor) Charles Markham called the design "utterly depressing" in a published letter to the *Durham Morning Herald*: "a pollutant to the visual environment of Durham." The newspaper complimented the interior sense of spaciousness and light, but found the Council chamber "chilly," perhaps "more suited to a panel of judges," and the exterior tending "to jar the eye. It suffers from being jammed in between the police headquarters, which it bulks over, and Trinity United Methodist Church. . . . The styles clash and the over-all appearance is one of clutter."

Problems also attended the opening in 1978 of the new Durham County Judicial Building, across Main Street from the 1916 Courthouse. A Bauhaus-eclectic building of six stories, it was designed by Archie R. Davis of Durham; his associate Balford Hackney was assigned to be project architect. Delays plagued construction; by August 1977 it was apparent that the original completion target of November 1 would be missed by months and that occupancy was still more than a year away. County Manager Ed Swindell acknowledged difficulties with weather and a plumbing contractor, but said the delay was ultimately due to the project's scale: "When you get into a project of this size, you sometimes run into problems of coordination," he told a reporter for the *Morning Herald*. By that point, however, Durham's legal community was already complaining that the building was too small to handle the county's workload. After it was finally occupied more than a year late, its elevators, locking system, and drains presented a succession of headaches for those working there, for Hackney, and for the lawyers who got to arbitrate conflicting claims between the county and the general contractor, W. J. Megin Inc.

Leaving Downtown

Problems were of course nothing new in downtown Durham. The commercial exodus that began in the 1960s accelerated through the 1970s with the expansion of Northgate Shopping Center into an enclosed mall in 1972 and the opening of the South Square Mall on the strategically vital Chapel Hill Boulevard—which had become a retail corridor linking the two towns. Sears, Thalheimer's, and Belk were among the downtown anchors that left for the suburbs, and some planners, citizens, and downtown interests—including the Downtown Revitalization Foundation—were ready to face the prospect that the area's retail career was over.

As far back as 1959, economic analysts predicted that downtown Durham, like other American downtowns, was fated to lose business to shopping centers more conveniently located for the buying public, and that its future lay in government, finance, and modest services for personnel employed in those fields. Others, with economic and emotional ties to downtown, kept the faith.

George Watts Hill Sr., chairman of the board of Central Carolina Bank, led the charge to save downtown Durham. The Durham Hotel and Motel (the erstwhile Jack Tar), in the center of the city, were owned by the Hill Family Foundation. For several years during the 1960s, Hill and his sisters, Frances Fox and Valinda DuBose, had financially supported the hotel as it experienced a low 30 percent occupancy rate, high operating costs, and taxes. During these years $300,000 was spent on renovations to the dining area and kitchen facility to compete with the new motels built in the area. Property taxes continued to reflect the high values of the very prosperous hotel of the 1940s and 1950s. In an attempt to reduce losses, Hill, in a meeting with Durham County commissioners, requested a reevaluation of the hotel and a reduction in property taxes to reflect the motel's present-day value. The commissioners rejected his request.

Property values continued to decline in downtown Durham through the later 1960s and 1970s as businesses fled to new shopping centers. The foundation continued to operate the hotel as it searched for new uses, such as a graduate center for Duke University or a senior center and senior residence for the city, with no success.

In 1974 Frank DePasquale was discussing downtown Durham's concerns with his classmate Richard Bell, a landscape architect in Raleigh. Bell likened downtown Durham to the beautiful medieval cities of Europe and expressed how its small size could allow it to become a pedestrian mall free of traffic. DePasquale, fascinated with the idea, introduced Bell to Watts Hill, who also was impressed. Hill then undertook the development of a new downtown Durham plan by Bell and his associate Wayne Taylor. "The Bull Is Back" became the official motto of the plan.

Bell's plan was published in the May–June issue of *NC Architect* magazine, a themed edition devoted to Durham and titled "What Has Happened to Our Downtowns?" For Durham, Bell stepped away from customary practice, which sees each project as an entity within itself circumscribed by property lines and budgets, and instead regarded downtown holistically. His plan was an attempt at social, as well as aesthetic, engineering (as is any project in "revitalization"): in its projected imposition of humane order upon human chaos, the plan even evoked the stylized utopianism of such nineteenth-century urban theorists as Jean-Nicolas-Louis Durand of the French École Polytechnique and the leftist Spaniard Ildefonso Cerdá y Suñer, as well as the "notional" urban cartography described in the study *Image of the City* (1960) by the MIT planner Kevin Lynch. The first of its four major projects suggested for Durham was grandly called a "Line of Life."

"Upon walking the streets of downtown Durham," Taylor wrote, "seeing the concrete bunkers with small trees in them decorating the streets, feeling the terrible danger in crossing streets filled with motorists fighting for parking spaces, noticing the beauty of many of the older buildings which remained, ascertaining the availability for urban renewal properties for open spaces and parks, discerning the cultural centroid of the downtown churches, upon groping through the terrible clutter of poles, posts, meters, directional signals and devices, and upon comparing the vacated stores with new financial institutions—we noted that all pointed to the fact that *somewhere* we, the designers and planners of this city—collectively were 'missing the boat.' We were building curbs, gutters, buildings, bunkers, poles, posts, and other new artifacts, yet *the city was dying.* Everyone knew it, a revitalization commission was created to study it, a report documented it, and another artifact—a civic center—was proposed to save it."

Like the advocates of the Tarrant plan of 1959, the Bell group emphasized pedestrian access and limited vehicular access. Bell's plan went further, though, advocating an urban park to surround the four downtown churches (First Baptist, Trinity Methodist, First Presbyterian, and St. Philip's Episcopal), and green space and residential development adjacent to the central "Bull Durham District" to the north and northeast. Within that district there would be plazas, fountains, sculptures—the "Line of Life"—with nightspots, restaurants, coffeehouses, and specialty shops as well as offices, all together creating the same sort of "mutual admiration society" that worked so well for suburban malls. "Traffic. Parking. Environment. People. Stimuli," the published plan concluded. "Each of the factors, when coordinated in a positive effort, can serve to create an efficient, productive and inviting climate for a strong central business district. To put it in a word, the Central Business District needs pizzazz."

With the published report, Hill announced that he would finance a section of downtown at the intersection of Corcoran and Parrish streets with fountains, landscaping, plazas, and lighting. In addition, he would completely renovate the hotel and motel, adding a major meeting room over Corcoran Street. Hill presented his concept to the Downtown Durham Foundation. A member of the board responded, "Watts, are you still trying to save that dead horse?"

A year later, on December 17, 1975, the Hills had the hotel imploded. That event, after years of discussion, finally attracted thousands of people to downtown Durham.

The Park

While the attention of Durham's movers and shakers seemed fixated—if not obsessed—on "bringing back downtown," through the 1960s and 1970s events were conspiring that would profoundly change the city and county economically, socially, geographically—and architecturally. If International Style and Modernism still ruled the "revitalizing" downtown, the Postmodernist future was taking shape on Duke's West Campus.

Edens Quad, Duke University (Courtesy of Amanda van Scoyoc and Eli Van Zoeren)

The Edens Quadrangle dormitories, opened in the fall of 1966, not only introduced undergraduates to the wonder of air conditioning but introduced to Duke building the use of pre-cast stone panels in place of laid stone, in an attempt to harmonize with the rest of the Gothic campus. The panels were something of a compromise, according to James Ward, Duke's architect from 1967 to 1983: not only was the stone supply at Duke's quarry near Hillsborough running low, but masons with the skill to use it were an all-but-vanished breed.

Along with the stone motifs, the Edens de-

Hanes Building, Research Triangle Park, photograph by Charles Cooper *(Courtesy of the Herald-Sun)*

sign applied verticality and human scale as well as other such Gothic features as narrow, recessed vertical windows and arched balustrades on upper-level walkways between the buildings. A more dramatic twist appeared on the red-brick Science Drive in 1968, with completion of the Paul M. Gross Chemistry Building. It employed large panels of Duke's characteristic Hillsborough granite and masses of concrete, offsetting its visual weight with repeated vertical lines of multistory windows and projecting service towers that rise a full story above roof level. A similar if more restrained Gothic-informed design went into the Nanaline Duke Research Center at the Medical School, completed the same year.

An even more remarkable, in places almost shocking, stylistic transformation was emerging at the Research Triangle Park. In 1959 construction began on the park headquarters, the Hanes Building. Finished in time for a dedication ceremony at Christmastime 1960, and housing the Research Triangle's own institute and foundation, the Hanes was designed by Lashmit, James, Brown and Pollock of Winston-Salem. It is an exercise in International Styling, two stories tall with emphatic horizontal lines, its white-brick exterior just slightly relieved by twelve shallow recesses for small windows and a glass-walled central entranceway recessed behind twin square columns. Tufted with low foundation plantings and surrounded by an expansive lawn, the Hanes Building makes a twenty-first-century viewer think of a hiccup on a putting green.

The Chemstrand Corporation Building, designed by Wigton-Abbott of New Jersey for the park's first industrial tenant and opened two months later, was a bit more adventurous: an elongated, two-story structure of 170,000 square feet, with glass dominating its brickwork and a three-story

section—for reception, administration, and a library—set asymmetrically
between the main wing and a cafeteria.

Before any buildings were occupied in the park itself, people who would
work in them were moving into the Parkwood subdivision. Just west of the
park and south of the city limits, Parkwood was innovative on several counts:
it had its own water and sewer system, and the developer offered Durham
County land on which to build a neighborhood school. Instead of the conventional grid, its modest homes were set along winding streets, with each residence adjoining woods or the neighborhood's twenty-six-acre lake.

Peace, quiet, and green spaces were part of the Research Triangle's pitch
from the start. The project, which began with 5,400 acres, was from the outset
conceived of as a vast college campus, with labs and offices separated by lawns
and woods. It was a novel idea at the time, but its sylvan tranquilities belied its
origin in the car culture.

The Burroughs Wellcome Building, a five-story, S-shaped, terraced and fac-
eted structure designed by Paul Rudolph in 1972, was sited so as to be a futur-
istic landmark from the Durham Expressway at Cornwallis Road. It was em-
blematic of new frontiers as conceived in Hollywood and was a backdrop for
the science-fiction movie *Brainstorm* (1983), which was set and mostly filmed
in the Triangle. The building's front and rear elevations slope at a thirty-degree
angle, such that each floor is smaller than the one below, while the ends display six-sided panels of beige limestone. Besides its "Spaceship" nickname, the
Burroughs Wellcome Building has been called "Cathedral" and "Acropolis"—
and represents Research Triangle architecture at its height of flamboyance. In
the Park and in Durham, it remains one of a kind.

Catching the wave, as the Park grew from twenty-one tenant companies to thirty-eight between 1969 and 1979, John Atkins III and two other Latimer architects, William L. O'Brien and C. Belton Atkinson, formed their own firm in 1975 and went after big jobs. Favored with Atkins's political advantage — "He knew all the governors," another local architect put it — by 2003, O'Brien/Atkins Associates had grown to 125 employees, headquartered in the Park, and its client list included such luminary firms as Glaxo, MCI, Cisco, and Biogen. In 1998 O'Brien/Atkins was named Firm of the Year by the state chapter of the American Institute of Architects.

Preservation

The Park continued to grow, reaching 7,000 acres and 108 tenant companies by the year 2000, but architectural innovation turned to architectural monotony — at least according to several architects commenting for a feature in the *Durham Sun* in 1987. One building after another was turned out in glass and brick, and the O'Brien/Atkins vice president for architecture, Philip Freelon, said, "We need to break out. In this market, there are cookbook applications on what is cheapest to build, [and that] contributes to buildings that look the same."

With the University Tower, a seventeen-story green-glass structure overlooking once–South Square Mall, and Peoples Security Building, a fifteen-story glass-walled structure downtown, stylistic tastes were taking another turn in Durham. Those buildings acknowledged the historical precedence of the longstanding Central Carolina Bank Building by topping out with spires, but they were far from Durham's cutting edge. That was squarely in the past.

Durham came late to historic preservation, a movement galvanized by the federal Historical Properties Act of 1966. It was 1974 before the disappearance of landmarks such as "Four Acres" and Union Station stirred citizens to form a Historic Preservation Society. Preservationists could only stand and watch as the landmark Durham Hotel was imploded in 1975, but early on they managed to have the eighteenth-century Stagville plantation in northeast Durham County preserved as a state historic property; they also began labors to save the St. Joseph's African Methodist Episcopal Church (1892), abandoned by its congregation in favor of a new, long, and low Internationalist home two miles farther out Fayetteville Street. However, with preservationist spirit running high in the wake of the national Bicentennial in 1976 and with the Durham County centennial approaching in 1981, the entire old business section was declared a National Register Historic District in 1978.

Durham was steadily growing outward, especially toward Research Triangle Park and Chapel Hill, the municipal population growing from just over 100,000 in 1970 to 187,000 in 2000 and the county's from 133,000 to 225,000.

New subdivisions flowed farther and farther from the city core, but at the same time venerable districts such as Trinity Park, adjoining Duke's East Campus, and Watts-Hillandale, between Watts Hospital (now the North Carolina School of Science and Mathematics) and the Hillandale Golf Course, became gentrified and highly fashionable.

A similar trend took hold in the newly historic business district, where "adaptive reuse" of distinguished buildings brought tax credits for the owners. In 1980 the Dutch investor Julius Verwoerdt bought the Kress Building (1933) on Main Street and left its Art Deco exterior intact while remodeling the space inside for offices and its penthouse for himself. The next year, a shopping mall, Brightleaf Square, replaced bulk tobacco in two of the red-brick warehouses, strategically located on the Gregson Street artery between the Expressway and Interstate 85 and a short walk from East Campus. Developed by the SEHED partnership—which included the Duke business professor W. Clay Hamner, President Terry Sanford of Duke and his son, Terry Jr., and Sanford's assistant Tom Drew—Brightleaf Square's renovation cost was about two-thirds that of new construction. At the same time Brightleaf opened, at Thanksgiving 1981, another local entrepreneur, J. Adam Abram, was turning another old brick

Courthouse detail
(Courtesy of Frank DePasquale)

tobacco warehouse into swanky condominiums across Duke Street from Durham High School.

"Durham's main asset downtown is its architecture," the director of Preservation North Carolina, Myrick Howard, said in 1985. "You need to capitalize on that." The Kress, Brightleaf, and Warehouse condominium projects were followed by a succession of adaptive renovations: the Durham High School and City Hall (1907) as headquarters for the Durham Arts Council and the Durham Hosiery Mill (1901) for elderly housing in 1988; the Courthouse (1916) for county offices in 1991; the Art Deco Durham Auditorium (1926) for the Carolina Theatre and, outside downtown, the County Prison (1925, later a tuberculosis sanitarium) on Broad Street for doctors and architects' offices in 1993; the Georgian Revival Public Library (1921) for offices in 1997; the Brodie Duke tobacco warehouse (1878) for the testing firm Measurement Inc. in 2000; and numerous others, including the American Tobacco factory complex, dating from 1874.

Adaptive restorations included residences, such as Sunnyside (1904) and the E. K. Powe House (1900), built for executives at the nearby Erwin Mills. Perched on a hilltop across Main Street and the railroad from East Campus, the stately homes had become rental hippie pads and an incubator for Durham's budding music and crafts scene in the late 1960s. Their condition, however, had deteriorated to the point of condemnation. At that point Brian South, a restoration specialist who had just moved to Durham from Charlotte, bought the houses and turned them into sparkling-fresh office condos.

Durham's embrace of adaptive reuse could be said to have started at Duke, where the Georgian East Campus Science Building was gutted and turned into the university's Art Museum in 1969. Designed by DePasquale, then of the Carr firm, the renovation is distinguished by its spiral staircase and a glass wall, which separates the lobby from the main gallery and allows a view into the main gallery from a second-floor balcony. The East Campus had its own fling with modernity in the Mary Duke Biddle Music Building, opened in 1974. It was designed by Edward Durrell Stone, the New York firm whose other credits include the Museum of Modern Art and the Kennedy Center. The low, partially subterranean building is distinguished by a surrounding patio, shaded by an overhanging flat roof, and backed by a colonnade of repeated archways.

E. K. Powe House
(Courtesy of Amanda van Scoyoc and Eli Van Zoeren)

(Below)
Mary Duke Biddle Music Building, Duke University *(Courtesy of Duke University Archives)*

Since then, however, Duke building has been characterized by variations on its signature Gothic, Georgian, and stone themes, from dormitories to medical labs and from football offices to parking garages—the last demonstrating that even the most utilitarian of structures, handled well, can still look classy.

"You can't assign a style" to Duke's late-twentieth-century architecture, said James Ward, whose office did not design buildings but rather functioned as the university's architectural critic and supervisor, with staff members assigned to each new project as "the eyes of the owner." Having established and nurtured good working relations with deans and department heads, Ward said, "We knew pretty much what their needs were," and by the time a program was ready to hand to a job architect, it was already well thought through and defined.

Duke's policy of the unitary Gothic look was established in the early 1960s, at the outset of the Fifth Decade growth and money-raising campaign. Henry Mayfield, of the Houston firm Caudell, Rollins, Scott, hired as supervising architect for construction at Duke, "had a real feel for what ought to take place," said Ward, whom Mayfield brought to campus in 1964. When Ward succeeded Mayfield, he sought to adjust to changing needs and rising costs without losing the architectural unity of the campus, and published a design manual for architects seeking to do business with Duke.

The Housing Boom

As the twentieth century came to a close, Durham had a plethora of commercial and institutional buildings in glass, brick, and steel, and myriad residential developments composed of winding streets, cul-de-sacs, and pseudo-traditional—"transitional"—houses that typically dwarfed their diminutive lots. Particularly after the economic dislocations of the 1970s, and the concurrently developing transience of the American workforce, the status of housing changed from a source of personal and familial identity—a source and symbol of stability—to that of an investment, purchased and often built with the expectation of temporary use, its design, siting, and marketing based on the promise of resale value as much as on livability. Financial institutions' lending policies, municipal zoning habits, the proliferation of by-the-numbers guides on how-to-build-a-subdivision, and the basic necessity for builders and real-estate salesmen to make a profit all encouraged the trend to buildings—residential and commercial both—that looked and functioned the same from coast to coast, as well as all through Durham and what was coming more and more often to be referred to as "the Triangle."

The economics of building and real estate brought geographic shifts to Durham. Construction crept north with the slow advance of water and sewer lines but flooded south toward the booming Research Triangle Park and the new highway corridors of N.C. 54 and Interstate 40. Durham filled in the formerly empty space between the park and Chapel Hill, and the two towns' limits advanced to meet from the 1952 Boulevard (U.S. 15-501) south almost to Chatham County. As the population bulk moved south, business followed. The area around the South Square Mall (1975) became for practical purposes the new downtown, as attorneys, accountants, bankers, realtors, and stockbrokers forsook the original business district. Architects and builders, though, must accommodate their work to changing times and tastes, and through the millennium's last thirty years those changes brought new and different demands.

Buildings, originally shelters and then shelters that made statements, increasingly became systems of climate control and communication, almost machines in themselves. The environmentalist movement, set off in 1962 by Rachel Carson's apocalyptic bestseller *Silent Spring*, and power prices, driven high by inflation and the energy crises of the 1970s, inspired demands for efficiency and conservation. The Americans with Disabilities Act (ADA) required designers—of new construction as well as retrofits—to provide ramps, doors, and restrooms that could accommodate wheelchairs. "Walkability" became an issue in the 1990s, leading designers to rethink the convention of surrounding buildings with parking lots and for-eyes-only lawns.

"Architecture reflects a lot of the contemporary mores," says Lucien Roughton, a former Latimer architect now head of his own firm in Durham. "When energy got to be a cause, passive solar popped up. [The Americans with Disabilities Act] was a big cause. Now we have 'green architecture': efficient, well-sited, energy-independent, 'high performance.' It's become the politically correct thing to do." Following "correctness" leads to neglect of other things, though, Roughton says. "Houses need to relate to their community. Maybe there is significant meaning, like a city hall. McDonald's is flashy to attract customers. A campus setting needs to respect the flow of people. Solar may run against other considerations, like keeping furniture from fading or a need for north light." Architects, after all, are artists deep down, and have values of their own. "The notion," Roughton said, "of just creating a box and sticking it on a piece of ground is just anathema."

Playing to the crowd has also led building in Durham to forms that are bizarre and darkly comic. The Southpoint Mall shopping center, opened in 2001 at Fayetteville Road and I-40, presented an imitation downtown, complete with statuary representing typically American townsfolk and billboards painted on the sides of buildings in the manner of the early 1900s. Supposedly a ploy to connect a generic shopping center with its location, the result is Bauhaus in drag, owing more to the fabricated nostalgia of Disney Inc.'s Main Street, USA, than to anything that ever existed in Durham, North Carolina—or anywhere else, for that matter.

Fin-de-siècle critics of American architecture and urban design, such as

James Kunstler in his *Geography of Nowhere* and the New Urbanist Andres Duany in *Suburban Nation*, have observed that developers of shopping malls and subdivisions attempt to deny the actual nature of their projects by naming them what they are not—"Commons," "Greens," and perhaps most absurdly, "Centres"—with the not-unreasonable expectation of attracting trade by invoking the mythic and nostalgic associations that those words have for generations that have never known the real thing.

Some other Durham developments reach for the past in ways that are more substantive and more reflective of the social-engineering impulse driven by the preservationist and environmentalist ethos and by reaction to the disasters of Urban Renewal. Trinity Heights is a mix of freestanding residences and townhouse condominiums that replicates, with remarkable success, the look and feel of its circa-1900 surroundings. With special dispensation from the city's zoning standards, houses are set close to the sidewalks; the result, in the view of the developer Bob Chapman, is that "someone standing on the sidewalk can converse with someone on the front porch in a normal tone of voice." Functional front porches, utilitarian alleyways for parking and trash collection, and "granny apartments" are other century-old amenities that con-

Trinity Heights townhouses *(Courtesy of Amanda van Scoyoc and Eli Van Zoeren)*

National Humanities Center *(Courtesy of Frank DePasquale)*

nect the new with the existing, all within easy "walkability" of the university and the trendy Ninth Street shopping and nightlife district.

To relieve traffic congestion and effect pedestrian safety, New Urbanist projects abandon the conventional wide, winding streets and cul-de-sacs in favor of the old grid layout. They also follow the principle of "mixed-use," setting offices, stores, and residences within walking distance, a pattern from pre-suburb cities that in theory reduces demand for vehicles and conserves green space by concentrating development in small areas. Designs for such "clusters" may follow Internationalist, Postmodernist, or other twentieth-century styles, but employ architectural unity and the functional as well as aesthetic relation of one building to another and buildings to open space to create the holistic sense of a village or campus. Examples are the Ninth Street Station and Triangle Center developments planned along an anticipated commuter rail line running from Chapel Hill through Durham, Research Triangle Park, and Cary as far as North Raleigh—and eventually, perhaps north through Durham County to Treyburn and the still-rural communities of Bahama and Rougemont.

Thus the latest in Durham design not only harks back to the city's early days but carries on the unitary (and, by implication, *com*-munitary) principle reaffirmed at Duke, in the 1960s, and by the even earlier Tarrant downtown plan and its Bell revision. "Back to the Future," however, is only a movie; golf-course spreads and so-called "McMansions" continue to go up as Durham expands; and whether the reactionary New Urbanism and Traditional Neighborhood will prove appealing to coming generations of homeowners, merchants, entrepreneurs, and financiers remains an open question for the next fifty years to answer.

Even as "tradition" informs building and design, one finds various plays on Bauhaus and Modernism. For example, the Hartman-Cox firm of Washington, D.C., designed the National Humanities Center in Research Triangle Park as a "monastic retreat for secular scholarship"—as described in the *AIA Journal* in May 1979. Though enclosing thirty thousand square feet, the building makes an understatement, nestled into woods at the end of a winding, sylvan drive, its glass-topped entrance almost hidden within a surrounding courtyard. While its white-painted brick walls give the center a clinical aspect, that impression is offset by a lavish use of glass, including a multitude of angled skylights that give the humanistic think tank the appearance of nothing so much as a greenhouse.

For the Burroughs Wellcome Fund Headquarters in the Research Triangle Park, the Charlotte firm of Perkins and Will went for a "regal and monastic" atmosphere, according to a case study prepared by the firm for North Carolina State University in late 2002. Like the Humanities Center, the building has an appearance that belies its 33,000-square-foot size. Nestled into landscaping that was part of its design from the outset, the building is clad in gray stone, with pink block inside a recessed entranceway that leads to a central interior courtyard. While the lines seem to hug the ground, the building's horizontals are relieved by the curved interior of its entranceway, dramatic verticals in columns and windows, and a circular opening above the entrance. The interior was designed for a "gallery feel," acknowledging its planned use for art exhibitions, and technical hardware is hidden to maintain the sense of austerity. All windows are operable, offices come in three arrangements, and conference rooms are designed for maximum flexibility in the face of changing tastes, times, and technology.

Meanwhile, in the face of changes, we may remember that it is not the rule but its exceptions, and not the ideologies but the people, who have the staying power. For instance, Clyde Lloyd's house on Nelson Street. At the time he built it, the style was already passé, the flat roof, curved walls, round windows, glass blocks, and overall look adapted from aircraft and automobile design. But the house has many stories to tell, best of all its own, and while many more structures that were stylish for their times have come, gone, and faded into anonymity, Lloyd's taste and handiwork were honored with a place on the Historic Preservation Society of Durham's tour of historic homes in 1998.

Sources

Bishir, Catherine W., and Michael T. Southern. *A Guide to the Historic Architecture of Piedmont North Carolina*. Chapel Hill: University of North Carolina Press. 2003.

"A Case Study of the Burroughs Wellcome Fund Headquarters, Research Triangle Park, NC." Charlotte: Perkins and Will Architects. 2002.

Hollingsworth, Harry D. *St. Luke's Episcopal Church, 1956–1981*. Durham: St. Luke's Episcopal Church. 1981.

Jacobs, Jane. *The Death and Life of Great American Cities*. New York: Vintage. 1961.

"What Has Happened to Our Downtowns?" *North Carolina Architect*, May–June 1975.

Phillips, Coy T. "City Pattern of Durham, N.C." *Economic Geography* 23 (October 1947): 233–47.

Roberts, Claudia. *The Durham Architectural and Historic Inventory*. Durham: City of Durham. 1982.

Rykwert, Joseph. *The Seduction of Place: The City in the Twenty-first Century*. New York: Pantheon, 2000.

Stephens, Robert Howard. "Down the Red Brick Road—and Back: Duke University Architecture 1948–1968." Master's thesis, Duke University, 1991.

Tilley, Doris B. *St. Paul's Lutheran Church, Durham, North Carolina 1923–1983*. Durham: St. Paul's Lutheran Church. 1983.

"You and Durham: City of Durham Annual Report," *Durham Morning Herald*, October 7, 1967.

4. Crafts

A CONDENSATION BY JILL WINTER
OF A LONGER VERSION
BY MARGARET PEPPER FLUKE

In the new, less stressful environment that accompanied the end of the Second World War, women in Durham and elsewhere, who had dedicated themselves so intensely to keeping their homes and families together, were drawn to the home arts. The artist Vivian Dai, who joined the Durham community in 1943, noted that women were "hungry to find something to do that would be fulfilling, useful, and creative." Through the GI Bill, postwar America also offered educational opportunities for returning servicemen and women. Many had time to rethink their career choices. In contrast to the repetitive, competitive process of mass production, the crafts process itself was appealing. The joy and satisfaction of work are restored when the maker creates a design and follows it through from raw material to finished piece. New opportunities for instruction were offered in all types of crafts, from pottery to woodworking to metalwork, and classes filled up rapidly.

Dai, Bob Black and Ormond Sanderson, Sid and Pat Oakley, and the seven women of Craft House were all instrumental in bringing the arts-and-crafts movement to Durham. Dai was the catalyst. Trained at the Newark School of Fine and Industrial Art, she founded the Creative Art Group for local painters in 1947. Vivian began teaching pottery and copper enameling classes in her home in 1953 and weaving in the early 1960s. At the time crafters were not considered artists, nor were they invited to participate in juried shows; but by 1971 she was able to say that "good crafts are now in the same category as art, and a tapestry will sell for as much as a painting."

The Creative Art Group became the Durham Art Guild in 1949, an organization instrumental in helping to form Allied Arts in 1954. Allied Arts (renamed the Durham Arts Council in 1975) was located in the Morehead Hills section of Durham, in a stately historic house called Harwood Hall, better known as the Watts House. It had no facilities for teaching pottery, weaving, or other crafts requiring special equipment. Nevertheless, the Art Guild sponsored a crafts fair there in 1958 as a fundraiser for Allied Arts, featuring demonstrations in woodworking, enameling, animal sculpture, wood inlay, jewelry making, and rug hooking. Known thereafter as the Allied Arts Fall Festival, the event was moved to the City Armory when its scope was expanded to include crafts from throughout the state.

In January 1961 Allied Arts bought and moved into the Foushee House at 810 Proctor Street. A ceramic studio was set up in the basement, with three Newton kick wheels and a Paragon electric kiln. The twelve members of a ceramics class taught there by Dai in the fall of 1965 eventually called themselves the Clay Club and met monthly in each other's homes. In 1966 Dai was asked to join the regional committee for a major juried exhibition at the North Carolina Museum of Art titled "Craftsmen Southeast '66."

Vivian Dai at her studio in Spruce Pine, NC *(Courtesy of Pepper Fluke)*

Durham artists whose work was selected for the show were Black (stoneware vase), Dai (rya rug), and Sanderson (stoneware, pewter and bronze "Standing Sarcophagus for Rejoicing Child": and "Sun Bird," a champleve enamel plaque with iron and gold deposit). Vivian's participation in that exhibition led her to urge Allied Arts to move beyond shows of the "bazaar" type to set new standards of quality, craftsmanship, and excellence. Juried selections would be unique pieces crafted from basic materials of clay, fiber, wood, glass, metal, leather, or paper—no kits, no manufactured molds, no pre-designed work.

With the assistance of fifty hard-working volunteers, Vivian Dai's vision became reality when the first Triangle Festival of Crafts opened in April of 1967, chaired by Virginia Osbourne and Pepper Fluke. The basement ceramics workshop at the Foushee House was transformed into an elegant craft gallery with special lighting, shelving, and plants by Jan Gregg and Ethel Bozarth. A large pottery division featured the work of Paul Minnis and Paul Hudgins. Florentina McKinney headed up the copper enameling division. Rugs, decoupage, silk screening, basketry, embroidery, silver jewelry, and mosaics were among the crafts exhibited and demonstrated. Candle making, rug hooking, creative stitchery, spinning and carding of wool, weaving, woodcarving, and violin making were all included. Susan Carlton Smith showed her miniature sculptures from natural, found materials—twigs, seeds, pods, fungus, butterfly wings. Janice and Richard Palmer organized a special section on children's crafts. The Triangle Festival of Crafts became an annual event. It was moved in 1978 to the new City Hall and then became a street fair, an event which continues to the present.

Craft Communities

By 1958 Bob Black and Ormond Sanderson had decided to stop their full-time teaching jobs and concentrate on craft arts as an alternative way of life. They created Straw Valley Gallery in a cabin, one of five buildings on property they rented from Ormond's uncle near the Durham-Chapel Hill Boulevard. Bob, an established potter, and Ormond, who did copper enameling, invited other local and nationally known craft artists to show their work.

Strawberry Fields Gallery, founded in 1969, was the creation of the potter, woodworker, and painter Sid Oakley and his wife Pat, whose talents included pottery, weaving, and stitchery. They wanted to build a campus that would be a crossroads for aspiring artists—a place to share ideas, learn, teach, or simply stop by for conversation. The Oakleys pursued their dream with hard work and personal sacrifice. They started with a $25,000 loan, sold all the furniture that Sid had made for their own home, and even slept on the floor. The property is now known as Cedar Creek Gallery and has fourteen buildings, including a state-of-the-art glass-blowing studio. The name was changed in 1973 when it became apparent that too many visitors thought they were coming to Creedmoor to pick their own strawberries.

Sid was best known for his porcelain oxblood red glaze pieces and pots with crystalline glazes. John Martin, a chemical engineer, came to Cedar

Sid and Pat Oakley at Cedar Creek (*Courtesy of Lisa Oakley*)

Creek around 1988 and joined Sid in research and design for crystalline glazed pots. John continues his pottery making at Cedar Creek today, and also serves as caretaker of the grounds, growing everything from orchids to herbs. In 2002 the Oakleys turned over management responsibilities at Cedar Creek to their daughter, Lisa, an accomplished artisan and glass blower in her own right.

Craft Guilds

Erwin Auditorium, the cultural and recreational center for West Durham's mill workers, became the home of the Durham Ceramic Guild. Organized around 1959, its goals were to promote and encourage ceramics as a hobby for its educational and therapeutic values, to foster creation of works of ceramic art, and to hold regular exhibitions. Annual competitions were held in the Old Armory Civic Center in downtown Durham. The expanding number of clay artists in the 1980s led to the formation of Triangle Potters Guild (1982), the Carolina Clay Guild (1985), and Clayworks Pottery Guild (1987).

Florentina McKinney spearheaded the formation of Carolina Designer Craftsmen Guild (CDCG), a designer craft guild officially launched in 1969. Founding board members were Jo Goulson, Helen Pratt, Priscilla Palmore, Sandy Milroy, Paul Minnis, and Pepper Fluke. Sid and Pat Oakley were strong promoters from the beginning. By 1989 CDCG membership had grown to over 150. Its twentieth-anniversary show, "See New Works!," was held at the Durham Arts Council and included Shirley McConahay's fabric trees complete with exotic fabric birds, Stu Martell's "wild" flowers of soft and supple leather, and O'Neal Jones's tables, fashioned from walnut and white corian, then one of the newest plastics.

Groups of Durham woodworkers include the Wood Spirit Carvers, founded by Ewing "Skeeter" Harris shortly after the Second World War; the Carvers Club; and Women with Knives, a club whose members use only hand tools (no machine work) for their creations. Members of the Chapel Hill Handweavers Guild, founded in 1961, and Triangle Weavers (1972) include many Durhamites.

Weavers, *left to right:* Helen Pratt, Dorothy Heyman, Vivian Dai, Sandy Milroy Jens, Silvia Heyden at Craft House, 1972 *(Courtesy of Pepper Fluke)*

Ruth Roberson and Connor Causey helped form the Durham Quilt Guild in 1977. Its growing membership soon necessitated a name change, and it became the Durham/Orange Quilters Guild. In 1998 Bertie Howard founded the African American Quilt Circle, whose first exhibit, "Lest We Forget: Preserving Our African American Quilting Heritage," was held at the Hayti Heritage Center on Fayetteville Street. In recent years this group has carried out an unusual project, making quilts as gifts for high school and college graduates living in public housing developments.

Craft House of Durham

When Florentina McKinney moved to Durham in 1958, there were no commercial outlets for crafts. A potter who eventually specialized in copper enameling, she held shows in her own home for several years. In 1969 she opened a small consignment craft shop at Lakewood Shopping Center, and in 1970 she became one of the seven founders of Craft House of Durham Ltd. These seven women shared a desire to establish an outlet in Durham for their own fine crafts and those of others in the area. Three were potters: Dorothy Davis, Pepper Fluke, and Jan Gregg. Myrtle Obrist made candles. Flo McKinney did copper enameling, and Priscilla Palmore was interested in both enameling and fabric design. Dorothy Bone, the seventh partner, brought strong interest in and appreciation of the crafts to the project and managed the office. The business was set up as a partnership with a small investment of capital ($200) from each of the seven.

Craft House opened in May, 1970, with the work of twenty-four craftsmen, selected by a standards committee and sold on consignment. In the following year Craft House moved across the street to a much larger house at 2713 Chapel Hill Road and the seven owners incorporated the business. With six display rooms, storage space, an office, and much more wall space for hanging weavings, batik, and stitchery, the facility made it possible to mount invitational shows that would broaden horizons and stimulate new ideas.

By 1973 Priscilla Palmore left the Craft House group to pursue new interests, and shortly thereafter Myrtle Obrist moved away from Durham. In 1974 Bob Black and Ormond Sanderson invited Craft House to join their new Straw Valley complex on Durham-Chapel Hill Boulevard. The five remaining owners were advised to seek a bank loan to upgrade from the consignment business to the wholesale purchasing of crafts. The bank readily agreed, but required the signatures of each of the five women's husbands. The women responded with a resounding "NO!" They all had property in their own names—kilns, tools, clay,

(Below, top) Craft House owners get their business license to open new gallery *(Courtesy of Pepper Fluke)*

(Below, bottom) First Craft House, opened May 1, 1970 *(Courtesy of Pepper Fluke)*

chemicals, copper, metal, yarns, and the objects they had created. The bank backed down, and Craft House came away with the loan.

On October 15, 1976, Mayor Wade Cavin cut the ribbon to open the new home for Craft House of Durham Ltd. at Straw Valley. The building featured a sycamore tree encased in a glass atrium, fourteen-foot ceilings, and wonderful wall space for displays. By now the business was representing more than a hundred craftsmen. In May 1980 the owners celebrated their tenth anniversary with a special showing of their own works. Blue Greenberg's review in the *Durham Morning Herald* offered a vivid glimpse of the event:

(Above, top) Second Craft House, opened in 1971 *(Courtesy of Pepper Fluke)*

(Above, bottom) Ribbon cutting, *left to right:* Jan Gregg, Flo McKinney, Dorothy Bone, Wade Cavin, Dorothy Davis, Pepper Fluke *(Courtesy of Pepper Fluke)*

Pepper Fluke's designs reflect her interest in the arts of primitive cultures. Her brown pots, heavily incised with deep blue designs, are the most satisfying for the collector who wants beautifully ornamented utilitarian objects. Jan Gregg['s] . . . gas kiln . . . give[s] her the translucence she seeks with her porcelains. For the heavier wind chimes, the electric kiln still works best for the sounds she wishes to capture. Dorothy Davis works in stoneware, and, besides lamp bases, she builds murals, clocks, planters and chessmen. . . . She is always experimenting with new glazes. Flo McKinney enamels bowls, plates and magnificent boxes of walnut. . . . Dorothy Bone collaborates with Dorothy Davis, creating hand woven lampshades for her beautiful stoneware lamps. What is most remarkable about these artists is the high quality of workmanship that they demand, first from themselves and then from their other artists.

The lengthy list of extraordinary talent shown at Craft House over the years calls to mind Silvia Heyden's tapestries, Mark Hewitt's pottery, Shirley Frey McConahay's masks and macramé, Katherine Shelburne's batik, George Danser's stained-glass boxes, and Carol Mitchell's silver jewelry. It includes leatherwork by Steve Brooks and Stu Martell, woodcarvings by Ginny Portwood, Rabbi Efraim Rosensweig's wood and enamel Menorahs, dollhouse furniture by Larry Myzner, wooden toys by Ty and Jeffryn Stevens, and cedar boxes by Larry Ballas and Betsy and Bill Hall.

Among the many shows hosted by Craft House was a highly praised traveling exhibition called "North Carolina Glass '80", which highlighted a renewed interest in the art and technique of glass blowing. In 1986 Craft House exhibited redware and salt-glazed stoneware by Mary Livingstone Farrell, a Durham native and Jordan High School graduate who with her husband, David, owns and operates Westmoore Pottery in Seagrove.

After Flo McKinney's health no longer permitted her to share in the activities of Craft House, the four remaining owners decided to close the business when their lease ended on January 31, 1987. Craft House had indeed fulfilled its two original purposes: to provide talented local designer craftsmen with a gallery of high quality in which to show and sell their work; and to help the public better understand what original, well-designed, unique handcrafted art is all about.

Crafts at Duke University

While the late William Stars was a member of the Duke University Art Department, he taught some pottery classes. He also suggested that Duke establish a craft center not leading to a degree program. In 1975 the Duke University Union took up the challenge. A planning committee was appointed by the union's director, William Osborne, and chaired by Peter Coyle, with funding assistance from the Mary Duke Biddle Foundation and the Duke Vice President for Student Affairs William J. Griffith. Krista Cipriano, a graduate of East Carolina University who taught pottery at the Durham Arts Council, was named director.

In the spring of 1976 Duke's president, Terry Sanford, presided over the opening of the Duke University Union Craft Center in Southgate Dormitory on East Campus. A highly qualified staff of teachers from the local community included the weaver Sharon Keech and the potters Conrad Weiser, Russell Knop, Barbara McKenzie, and Sarah Howe. A West Campus facility on the lower level of the Bryan Center was added in 1982, providing studios for weaving, photography, jewelry making, and other disciplines. Pottery and woodworking classes continued to be offered in Southgate Dorm.

In 2002 administrative responsibility was transferred to the Office of Student Activities, and the center was officially renamed the Krista Cipriano Craft Center. Studios and equipment were consolidated on East Campus: one for pottery, jewelry, and woodworking in Southgate, another for photography and multipurpose use in the Ark Annex. For lack of space, the weaving studio was eliminated. The Craft Center closed in May 2004. For nearly thirty years it had been an essential element in the life of Duke

University, providing an outlet for creative expression amid the stress and competition of the academic environment.

Community Programs

In 1967 John Bell taught a first-time course in woodcarving at Erwin Auditorium under the auspices of the Durham City Recreation Department. Students learned to use a chisel and mallet to shape bowls and other beginning projects. Classes in ceramics, pottery, and sculpture were offered at the Edison Johnson Craft and Recreation Center, which was constructed in 1971–72. By 2005 all ceramics classes (using molds) were moved to the W. D. Hill Recreation Center. Maggie Guion, who moved to Durham in 1944, taught crafts at city playgrounds and recreation centers. Her pine-needle baskets, which she first began making in the 1930s, were exhibited and sold at Craft House during the 1980s.

The Lowes Grove School of Design in Durham County was funded by a three-year federal Title III grant (1967–70). The program's goal was to motivate academically underachieving junior high students through exposure to the arts, giving them solid training in good work habits to help them select a career of their choice or go on to a school of higher education. Supported by an extensive arts and crafts library and well-equipped studios, the curriculum included ceramics, jewelry, silkscreen printing, photography, painting, printmaking, weaving, interior design, and dress design. In those days, when county schools were not completely integrated, the program was also a model for the future. Students from Merrick-Moore (a black high school) and Jordan and Southern (white high schools) were bused to the School of Design. The Durham County Schools chose not to fund the program when the grant expired.

The Durham School of the Arts occupies the former Durham High School complex. Larry Downing, a teacher and local artist working in ceramic and mixed-media sculpture, views the school as a unique training ground for students interested in the cultural arts. One look around his classroom is an inspiration in itself. He sets the tasks to be accomplished, and the students follow through using their creative instincts.

In 1982 Dr. James Semans proposed the establishment of small professional development grants for individual artists. His idea led to the formation of the Emerging Artists Program by the Durham Arts Council. Craft artists in clay, woodworking, weaving, mixed media, metalwork, glass, and fiber have been recipients of these grants.

SeeSaw Studio, a nonprofit after-school design and business program for Durham teenagers fourteen to eighteen, was created in 1998, the brainchild of a retired Duke zoology professor, Dr. Stephen A. Wainwright. He based his idea for the organization on the Kuzari Bead Company, started in 1975 in Nairobi, which gives employment to financially struggling women. The studio accepts commissions designed by teams of students who carry out a project from conception to finished product, including marketing and sales.

Moving Downtown

In 1985 West Brothers Moving and Storage purchased the Venable Business Center and Prizery Building at the corner of Pettigrew and Roxboro streets. Barney West offered space in the renovated building, considered Durham's first "arts incubator," to local artists and small businesses. Dan Ellison, a lawyer, started another "arts incubator" in 1996 with the purchase of the Palms Restaurant, now called Durham Arts Place, to create spaces useful for artists.

Since the mid-1990s the restoration of Durham Central Park has led to an exciting emergence of arts activities and businesses in and around Foster Street. The former home of the Durham Awning Company became Claymakers in 2000. The renovated building has individual studio areas, a teaching studio, a retail store for the sale of clay, ceramic tools, supplies, and equipment, and a gallery for the exhibit and sale of ceramic art and pottery.

Walker Stone opened his tobacco Liberty Warehouse to artists and nonprofit arts organizations, including ARP Design Studio, the Durham Arts Council Clay Studio, and Liberty Arts Inc., a nonprofit corporation whose purpose is to provide the industrial equipment and space that individual artists in metalwork could not afford. Vega Metals is around the corner on Hunt Street. The Scrap Exchange moved to the Liberty Warehouse in 2000 from its former location in Northgate Mall. This nonprofit organization, founded in 1991, collects clean, reusable industrial discards for practical and artistic reuse, thus promoting both creativity and environmental awareness. Donated "scrap" items include fabric, colorful foam pieces, textile cones and tubes, holographic adhesive paper, baskets, and boxes.

The revitalization of Durham's downtown in "the City of Medicine" depends on the arts and culture, expansion of the efforts going on in Durham Central Park, and more and continued support for local artists. Our neighbors who are craft artists make our lives richer and better right here in Durham, because art is indeed "good medicine."

5. Dance

LINDA BELANS

When the late Pearl Primus performed at the North Carolina College for Negroes (now North Carolina Central University) about a half-century ago, it would have been hard to imagine what the future would hold—for dance or for Durham. Those fortunate to have seen her at B. N. Duke Auditorium still remember the performance. She was costumed in white, leaping high, moving from her heart, from her experience, and from her social convictions. She was free to dance in the black community where she was well known, but not free to choose a hotel in the segregated city.

By the time Primus, an anthropologist and scholar, returned to Durham in 1991, she was considered one of the prime forces in modern dance internationally, with a penchant for using the art form to comment on social and cultural conditions. This time, however, she was working across town at Duke University, feted by the American Dance Festival (ADF), where she was awarded its first endowed Balasaraswati/Joy Ann Dewey Beinecke Chair for Distinguished Teaching. This time Dr. Primus had her choice of hotels.

Much has changed in Durham in those intervening years, not only in social and cultural politics but in dance as well. Duke, where according to its archives social dancing was prohibited on campus until 1935 because of the school's strong Methodist ties, is now considered a mecca for dance. That is because in 1978, the American Dance Festival relocated from Connecticut College to Duke, bringing its historic program with a rich modern dance

Pearl Primus in "Hard Times Blues," photograph by Gjon Mili (*Courtesy of American Dance Festival*)

tradition. The university was intended to be a temporary home to ADF, as executives at the Durham corporate headquarters of the Liggett Group promised to find a new space for the growing dance organization. But the tobacco company left town, and today ADF is still one of Duke's annual summer tenants, flooding the campus with about five hundred dancers, choreographers, musicians, critics, and scholars from around the globe, who meet at the intersection of dance and the humanities. ADF's twenty-five-year search for a permanent home may soon end with the construction of the Durham Center for the Performing Arts, where the festival is likely to be an anchor tenant. The evolution of the American Dance Festival is part of the history woven through Durham's storied tapestry of dance.

Earliest Stirrings

In 1935 a modern dance group was formed at Duke whose purpose was "to promote dance on the campus," according to a document called "Durham's Assets in the Arts," compiled and published in 1965 by the Durham Community Planning Council. The group later became the Terpsichorean Club under the direction of the late Julia Wray and the accompanist Pat Greyer, who sponsored dance performances on campus as well as exchange programs with the North Carolina College Dance Group (of the North Carolina College for Negroes). Wray was one of many who would play a pivotal role in helping to establish modern dance as a force to be reckoned with at Duke. Another of those mavericks is Ella Fountain Pratt, former dancer and teacher, who later became the first director of cultural affairs at Duke. She notes that in the 1940s the Ballet Russe de Monte Carlo was invited to perform at Duke by J. Foster Barnes (referred to as "Bishop"). Performances over the years were produced by the Duke Artists Series, which in 2004 was folded into the reorganized Institute of the Arts and renamed Duke Performances.

In the 1930s and 1940s, just down the road from Duke, an entirely different cultural phenomenon was taking place. When farmers brought their tobacco leaves to sell at the warehouses, buck dancers, musicians, and other street performers both white and black, including Blind Boy Fuller and Sonny Terry, would play for tips. Buck dancing, a relative of tap dancing, was made most visible and popular by the legendary buck dancer and long-time Durham resident John Dee Holeman. Born in 1929 in Orange County, Holeman was a self-taught musician who is still considered one of the preeminent blues guitarists in the area.

Many things about the growth of dance in Durham would have been hard to imagine in previous decades. No one could have predicted the enor-

mous presence that African dance has assumed. Before Chuck Davis established his African American Dance Ensemble (AADE) in 1984, first managed by the Duke graduate Pamela Green, African dance was primarily
considered the domain of anthropologists and scholars like Primus and the
late Katherine Dunham, who received the Scripps / American Dance Festival award in 1986. But that all was changed by Davis, a charismatic figure
standing six feet five who is affectionately known as Baba Chuck to the
thousands of children and adults he has influenced across the globe.

Born on January 1, 1937, Davis continues to call Durham home for himself and his company, and AADE continues to influence dance: Ava Vin-
issett is on the dance faculty at Duke; and Sadiyah Shakur (originally a
member of Davis's company in New York before she moved to Durham
in the 1980s) directs her twenty-two-year-old Collage Dance Company, a
successful training and performing group for children and youth in Dur-

African American Dance Ensemble, Dancers: Gail Martin, Venita Ashford, Lou Carter; Musicians: Khalid Saleem, Hashim Salih, Beverly Botsford, photograph by Jay Anderson *(Courtesy of American Dance Festival)*

ham. Collage has launched the careers of numerous professional dancers and drummers. Other original members of the company include Venita "Ashford" Allen, Thadeus Bennett, Ivy L. Burch, Lavender "LD" Burris, Lou Carter, James "Jimmie" Green, Toni K. Hall, Brenda Hayes, Gail "Martin" Rouse, Gloria "Muldrow" Bailey, Sherone Price, Leah Wise, and the late James "Jimmy" Williams. Drummers for the African American Dance Ensemble have included Beverly Botsford, George Glenn, Hashim Salih, and the musical director Khalid Saleem.

No one could have predicted that a geographic area where few visiting ballet companies performed anything more than "ballet's greatest hits" would become home to Carolina Ballet in 1997. Within its first five years of existence, the company assumed international notice. Although based in Raleigh under the artistic direction of Robert Weiss (former soloist with the New York City Ballet under George Balanchine), the company has given premières of works at Duke in collaboration with music commissioned by the Ciompi Quartet, and is doing for ballet regionally what ADF has done for modern dance.

It is also hard to imagine a time when there was such a dearth of dance in Durham that there was virtually no coverage or calendar listings in local newspapers. The *North Carolina Anvil* (now defunct), the first paper in the Triangle to run a weekly arts calendar, placed dance under "Shorts," while all the other art forms enjoyed their own headers; even "Poetry" had its own calendar column. In 1977 Linda Belans wrote a letter to the editor entitled "Wake up! Don't you know America is dancing?" and was soon writing about dance for the paper.

Ballet companies had a long history of performing primarily at Duke, and while modern dance began taking shape in Durham in the form of classes and small performing groups, there wasn't much professional modern dance. But what there was foreshadowed the future. In the early 1970s Ella Fountain Pratt helped bring one of the queen mothers of modern dance to Durham. "If Martha Graham ever decides to travel, we want to be first on the list," she recalls saying. A friend of Pratt in New York who knew the famed impresario Sol Hurok arranged a visit. It seems that the author and Duke professor of romance languages Wallace Fowlie (who had known Graham at Bennington) was in the audience and asked to see her after a sold-out concert at which she performed "Seraphic Dialogue." Pratt took Fowlie through an underground passage and knocked on the diva's door. "She had three-foot-long eyelashes, antennae that protruded from the top of her head, resembling one of the better beetles," Pratt recounted. "Miss Graham," she said, "there's someone here to see you that you may remember." "Remember him?" Graham replied in her affected speech after laying her exotic eyes on him, "I stole from him!" Pratt describes Graham as few others ever would: "She was darling."

There was a succession of serious dancers after that, including Alwin Nikolais, Murray Louis, Indian dancers, and African groups, among them a troupe of dancers and singers from Sierra Leone who gave Duke's first topless show. (Pratt was asked in advance if the dancers should cover their torsos, but she insisted that they perform as they would in their own country.) But it took a long time for modern dance to flourish in Durham and for audiences to have a vocabulary to talk about it, to feel confident enough to say or trust what they liked. Now, at intermissions, viewers can be overheard conversing, even arguing with authority about their favorite companies, or which dancer performed the same role better, or bemoaning the return of some of the "regulars" at ADF, wishing for room on the roster for more, untested companies.

How did Durham go from a place where local newspapers had practically nothing to write about dance to a place with such a reputation that the dance writers at the *New York Times* could converse as knowledgeably about the Regulator Bookshop on 9th Street as about the newest ADF première from New York, France, or China? A place that has become one of the coveted spots to perform because of its intelligent dance audiences? A place where the famed Savion Glover (whom the late Gregory Hines described as "the greatest tap dancer who ever lived") could make a surprise appearance at the Carolina Theatre to perform with his adopted and celebrated North Carolina Youth Tap Ensemble, founded by Gene Medler? On his visits to Durham, Glover would swoop up a dancer or two from its company to perform with him in New York, including Michelle Dorrance, daughter of M'Liss Dorrance (member of the Duke dance faculty and co-founder of the New Performing Dance Company) and Anson Dorrance.

The area has nurtured the careers of other dancers who have gone on to perform with major companies. Jack Arnold auditioned for the modern-dance company Pilobolus several times: the first was on a lark, as he had no intention of leaving Durham, where he was enjoying a career as a dancer and choreographer. But as Pilobolus's interest in him grew, the stakes suddenly got very high and his anxiety rose. Eventually, after several arduous auditions, he made the cut and joined the company from 1987 to 1990. He also taught at ADF from 1991 to about 1998, and served on the board from the end of his teaching run to 2002. He is still a guest choreographer and occasional performer for North Carolina State University's dance program, where his wife, Robin Harris, is director.

Shen Wei, one of ADF's International Choreographers in the summer of 2000, selected Jessica Harris, a graduate of Carolina Friends School in Durham, to join his newly forming company. Little did Harris know that Shen was soon to become a star and that she would share the limelight with one of the hottest choreographers in the country.

Durham has become so dance-rich for a city of its size that celebrities have made it their home; among them are the internationally important Laura Dean, famous for her signature spinning choreography, and Carlotta Santana, who moved her acclaimed Carlota Santana Flamenco Vivo from New York to Durham. Carol Parker, a ten-year veteran with Pilobolus, where she was dance captain, toured with Baryshnikov after she left the company and lives in Durham. (Parker was formerly married to Jack Arnold, whom she met while dancing with Pilobolus). Ronald K. Brown, one of the country's most sought-after choreographers, is managed by Pamela Green of Durham, Chuck Davis's first manager. Durham native Tyler Walters, former student of M'Liss Dorrance, returned home after a successful career with the Joffrey Ballet; he is currently a resident guest teacher with Carolina Ballet and on the dance faculty at Duke.

Before the modern dance boom of the 1970s filtered to Durham, there was Ella Fountain Pratt, Jacqueline (Erickson) Morgan, Vicky Patton, Nancy Pinckney, Kaye Sullivan, Julia Wray, Dot Borden, Dot Silver, Rosemary

Howard, Lee (Wenger) Vrana, M'Liss Dorrance, Barbara Busse, Betsy Buford, Betsy Blair, and others. Each of these women had, in her own way, the vision, the energy, and sometimes just plain chutzpah to help place Durham on the international dance map.

Dance itself is rooted in a legacy of individual movers and shakers. It is a very personal art form, and those who have propelled it forward are generally referred to by their first name or a nickname: "Martha" (Graham), "Savion" (Glover), "Merce" (Cunningham), "Alvin" (Ailey), "Bill T" (Jones), "Mr. B." (Balanchine), "SandMan" (Sims). These innovators seem immediate and approachable, even if they are no longer alive, and even if the dancers who seem to be on familiar terms with them never actually had contact with them. Perhaps it's because dance is the one art form in which people must touch each other physically. And in that touch, there is intimacy. Before film and video, dance was passed down through the generations by touch and through the oral tradition. With the exception of ADF's video archives, photos, and newspaper reviews and previews, there are no scripts, buildings, paintings, scores, or other tangible traces of the history of this ephemeral art form in Durham. As a result much history is lost, most is told through stories, and some has morphed into apocryphal tales, which make the telling of history a bit of a dance itself.

There are, however, markers along the way that help tell the city's story

M'Liss Dorrance directing her dance, "Road to Killarney" (Courtesy of Jacqueline Erickson Morgan)

Ella Fountain Pratt with Steve Feldman (Courtesy of Ella Fountain Pratt)

of dance. In 1956 Mrs. Pratt was asked by Deans Bill Griffith and Herbert Herring to do something cultural with students, "Anything." It was a time when opera and theater could sell a house, but modern dance struggled here as it did nationally. It all depended on good friends to pull it off; so supporters such as Arthur Larson, director of the World Rule of Law Center, and his wife Florence, an accomplished sculptor, gave parties for the Artists Series. "Really swinging parties," Mrs. Pratt recalls. "You can't have dance without a good party." The tradition continues: today, after ADF performances, a patron or

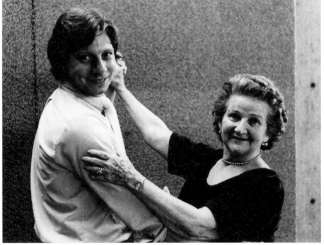

enthusiast throws a party to feed the dancers and keep the other patrons engaged.

Meanwhile, North Carolina Central University (NCCU) launched its dance program in 1955 as part of the physical education department. Soon step dancing and drill dancing found their place in fraternities and sororities on the campus, making dance a competitive sport. Step teams found their way into black churches. In 1966 Kay Sullivan arrived in Durham from Detroit, and out of concern that there was no dance for children in the black community, began teaching in the basement rec room of her home at 2509 Weaver Street. The school grew so quickly that she moved to Durham Business College's large all-purpose room on Fayetteville Street, but the school soon outgrew that space as well. Sullivan purchased a space on South Roxboro Street, down the corner from Bumpass' Grocery, and created her own flexible dance floor out of plywood and duct tape. Eventually she outgrew that space as well and finally found a permanent home big enough to accommodate the thousands of students she taught, including Sherone Price, who was also studying with Annie Dwyer in a high school in Pittsboro. (Price went on to have a long career with Chuck Davis's AADE

Kay Sullivan *(Courtesy of Kay Sullivan)*

and teaches at ADF.) The W. D. Hill Recreation Center opened its doors to Sullivan and designed a proper dance space: they laid a raised wood floor over the tile and painted the ceilings black. The highest honor came when the center named the space the M. K. Sullivan Dance Studio, which it is still called today. Sullivan also taught at NCCU and collaborated with Linda Norflett of the drama program on dinner theater productions. Sullivan left Durham in 1987 for Mississippi, where she developed a thriving dance program and taught in the public schools. She recently returned to the area, but her interests are now focused on the study of the environment through the arts, and she has no plans to teach dance again.

A major force in the development of dance at NCCU has been Nancy Pinckney, who recalls that before the civil rights movement shifted the dividing lines between races, dance in the black community was largely isolated. St. Joseph's Church, the one major performing space in Hayti and home to the Ebony Dance Company, was moved when the Durham Expressway cut through and forever changed the community. Pinckney's parents would have been the last to imagine that their daughter would become the director of the NCCU Dance Group in 1971, the national Black College Dance Exchange, and an assistant professor of physical education, recreation, and dance at the university. As a child she wasn't allowed to dance at home; it was "the devil's workshop," her parents would say back in her hometown of St. George, South Carolina. But Pinckney continues to influence legions of students. She has been recognized for her contribution to dance in the black community with a Disneyland award for founding, promoting, and supporting dance in historically black colleges and universities (2003), and by the International Association for Black Dance.

"If they were anywhere near Central's campus, they were dancing with Ma [Pinckney]," says Chuck Davis, whose own company was drawn from dancers at NCCU and from children in surrounding neighborhoods, including Few Gardens and Mc-Dougald Terrace. "It was said that anyone living in this area could only rise to a certain level." In spite of all the limitations and doubt imposed on the company internally and externally—the undisciplined kids whom Davis had to press into shape, initial prejudice, and lack of funds—the company has grown to international importance. For example, the performance by his African American Dance Ensemble (AADE) of Donald McKayle's classic "Games" at the American Dance Festival in 1987 launched ADF's Black Traditions in American Modern Dance, a project that spanned several years and eventually led to an award-winning television program. Among Davis's other impressive accomplishments are his founding of Dance Africa in New York in 1977, an annual international event held at the Brooklyn Academy of Music, and of Dance Africa in Chicago, which he initiated twenty years ago. Locally he produces an annual Kwanzaa celebration.

Davis's company first began traveling internationally in 1982 when ADF charged it with creating an arts-in-education program. In 1983 Julia Wray, Duke's first dance program director, brought Davis to teach at the univer-

Nancy Pinckney at the celebration of the 95th anniversary of NCCU *(Courtesy of Nancy Pinckney)*

sity with the drummer Khalid Saleem; Davis still appears there occasionally as a guest teacher. Davis has been awarded an honorary doctorate of fine arts from Medgar Evers College and in addition to touring, teaches movement for actors at NCCU.

A Change of Pace

There was a dance boom in America, and Durham felt its aftershocks. Jacqueline Morgan, then Jacqueline Erickson, arrived in Durham on January 1, 1971; she quickly discovered that there were few dance companies and schools, and that those few felt isolated from each other. "Everyone was an island," she recalls. But there were several women who were at work pulling dance together. The first phase was launched by Wray, Pratt, Suzanne White Manning, Busse, Barbara Bounds, Pinckney, Nina Wallace, Dot Borden, and others. Dot Silver filed for nonprofit status to create Dance Associates, a big first step in fostering a new creative, cooperative spirit. There was an organization in place but no money to advance the cause for local dance, and few had time to actively and consistently pursue it. That's what Morgan had—time. She raised money for a remarkable day in the history of dance in Durham: March 1, 1975, to be called a Day for Dancing. Morgan organized a daylong series of classes, but it needed a space, and at that time the Durham Arts Council was too small to house the event. Morgan created a collaboration between the city and the council, making it possible to hold the event at the Edison Johnson Rec Center. "I recall," Morgan says, "driving to the Edison Johnson Rec Center on the morning of the first Day for Dancing. I passed two women riding their bikes. I remember thinking, 'Wouldn't it be great if they were going to the Day for Dancing,' hoping that at least two people would show up."

As it turned out, those two women did show up, along with hundreds of others. "It was so crowded that we couldn't handle the group and we just told them to go to a class of their choice. If there was room, they could attend, and to come back afterwards to pay for the class." Most of those who were asked complied and returned to the front desk to pay—fifty cents per class. Morgan did not have to foot all the bills for this event but did pour a lot of her own money into dance in Durham at the time, as did many others. The Day for Dancing lasted another four years, alternating between UNC and Durham sites. Several small dance companies were formed through the experience, including Allied Arts Dance Company, under the direction of Beth Corning. Morgan recalls performances for children presented by Dance Associates, including adaptations of Leo Leonni's *ABC Book* and *Noanna, the Animals on the Ark*, directed by a Duke student, Linda Usdin. White-Manning formed the aptly named Synergy Dance Company.

Carol Richard and Diane Eilber formed the Carolina Dancers, a company based in Chapel Hill, which offered mostly original choreography at well-attended performances around Durham.

Day for Dancing *(Courtesy of the Herald-Sun)*

Modern dance, and its fine quality of dancers, teachers, and choreographers, had entered Durham's consciousness, and with them enough enthusiasm for a second phase of growth. Rosemary Howard, providing the primary energy along with Morgan, M'Liss Dorrance, Lee (Wenger) Vrana, and Marian Turner, launched the New Performing Dance Company (NPDC) in 1975, rehearsing at Bounds Dance Studio in Chapel Hill, with Barbara Bounds an avid early supporter. The original company was a project of the Dance Associates of Allied Arts. Silver, a former dancer with Martha Graham now residing in Chapel Hill, along with Turner from UNC, Susan Jones, Howard, and Dorrance, were NPDC's first choreographers. The artistic directors were Dorrance and Bounds, with Howard as company manager. Three years later Vrana became the artistic director and soon after, NPDC established its home and the affiliated school in downtown Durham

on Main Street. Howard, a co-director, and her late husband Michael had helped refurbish the space above the Book Exchange into several beautiful studio and rehearsal spaces. It had all the characteristics of a successful venture, but when Morgan returned from a year away, she again saw the need for someone with time to develop the school into a profitable business. Soon her intuition paid off, and under her leadership enrollment

New Performing Dance Company, Linda Sobsey, Rosemary Howard, photograph by Alan Schueler *(Courtesy of Jacqueline Erickson Morgan)*

Rehearsal of "Morning Song," choreographed by Lee Wenger *(Courtesy of Jacqueline Erickson Morgan)*

in the school increased significantly. The space was used frequently, especially in the early years, by ADF companies, as a rehearsal and audition space. Pilobolus worked on *Molly's Not Dead* daily in the studio before its ADF performance that first year. The NPDC school was also the site of many good after-performance parties for the visiting companies. The company generated enough revenue to pay fees to teachers in line with the industry standard and to cover company expenses.

New Performing Dance Company made its début on December 1 and 2, 1975, at Page Auditorium and enjoyed a successful run, performing to large, enthusiastic audiences at Duke, Durham Academy, and other venues, and offering master classes in schools. The company's eclectic repertory of original choreography by the directors and others, including Silver, helped make it accessible to all tastes. Jazz, modern dance, ballet, and tap were all standards on the program. Morgan, who stayed involved in dance until 1982, credits the generosity of Duke University with the early success of dance in Durham. "In large part, dance blossomed because of the support and cooperation from Duke and its faculty," she says. "They gave fledgling groups a stage, a lighting designer, and some credibility." Dance schools began to appear, including Nina's School of Dance under the direction of Nina Wheeler, which continues to produce an impressive number of commercial dancers. Carolina Friends School has a strong dance program, founded by Dot Borden. Sue Stinson, Linda Belans, Donna Faye Burchfield, and Annie Dwyer (since 1990) have successively directed the program. Durham Academy's dance program flourished as well, under Jennifer Potts's longtime direction. Most recently, the Durham School of the Arts, where Vrana has been curriculum specialist since 1995, has produced dancers under the tutelage of Sarajo Berman and others. Community dance classes have been part of the offerings at the Hayti Heritage Center and the Durham Arts Council as well as recreation centers throughout the city. Over the years, participatory dance groups have offered clogging, contra dancing, and English country dancing (thanks to Alan Troxler). More recently, swing dance and salsa dancing have taken on a life of their own in the city's clubs and recreation centers.

Rosemary Howard, ca. 1975, NPDC *(Courtesy of Lee Vrana)*

In 1981 the Institute of the Arts at Duke opened its doors, and in the 1985–86 academic year, while under the direction of Michael Cerveris, the institute cooperated with the dance program to produce "Six Choreographers: Turning Points." That same year, Barbara Dickinson came to Duke as an artist-in-residence in the dance program; she assumed its directorship on March 29, 1989, after the death of Julia Wray and went on to become the director of the dance program and associate professor of the practice of dance. Wray was a vital force at Duke, developing the dance program. She was determined to entice Clay Taliaferro to join the faculty. "How can we get you to come be with us?," he recalls Wray asking him. "You could teach swing, with tap dancing 101 on the ceiling if you like, or anything else you want, we just want you here." Cerveris followed up by going to New York to see him teach and rehearse. When Taliaferro arrived at Duke in 1987, he received an enthusiastic welcome: the university had landed a star to teach in their dance program—the heir apparent to José Limón, one of America's modern dance pioneers and legends.

Durham had come a long way since Taliaferro's first visit to Durham thirty-two years earlier—when there was no celebration, no welcoming committee, and no fanfare. He had come with his tennis team from Lynchburg, Virginia, to compete in a regional tournament. The team was accompanied by his coach Dr. R. Walter Johnson, a mentor and teacher to Arthur Ashe and Althea Gibson. But segregation had drawn the line on Durham's public courts, one which Taliaferro's team was not permit-

NPDC, Lee Wenger *(top)*, Bruce Vrana *(left)*, Ron Paul *(right) (Courtesy of Lee Vrana)*

ted to cross. Duke, although still segregated, offered its courts to the team over the weekend. Taliaferro's return to Duke three decades later began a nineteen-year relationship with the university that lasted until he retired as professor of the practice in dance in 2007.

Over the years, Taliaferro collaborated with Kathy Silbiger, who started as the coordinator of programs and administration for the Institute of the Arts as well as administrator to the dance program, her first exposure to dance. "I looked at everything that moved," she said, "and got excited." When Silbiger became director in 1990 she craved more unusual movement, thinking that ADF wasn't adventurous enough; in 1988 she founded the New Direction series, which has introduced dance from parts of the globe that most of us will never visit. Silbiger became the most daring dance programmer in the area. She brought the avant-garde choreographer and performer Lucinda Childs to Durham, as well as community-based performances directed by the former Balanchine ballet star Jacques D'Amboise. She fostered

Clay Taliaferro (*Courtesy of Clay Taliaferro*)

strong local talent such as Killian Manning, and challenged audiences with Kathak Dance, Blondell Cummings, Li Chiao Ping Dance, Rennie Harris, and the Urban Bush Women. She blurred the line between dance and theater with "She Didn't Like the Moon without Clouds," by the Archipelago Theatre of Chapel Hill, and Mark Dendy's "Busride to Heaven." She gave respectability to club dancing, collaborating with the dance historian and former faculty member Sally Sommer to feature Savion Glover and other hoofers and tap dancers as part of a humanities seminar. She presented Rennie Harris, Twyla Tharp, Kim Irwin's "Wanted: X-Cheerleaders," and Sam Piperato's one-person show "Ten in Ten," all within the same 1996–97 season.

Silbiger produced the José Limón Dance Company, supplemented by local dancers, in a weeklong residency culminating in performances of "Missa Brevis" in the Duke Chapel in April 1989. (This had been a dream of Julia Wray, who unfortunately did not live to see it.) Coming full circle, as Taliaferro prepared to retire in 2007 he performed at Duke with the Limón Company, reprising his title role in the "Moor's Pavane," the company's signature piece, in February 2006. From December 1 to 3, 1989, Silbiger produced the first Julia Wray Memorial Dance Concert, involving fourteen North Carolina dance companies. She brought swing dance to the stage, merging community dancers with professionals, followed by a raucous dance party for the audience. Silbiger launched the Living Traditions program with the Lhama Folk Opera of Tibet with Dance in 1991, and has broadened audiences' cultural understanding through dance and music ever since.

In 1998 Duke's dance program celebrated the one hundredth anniversary of the glorious Ark, which coincided with Silbiger's last year as the administrator for the dance program. She then restricted her work to producing at Duke, bringing in Eiko and Koma, Doug Varone, and Carolina Ballet.

Julia Wray *(Courtesy of Davis Wray)*

Silbiger retired in December 2006. Over the years dance had come alive in Durham, and Morgan credits Dance Associates with its birth. It "pulled people together for a common cause." And the North Carolina Dance Alliance gave it respectability.

American Dance Festival

Before Silbiger began advancing dance, ADF made its storied move to Durham in 1978. The plan to attract ADF to Durham began in the summer of 1975 through the efforts of Vicky Patton, a local dance aficionado and special projects assistant to the late Terry Sanford, then president of Duke University. She was looking for "fun, creativity, arts in Durham in the summer." At the time East Campus in the summer was like a ghost town, and Sanford allowed her to start a dance program there that she named Loblolly, after the Carolina pine. But she soon found that it was harder to get a dance program going than she had imagined, as she found herself jumping from community classes to boarding students. Sanford suggested that she speak with Nancy Hanks, a Duke trustee and head of the National Endowment of the Arts, who in turn suggested that she speak with Charles Reinhart, director of the American Dance Festival in New London, Connecticut. Patton trekked up there and stayed with her friend White-Manning, a member of the Duke dance faculty who was studying at the ADF school. "I fell in love with ADF," Patton says, "but knew I could never do anything like that in Durham. After all, there was only one ADF."

The next spring, Patton was lying in her hospital bed after the birth of her son, when someone brought the office mail to her. Buried in the stack was a mass mailing announcing that ADF was considering leaving New London and would entertain proposals. In partial jest she said to White-Manning that the festival should come to Durham. Soon Patton, in her typical can-do manner, kicked into action. Begging Sanford's secretary for five minutes to see him during a fully-booked day, Patton stood in his doorway between appointments and asked one pressing question: "May I invite the American Dance Festival to Duke?" And characteristically for Sanford, he gave her an easy and quick "yes." Patton got busy.

The American Dance Festival, Patton recounts, had a long list of requirements, including large dance spaces with wooden floors, high ceilings, and good ventilation. Duke could offer all those on East Campus. The university had unused dorms and dining halls as well. Increasingly, it looked as if Duke had what ADF needed. But it also became increasingly apparent that the staff in ADF's home office in New York wasn't paying much attention to Patton. "We had an incredible proposal, but they were not considering coming south," Patton said. Several things helped convince them.

First, Patton and her husband, Bob Chapman, went to New London to make sure that ADF knew Duke was serious. Reinhart still wasn't interested and barely made time to see the couple, according to Patton. Then, as they were dismissed, Chapman asked, "If we send a private jet to pick you up and then return you to New York City, would you come spend twenty-four hours at Duke and see what we've got?" Unaware of how her husband would produce a jet, Patton recalls: "I almost fell over." Reinhart laughed and agreed. Chapman later explained that he had become good friends with the administrators at the Liggett Group, and remembered that they had a jet. He counted on them to participate in the adventure.

Patton went home, made a scrapbook about ADF, and took it to Bob Fasick at Liggett, who immediately agreed; and corporate jet delivered Reinhart to Durham. "We snowed him," Patton says.

Reinhart put together a committee to study the proposal. They narrowed the search to Minneapolis and Durham. "In so many ways," says Patton, "Minneapolis had the edge, but we had June Arey." The efforts of Arey were the second thing that helped persuade ADF to come to Durham, although not immediately. Arey, a longtime friend of Reinhart, was at the time director of the Dance Division of the NEA and head of the proposal committee. She was also from Winston-Salem and loved central North Carolina. According to Patton, she "had great faith that [the state] was the up and coming place to put a festival." Things were looking good for Durham, but there was one hitch. It seems that a board member or two in New York were leery about moving to the South. Jake Phelps, then head of Duke Union, remembers being called out of a meeting to take an urgent call from Reinhart in New York. He expressed to Phelps his board members' concern that bringing the festival to the Bible Belt might present problems for dances that contained nudity. Phelps, who has successfully lured many national performing programs to Duke, assured Reinhart that although a recent production of "The Robber Bridegroom" contained nudity, and even a student production of "Hot L Baltimore" contained partial nudity, no one blinked an eye. Reinhart, according to Phelps, was finally sold on Durham.

The American Dance Festival launched its inaugural season and school in Durham in the summer of 1978 with a program called Gala Performance at Page Auditorium, celebrating the heritage of American dance. It featured the work of the late Isadora Duncan and Mary Wigman, in addition to Paul Taylor's "Aureole," José Limón's "The Moor's Pavane," and Pilobolus's "Ciona."

The morning after Pilobolus's début, however, a headline in the *Dur-*

Page Auditorium, Duke University, June 1984, photograph by Jay Anderson (*Courtesy of American Dance Festival*)

ham Herald across the theater page proclaimed: "Nude Dancing Comes to North Carolina." So much for audiences that would not blink an eye. But the company has been a popular staple of ADF in Durham ever since, winning the Samuel H. Scripps / American Dance Festival award in 2000. Little did anyone know that a student at ADF that first summer would go on to boast her own controversial headlines several years later: Madonna was a scholarship student in the six-week school, which was directed by Martha Myers.

Arey left the NEA to become Reinhart's public relations coordinator. One of her first acts was to set up a group called Friends of ADF in the Triangle. This was a strong, dedicated core of people, who took on leadership roles and were instrumental in launching ADF in Durham. The list of Friends and other supporters is long; it includes Sanford, Mary Duke Biddle Trent Semans, Betsy Buford (now head of the North Carolina Museum of History), Dot Borden, Jacqueline Morgan, and Ella Fountain Pratt.

The American Dance Festival is an event at which "firsts" happen regularly and careers are launched. In 1979 Martha Clarke's new company, Crowsnest, made its début, and, much to everyone's relief, air conditioning was installed in Page Auditorium. In the following year PBS brought its series Great Performances in America to Page Auditorium to film Pilobolus. That was the year the $25,000 Samuel H. Scripps award was established to honor choreographers who have made a significant contribution to dance. Martha Graham received the first award, presented to her by First Lady Betty Ford, a former dancer in Graham's company. Also in that year, the North Carolina native and future modern dance and theater maverick Mark Dendy was a student at the ADF school, along with Donna Faye Burchfield, who became dean of the ADF school in 2001. Burchfield has since established a joint MFA program with Hollins University, where she is a professor of dance and director of the dance program.

In 1982 the Japanese Butoh company Dai Rakuda Kan set down the great camel battleship for which it is named on the stage of Page Auditorium for its United States début. It was a spectacular and groundbreaking performance on a massive multilevel set that is still talked about as one of ADF's landmark performances. Also in that year, the festival established its Reynolds Theater series, launched the Young Choreographers and Composers program, and established year-round headquarters in Durham (ADF still maintains its office in New York). Reinhart has residences in New York and Durham as well.

Eiko and Koma, both MacArthur fellows, made their début in 1983 and have returned numerous times over the years, taking their meditative, Zen-like work out of the theater and into the pond at Duke Gardens, under a magnificent magnolia tree on East Campus, onto the diamond at the old

Durham Bulls Park, and to the grounds of the Nasher Museum at Duke. In 2006 they broke new ground, performing a moving five-minute dance at patients' bedsides at Duke Hospital, sponsored by Health Arts Network at Duke (HAND). In 1984 Ruby Shang presented the Small Wall project, which was performed all over the Duke campus, including Duke Gardens, with about eighty performers drawn from her company, ADF staff, and students. The performance was commissioned to celebrate the festival's fiftieth anniversary, although there is some dispute over ADF's actual birth date.

The American Dance Festival links its roots to the Bennington School of Dance at Bennington College, conducted over six weeks in 1934 under the direction of Martha Hill and Mary Josephine Shelly. In 1947 the program moved to Connecticut College, and in the following year it became known as the NYU–Connecticut College School of Dance. At the conclusion of the 1948 season, when the school presented a series of performances called an American Dance Festival, the summer ADF was

Charles & Stephanie Reinhart, 1993, photograph by Rebecca LeSher (Courtesy of American Dance Festival)

essentially born, though the formal incorporation of the American Dance Festival did not occur until 1976. The year 1950 marked the end of the partnership with New York, and Reinhart became director of the program in 1969, with Martha Myers as dean of the school. Doris Duke attended a festival performance in Newport, Connecticut, in 1977, the same year that Stephanie Reinhart became administrative director. Reinhart became co-director in 1993.

The marriage of Stephanie and Charles Reinhart was a partnership that intertwined their life and work, dedicated to seeking out modern dance, established and unknown, at home and abroad. Stephanie Reinhart was an avid and successful fundraiser. At the time of her death from leukemia in 2002, she had helped to produce more than three hundred North Carolina premières, nurtured the careers of many emerging choreographers, and brought thousands of choreographers and dancers together from around the world to study, exchange ideas, and perform at ADF on the Duke campus.

The festival's search for a permanent

home has been a long, sometimes puzzling, and frequently frustrating one. In the mid-1980s members of the ADF staff, including its architect Nagler, considered many potential buildings in Durham, but there was generally something missing from the equation, such as adequate space, or good sightlines in existing theaters. Additionally, the Reinharts placed most of the responsibility for finding a home on the city and various influential people. In 1986 members of the Durham City Council, flanked by the local media, arrived at the festival's summer administrative home at Epworth dorm for their scheduled tour of the school and rehearsals. The Reinharts seemed reluctant to accompany the entourage around the campus, but did so upon prodding from the staff. Several years later a group of influential community members, led by the former Duke president H. Keith H. Brodie, actively pursued sites for an ADF home. But the ball was dropped along the way again. Perhaps most revealing is the fate of a $2 million dollar appropriation by the North Carolina legislature toward the purchase of a facility. The funds were eventually withdrawn because of ADF's inability to find a site.

To the Reinharts' credit, the American Dance Festival has grown well beyond the original vision of Bennington College in 1934. The largest festival of its kind in the world, ADF has become an internationally important presenting organization and school, and has helped launch the careers of numerous dancers and choreographers. Its success in Durham is directly linked to the hard work of many dedicated people before ADF moved here, and who have helped nurture it ever since. Equally important, ADF set the stage for other major art festivals to take root in Durham: the Blues Festival, the Full Frame Festival, the Jewish Film Festival, the Gay and Lesbian Film Festival. As of this writing, NCCU is planning the first summer jazz festival (2007) in a new partnership with the African American Jazz Caucus.

Dancing into Tomorrow

What will the future of dance hold for Durham? Many small dance companies have emerged over the years; some have folded, several still perform occasionally, and others are on the rise, all of them frequented by smart dance audiences seasoned over the last several decades. On the horizon is the highly anticipated production of Carlota Santana's "Carmen," directed by Rafael Lopez-Barrantes, to celebrate her company's twenty-fifth anniversary. It is scheduled to have its première at the Joyce Theater in New York in 2008. Duke, which has dramatically transformed its programming since social dancing was legally permitted on campus in 1935 and the first modern dance group was formed, will include in its 2007 Strategic Plan the integration of the arts into campus and academic life. Other new additions are Provost Peter Lange's Council for the Arts, formed in 2006 to help guide the integration, and the appointment of Aaron Greenwald as interim director of Duke Performances after Silbiger's retirement. It remains to be seen how all of this might continue to influence dance in Durham, particularly as Duke builds the arts into its new Central Campus. If Duke can lure David Dorfman from Connecticut College, he could be a charismatic and talented link to a community that is familiar with him through his performances at ADF. It is poetic coincidence that Duke is again looking to Connecticut College to make its mark on the dance world, as it did when it lured the American Dance Festival here in 1978.

With the rapid growth of the Hispanic population locally, and its influence on many facets of community life, including fashion and food, one wonders how the mixture of cultures might influence a next wave of dance. Greater influences on the growth and health of dance, however, are economic peaks and valleys and the availability of public and private funding. Currently dance companies are struggling, and producers and presenters express concern. In addition, the response to terrorism has forced the cancellation of some visits from foreign companies, including those from Nigeria, India, and Cuba, that were scheduled to perform as part of Duke Performances. One thing seems certain: dance has developed roots that run deep into the Carolina clay. It is now impossible to imagine Durham without dance.

"Deep Vermillion," by Nancy Tuttle May, photograph by Diane Amato *(Courtesy of Nancy Tuttle May, from the collection of Paula Sims)*

"Yellow Can #1," oil/
paper 1989 by Elizabeth
Lentz (Courtesy of Chris-
tine Lentz)

"Secret Place," by
Edith London, oil on
canvas (Courtesy of
Lee Hansley Gallery,
Raleigh)

"Gathering Twilight,"
2007 by Jacob Cooley
(Courtesy of Jacob Cooley)

Stained glass window at White Rock Baptist church, photograph by Frank Hyman *(Courtesy of White Rock Baptist Church)*

Stained glass windows at Duke Memorial Church *(Courtesy of Duke Memorial Church)*

Stained glass windows at St. Stephen's Episcopal Church *(Courtesy of Amanda van Scoyoc)*

St. Luke's Baptismal Font, designed and constructed by Frank DePasquale, photograph by Amanda van Scoyoc *(Courtesy of Frank DePasquale)*

"Homage to Atget," 1989–93. Wall-to-floor construction incorporating stock and salvaged building materials and found architectural elements made of maple, fir, walnut, pine, steel, stainless steel, galvanized steel, brass, aluminum, and Plexiglas, by William Noland (*Courtesy of William Noland*)

"falling bodies blanket me," by David Solow (*Courtesy of David Solow*)

"Dance to the Cadence of Flutes and Drums," saw dust fired clay, terra sigillata, and acrylics by Ellen Kong *(Courtesy of Ellen Kong and Tyndall Galleries)*

"Guardian of Generations," quilt by Selena Sullivan, African American Quilt Circle, photograph by Frank Hyman *(Courtesy of Selena Sullivan)*

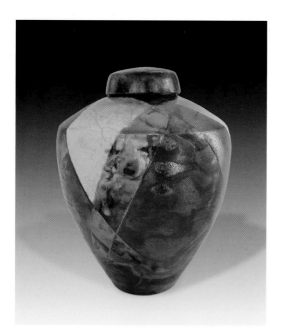

"Large with Diagonals,"
raku by Conrad Weiser
*(Courtesy of Conrad Weiser
and Tyndall Galleries)*

Pot by Pepper Fluke
*(Courtesy of Pepper
Fluke)*

Hinged Treasure
Boxes by Julie Olson
*(Courtesy of Julie
Olson)*

Copper teapot, 2005
*(Courtesy of Andrew
Preiss)*

"Parting Ways," acrylic
on canvas by Ernie Barnes
(Courtesy of Ernie Barnes)

"Father and Son," by Robert
Broderson *(Courtesy of Carol
Broderson and Gallery C)*

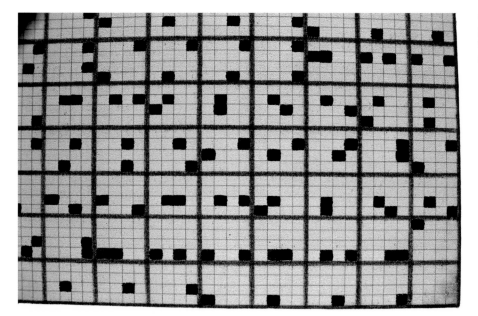

"Possibilities of Filling in Sixteenths," by Vernon Pratt *(Courtesy of Deborah Pratt)*

Untitled by John Menapace
(Courtesy of John Menapace)

Two Callas, 1980 © Caroline Vaughan *(All rights reserved; courtesy of Craven Allen Gallery and RippleSphere, LLC.)*

"Can You Hear My Silent Scream," oil on canvas by Beverly McIver *(Courtesy of Beverly McIver and Tyndall Galleries)*

"Woman with Guitar," 1947, by Elizabeth Catlett, photograph by Barbara Williams *(Courtesy of NCCU Art Museum)*

"Appassionato," tapestry by Silvia Heyden *(Courtesy of Silvia Heyden and Tyndall Galleries)*

"Southern Highlands Man-
dela," in process 2007 by
Bryant Holsenbeck (Courtesy
of Bryant Holsenbeck)

6. Music

NONNA SKUMANICH

Music has always been a part of the Durham community—in the beginning perhaps not the refined music that developed in the royal courts and lofty churches of Europe over the centuries, but music nonetheless. Whether it was Dr. Bartlett Durham and his cronies in the 1850s serenading the town on bright moonlit nights, or the Reverend Gary Davis in the 1930s playing his guitar outside the tobacco warehouses, worshippers in their churches, workers in the mills and factories, students in their schools, or members of the academic, professional, and industrial sectors of society— all have been involved in the making and appreciation of music. Not even the Ku Klux Klan was immune: when C. P. Ellis attended a rally of the local chapter of the Klan in 1963, there was a musical ensemble playing on an open-air stage. From these different quarters came the many people who helped shape the unique musical forms that make up the fabric of American culture: from hillbilly songs to avant-garde chamber music.

The Universities

The Second World War was a watershed in Durham as in the rest of the nation. Returning veterans swelled the enrollments of Durham's two universities, Duke and North Carolina College for Negroes (now North Carolina Central University, or NCCU), and brought to Durham new populations and new wealth. A few years later the establishment of Research Triangle Park significantly increased the proportion of well-educated and well-paid residents in the area. From increased population and surplus wealth came demand and support for the arts. As a result, Durham experienced a burst of artistic activity in the decades after the war. Music was the art form that saw the most activity, reaching into every segment of society.

While schools, churches, and civic organizations have contributed their share, one cannot overestimate the influence of the universities in nurturing and supporting musical appreciation and taste, not only by establishing concert series that have regularly brought internationally known artists to Durham, but through their educational curricula. The presence of world-class music educators and performers has played a significant role in putting Durham on the map. Without them it might well have remained—musically speaking—a cultural backwater.

North Carolina Central University (NCCU)

From its beginning as the National Religious Training School and Chautauqua in 1910, music played an essential role at NCCU. The founder and first president, James Edward Shepard (1875–1947), was committed to a classical liberal arts curriculum that included training in the arts. As early as 1911 and 1912, school bulletins reveal studio classes for piano and voice as well as orchestra and brass band ensembles. Also present, though unlisted, was a chorus. Composition, instrumentation, and orchestration also appeared in the catalogues from time to time in the early years. Training was rigorous and based on classical European works and methods. One of the goals at the college was to produce music educators, and thus it had a music curriculum long before Trinity College established similar classes.

By the time the college became a four-year liberal arts institution in 1925, it was listing these courses in a Department of Music. Catherine Ruth Edwards was designated the first chairwoman of the music department in 1928 and held the title until her retirement in 1958. When the music build-

Nell Pierce Hunter
*(Courtesy of St. Joseph's
A.M.E. Church)*

ing was erected in 1976 it was named in her honor. Nell Pierce Hunter (1889–1992), wife of a Durham physician and a graduate of NCCU (1947), was another distinguished teacher who later chaired the department. Hunter had studied music and voice pedagogy in the 1920s at the Chicago Musical College, after which she performed and received further voice instruction in Europe and the United States. She returned to the Chicago Music College to receive her M.A. in 1951. Hunter was the choir director at St. Joseph's A.M.E. church and a community force for bringing people together to sing. During the Depression she was assistant director of the Federal Music Program of the WPA in North Carolina and later state choral director for the National Youth Administration. Her choirs at NCCU served as ambassadors for the university by performing recitals throughout the country. She returned to Chicago after her husband's death in 1957.

With Hunter's departure, Samuel Washington Hill (1909–1998), another prominent choir director, took on the role of teaching and of promoting the school and attracting applicants through extensive East Coast tours. Gwendolyn Tait Haskins directed the chorus after Hill. In addition to continuing the concert touring tradition, she was a noted artist who performed at Carnegie Hall. The chorus's national performances brought attention to the outstanding vocalists at NCCU. Two graduates of the music department, Hilda Harris and Elvira Green, later sang leading roles with the Metropolitan Opera Company. While the chorus was receiving national recognition, Dr. Robert John, chairman of the music department, the faculty member

Charles Gilchrist (*Courtesy of Charles Gilchrist*)

Paul Koepke, and several other local artists performed regularly on campus in a Sunday afternoon chamber music series.

Coincident with the nationwide civil rights movement were new springs of creativity and a revived interest in old popular musical forms such as gospel, blues, and jazz. The new emphasis on inclusion spurred the black community to engage in a cultural revival, and Durham and NCCU were rich in resources. Music once considered unacceptable by the "respectable" sectors of the black community was now listened to with interest. It was no accident that this change occurred during the civil rights movement. Blacks with pride in their own culture and white collegians with sympathy for their civil rights struggle shared an enthusiasm for the rediscovered genres. Black popular music became a common ground for the young of both races. Jazz in particular was picked up by a number of universities across the country, including NCCU and Duke.

During Eugene Strassler's tenure as chairman of the music department in the 1960s, these new popular forms of music became recognized as legitimate subjects for study. Strassler brought Donald Byrd, the renowned jazz trumpeter, to the faculty. The trend increased when Charles Gilchrist (1939–1996), a graduate of NCCU (1961), joined the faculty in 1968, and again when Byrd returned to the faculty in 1976 and directed the degree program in jazz studies until the early 1980s. Dr. Ira Wiggins (1955–) joined the faculty in 1986 and further built up the jazz curriculum. Born and raised in Kinston in a family interested in jazz, he had taught music in the public schools after earning a B.M. (NCCU, 1977) and an M.M. (Virginia Commonwealth University, 1983). While teaching and developing many student jazz ensembles at NCCU, he went on to earn his Ph.D. (UNC-Greensboro, 1997). In 1990 he instituted the NCCU / Grady Tate Jazz Festival as an annual event. It exposes students to the best of jazz musicians, such as Clyde Hampton, who came to campus to perform and to critique student work in jazz arrangement and composition. Grady Tate also took part more than once.

By 2005 NCCU's jazz program included thirty-four jazz majors, two large bands, four combos, and one vocal ensemble. One of the two jazz ensembles had already won an international reputation, having performed at the Montreux Jazz Festival in 1996, in the White House for President Clinton, and at other coveted venues. Two graduates of the program, Stanley Baird and Chip Crawford, remained to teach and established a summer camp for middle school students, the Shepard Jazz Camp. The children join the all-student ensemble as well as smaller combos and are taught music theory in addition to arranging and composing. NCCU supplies rehearsal space and faculty to conduct the combos. Byrd has taught at the camp, and the versatile and equally renowned musician Branford Marsalis, now settled in the Durham area, has lent his talents by performing, teaching, and coaching on occasion at both NCCU and Duke University. Alumni of the Jazz Camp have garnered awards, among them Chris Pattishall, who received a Young Jazz Composer Award from the ASCAP Foundation in 2005.

Gilchrist, chairman of the music department from 1985 until 1995, continued to diversify the music curriculum in his work as choral director. No doubt he recalled and had not relished his experience as a student, when he was chased out of the practice room for playing jazz instead of Mozart. He expanded the repertory of the chorus and produced records of a number of its performances while leading it to greater prominence in the national collegiate community. Gilchrist had grown up in a poor but close-knit minister's family, where his mother instilled in him a love for the Negro spiritual and gospel music and taught him to play the piano. Forced to forgo sports in school, he found an outlet in music. He played trumpet in the school band while developing his vocal and piano-playing skills. Gilchrist began his teaching career at Laurinburg Institute, directing instrumental groups. After obtaining a master's degree in choral directing from Indiana University in 1967, he returned to NCCU. He received a Ph.D. from UNC-Greensboro in 1980, meanwhile studying keyboard improvisation at the University of Miami, Coral Gables. While gospel and Negro spirituals were closest to his heart, Gilchrist loved all forms of music and exposed his students to its full range from around the world and across the ages. He became a noted music arranger and was music director of St. Joseph's A.M.E. Church. He was also guest conductor of the North Carolina Symphony and played at many weddings, parties, and community affairs. NCCU established a scholarship and endowed chair in his name.

The violinist Dr. Earl Sanders joined the music faculty in 1960 to teach music history, theory, and stringed instruments, while also directing the student string ensembles groups. He performed with many orchestras in North Carolina and with the Lynchburg (Virginia) Symphony. For a number of years, Sanders and the NCCU faculty members Lilian Pruett, pianist, and Mary Gray White, cellist, performed as the North Carolina Piano Trio at NCCU, Duke, and UNC-Chapel Hill. Sanders also performed in

faculty recitals at NCCU with the organist David Pizzaro and at Spelman College with the organist Joyce Finch Johnson. He was a member of the North Carolina Theatre Orchestra and concertmaster for the Durham Savoyards and the Long Leaf Opera Company. He performed in many jazz ensembles with such luminaries as Isaac Hayes, the Modern Jazz Quartet, Dave Brubeck, Benny Goodman, Dizzy Gillespie, Ella Fitzgerald, Boots Randolph, and Floyd Cramer. He played bluegrass with several ensembles and gospel with the Happy Goodman Family.

As director of the NCCU Lyceum Series from 1968 to 1988, Sanders expanded the variety of visiting artists. The Lyceum Series was an outgrowth of the tradition established by Dr. Shepard, who regularly hosted nationally and internationally known performers and speakers. While it was under his supervision, Dr. Shepard's personal letters of invitation to prominent town residents and leaders insured community participation, and all students were required to attend. Such singers as Roland Hayes and Marian Anderson appeared more than once, as did the Russian-born pianist Benno Moiseiwitsch and the American cellist Mary Fraley. Year after year the series introduced notables in the world of the arts to the community. As musical tastes changed over time, embracing popular black music by whites as well as blacks themselves, the series included artists such as the gospel singer Shirley Caesar and other jazz musicians.

Over the years other musicians visited NCCU and made their mark on the college and community. Through the philanthropy of Benjamin N. Duke, the college had obtained a thirty-six-rank pipe organ of high quality, which attracted noted faculty in keyboard studies—Celia E. Davidson (1929–2002) in the 1950s and later Paula Harrell, who was chairwoman of the department in 2005. As a result, NCCU's program as a whole grew in importance and variety. Student ensembles expanded to include the jazz and choir groups and later the university band, which began playing at athletic and civic events and local and out-of-state parades, as well as the string, brass, and wind ensembles. The band was originally established in the 1940s by Steven Wright and later directed by the music faculty members Wesley Howard and Joseph Mitchell.

Duke University

Over many years Duke University has been a vital source of music and musicians, although it was slow to recognize the value of music and the other arts in higher education. The emphasis of Trinity College, the predecessor of Duke University, was instead on academic and scholarly achievement. The arts seemed to these early educators only activities to fill leisure time. In addition, Trinity's tie to the Methodist church (which then had conservative moral views) slowed its acceptance of the arts as subjects of study. It was therefore as extracurricular activities that the arts first made their appearance on the Trinity campus. Amateur theatrical groups, glee clubs, and

Glee club, Trinity College *(Courtesy of Duke University Archives)*

instrumental musical groups were the harbingers of the musical arts on campus. Attitudes began to change in the 1920s after Trinity College had become Duke University and the spacious new campuses could accommodate a variety of performances.

While he was not the first to be hired to train voice ensembles at Duke, J. Foster Barnes, who joined Duke in 1927 to direct student glee clubs and social life, was given greater scope to develop music programs. He initiated the Chapel Choir for the newly built Duke Chapel in 1931 and established a subscription series, much like the Lyceum at NCCU, of visiting first-rank artists for performances in Page Auditorium soon after it opened. The first concert in 1931 brought Ignace Paderewski, the world-famous pianist, and performers throughout the years ranged from soloists such as Kiri Te Kanawa to groups as large as the Royal Philharmonic Orchestra of London. On Barnes's death in 1956, William Griffith took over administration of the Artists Series and Page Auditorium as part of his responsibilities as the first director of student affairs and the Student Union. During his term as director, segregation in Page Auditorium was abolished. He also brought Ella Fountain Pratt to campus to manage the arts performances; she became an invaluable leader and promoter of the arts for both the university and the larger community.

J. Foster Barnes (*Courtesy of Duke University Archives*)

Alice M. Baldwin, the first dean of the Woman's College which had been established with the new university, added Julia Wilkinson (later Mueller) to the faculty in 1939 to teach music history and instrumentation. Mueller also directed the women's orchestra. In 1941 Duke set up the Department of Art, Aesthetics, and Music (predecessor of both the art and music departments) under Katherine Gilbert's direction, introducing the arts to the curriculum. Gilbert, an eminent scholar, brought in music faculty not to train professional musicians but to provide a broad education in the arts. This addressed Dean Baldwin's concern that Duke not be in the business of training music teachers, considered a genteel occupation for southern ladies, at a time when Duke faculty women were working hard to be recognized for their academic accomplishments.

With the appointment to the department

Katherine Gilbert *(Courtesy of Duke University Archives)*

(Right) Allan Bone *(Courtesy of Duke University Archives)*

in 1944 of Allan Bone, who was responsible for the band and later the orchestra, music at Duke took on the role that it has consistently played ever since. That was characterized by an increased presence and importance on campus and encompassed service to the community as a whole. Despite segregation, which did not officially disappear until the 1960s, Bone bent the rules to break down the racial division. He insisted that Earl Sanders from NCCU be allowed not only to rehearse but also to perform with the Duke Symphony. Bone also thought that the black and white high school bands should not parade separately at Christmas; consequently he combined them into one parade, enduring much criticism as a result. Mueller and Bone worked well together, creating a strong base for musical studies at the university. In 1951 Paul Bryan, a specialist in brass instruments, was added to the faculty to conduct the student concert and marching bands. He also increased the opportunities for instrument study and performance.

It was an uphill battle for the music faculty to establish an independent department of music. The administration was resistant, one dean questioning the difference between piano playing and typing. There was also

Joaquin Sorolla y Bastida, *Portrait of Mary Lillian Duke (Mrs. Mary Duke Biddle 1892–1960)*, 1911, 83 x 44 ⅜ inches. Collection of the Nasher Museum of Art at Duke University, Gift of Nicholas Benjamin Duke Biddle. © 2008 Artists Rights Society (ARS), New York/ VEGAP, Madrid

prejudice against faculty members without Ph.D.'s, which many professional musicians and music educators lacked. But through the efforts of the music faculty, particularly Bone and Mueller, and with the support of Mary D. B. T. and James H. Semans, the Department of Music was established in 1960. A granddaughter of Benjamin N. Duke, graduate of Duke, and trustee and past chairwoman of the Duke Endowment, Mary Semans has been, with her husband, an untiring supporter of the arts.

In 1956 Mary's mother, Mary Duke Biddle, herself a musician and opera singer who had always wanted the university involved in the arts, established the foundation that bears her name. After her death the Semanses directed its philanthropy toward the activities that Mrs. Biddle had embraced, primarily the arts and particularly music. Hence the foundation played a major part in the creation of the Mary Duke Biddle Music Building, built in 1972, by substantial contributions to its planning and construction. It was dedicated in 1974 with great fanfare. Isaac Stern and Dizzy Gillespie were guests, and the resident composer Iain Hamilton wrote a *te deum* for the occasion, performed by the Duke Chorale and the Duke Wind Symphony in the new building's rotunda.

The foundation also encouraged the Music Department to consider and determine its future direction in a manner consistent with the goals of the university. The foundation's support has been available for many important projects, such as funding the first several years of the Ciompi Quartet and commissioning new compositions by Norman Dello Joio and Louis Mennini for the Duke Symphony and Duke Wind Symphony. The Mary Duke Biddle Foundation has also encouraged and sponsored many nonuniversity groups, including the Mallarmé Chamber Players in Durham and similar organizations elsewhere.

With the growth of the university and its music faculty, musical organizations proliferated. The Duke University Symphony was a reformulation and continuation in 1938 of the earlier men's and women's symphony orchestras led by Robert Fearing, who left Duke to join the army at the outset of the Second World War, and by Julia Wilkinson Mueller. After Allan Bone's arrival in 1944, he conducted the orchestra until 1980. Because Bone budgeted sufficient funds to hire a core of mature string players that supplemented the meager number of Duke students and town players, the orchestra was really a university-and-community institution. He also hired professional soloists and was able to perform an impressive portion of the standard orchestral repertory from Mozart to Mahler with an orchestra of symphonic proportions.

Under the leadership of Harry Davidson, the current conductor, the number of string players has significantly increased, especially helped by the recruiting efforts of the Ciompi Quartet, now a resident ensemble. The orchestra is now larger and plays standard repertory works by master composers, occasionally with professional soloists, and attracts large audiences. The Duke Wind Symphony, the new name chosen by the Duke students for the concert band, became a separate entity in 1974 when its members wished to distance themselves from marching and pep bands. They were playing serious music and hoped that their musical purpose might be recognized and accepted in the classical community. Professor Paul Bryan led the group from 1951 until 1988, when he retired. During those years the Wind Symphony performed a variety of music in regularly scheduled concerts. They also played the first concert given from the stone platform in front of the fishpond in the Duke Gardens. Over the years the Duke Wind Symphony has commissioned and performed many new works. The highlight of each year is the spring tour—north or south along the eastern seaboard. It offers an opportunity to spread the word about music and excellence at Duke University. For the students, one important side effect of the organization is a social one, much like that of a fraternity or sorority.

Members of the Wind Symphony have also traveled to Europe. In the 1970s Professor Bryan initiated the first Duke study-abroad music program. He directed the Duke Wind Symphony in five semester-long programs during which they performed in Austria, Germany, Italy, and Czechoslovakia. A lasting result of these programs has been an annual formal Viennese ball, held in the old city armory, where the Duke Wind Symphony plays traditional waltzes and polkas.

The Duke Madrigal Singers, under the direction of Eugenia Saville and the Duke Opera Workshop, was the inspiration of Professor John Hanks and came into being in the 1950s. A trained singer and art song specialist and

Madrigal singers at Duke University (*Courtesy of Duke University Archives*)

John Hanks (*Courtesy of Ella Fountain Pratt*)

a member of the faculty from 1954, Hanks produced graduates of the Opera Workshop who went on to illustrious careers with the Metropolitan Opera Company, including Michael Best and William Stone. Stone has had a particularly noteworthy career, having sung at La Scala and with the New York City Opera and the Chicago Lyric Opera.

Music composition became an established part of the curriculum with the appointment of William Klenz, a cellist and musicologist, in 1946. During his tenure he founded the Collegium Musicum, which performed medieval and Renaissance music. This effort reflected a revival of interest in classical music circles across the United States of learning and mastering early music performed on historically authentic instruments. In the early 1970s Frank Tirro, chairman of the music department, who was very well attuned to current trends, reinvigorated the organization, and it continued to thrive, presenting well-attended concerts in the Duke Chapel and the Nelson Music Room in the old East Duke Building. The Music Department lent the group original instruments from its collection. In the 1970s a number of groups were spun off the Collegium Musicum, including the Byrde Fancyer's Delyghte and Sinfonia. The Caldwell Ensemble emerged in the late 1980s, followed by the Taurus Ensemble in the 1990s. These groups were made up of Duke students as well as members of the community. The Triangle Recorder Society and the Feathered Fipples, also spinoffs, were entirely community entities.

At about the same time that other universities were incorporating jazz studies in their music curricula, Tirro, whose main scholarly interests were the unusual combination of jazz and Renaissance music, established a jazz studies program at Duke in 1977 (the same year he published a history of jazz) and recruited Mary Lou Williams to direct the new program. She also assumed direction of the Duke Jazz Ensemble, originally formed by Paul Bryan and Jessie Holton in 1969. Upon Williams's death in 1981, Paul Jeffrey succeeded her as professor of jazz studies at Duke. While on the faculty he established the annual spring North Carolina International Jazz Festival and the fall Duke Jazz Series. Both pro-

grams brought to Durham a number of jazz performers from throughout the United States and around the world. He retired in 2003.

In 1961 music composition was further promoted when the internationally known British composer Iain Hamilton was persuaded to join the newly created department. His appointment and retention over seventeen years were made possible by the Mary Duke Biddle Foundation. Among his many works during those years was an opera commissioned to commemorate the four hundredth anniversary of Sir Walter Raleigh's discovery of America; *Raleigh's Dream* was initially performed at Page Auditorium on June 3, 1984.

Through the efforts of the Semanses in 1979, Robert Ward, the well-known American composer and former director of the North Carolina School of the Arts in Winston-Salem, was persuaded to come to Duke. In contrast to Hamilton's atonal work, Ward's music adheres to the melodic classical style in its tonality, and its rich orchestration. Ward has written a large number of compositions for orchestra, chamber works, church and choral music, and operas. He is probably most widely known for his opera *The Crucible*, a musical setting of Arthur Miller's play, for which he won the Pulitzer Prize for music in 1961. Among his notable compositions while at Duke is *Music for a Great Occasion*, written for the inauguration of Terry Sanford as president of Duke. His *Images of God*, a liturgical choral play with its roots in a Biblical story, was also written during his years at Duke and performed in Duke Chapel.

Robert Ward *(Courtesy of Robert Ward)*

Ward was honored on his seventieth birthday by a performance of his works at Carnegie Hall by the North Carolina Symphony. Ward retired from the university in 1987 but continues to live in Durham and compose prolifically. His most recent works have been *Beginnings* (2007), commissioned to commemorate the founding of the North Carolina Symphony, his Seventh ("Savannah") Symphony, given its première by the orchestras in Augusta, Georgia, and at the University of South Carolina in March 2004, and music for the opera *A Friend of Napoleon*, given its première in 2005 in Wooster, Ohio.

A number of Ward's students have had successful careers. Michael Ching has worked variously as a conductor and artistic director with opera companies in Miami, Richmond, Memphis, and Houston, as well as with the Triangle Opera in Durham. Anthony Kelly, a composer now on the Duke music faculty, has a gospel music background, and his music has won many awards. Patrick Williams has written many scores for Hollywood films.

Currently, the distinguished composer Stephen Jaffe leads the composition program. He joined the Duke Music Department in 1981. Writing music that is both decidedly original and complex, he has won many awards. He composed his First String Quartet for the Ciompi Quartet, for which he was given the Kennedy Center Friedheim Award.

Because the university has a magnificent Gothic chapel at its center, and in accord with James B. Duke's instructions, music in the chapel is a vital part of Duke's service to the community. First used in 1932, and completed and dedicated in 1935 with the installation of its windows, the chapel was from the start ecumenical and designed to serve the entire university community. It grew over the years to take a prominent place in the spiritual life of the city as well. The chapel has three pipe organs of international cali-

Aeolian Organ, Duke University (*Courtesy of Duke University Archives*)

ber, and Duke Chapel and the Department of Music sponsor an organ recital series featuring the world's finest organists on these renowned instruments. The Æolian organ, which has four manual keyboards and a pedal keyboard with 6,900 pipes, was built and installed in 1932. The massive Æolian's appeal to a wide range of concert organists from around the world over many years was largely due to the tireless efforts of Mildred Hendrix (1905–1985), Chapel organist and university organist from 1944 until 1967 and professor of music from 1944 until her retirement in 1969. Not only was she able to cope with the increasing unreliability of the organ, but she was sensitive to its tonal idiosyncrasies and made it perform to its best po-

tential throughout the years. It was also during Hendrix's tenure that the Chapel organ program began to develop.

Recognizing that the Memorial Chapel was used for many smaller services, Hendrix and James T. Cleland, then dean of the Chapel, set about to secure an instrument for it as well. With the assistance of the Mary Duke Biddle Foundation, a contract was signed with the Holtkamp Organ Company of Cleveland and an instrument was installed in 1969 as the Mary Duke Biddle Organ. It was the first step toward obtaining a neo-baroque organ in Duke Chapel.

The Brombaugh organ was commissioned in 1995 and built by John Brombaugh, one of the world's most distinguished organ builders, as a replacement for the Holtkamp organ in the Memorial Chapel. The Holtkamp Organ had been given to Wofford College as a memorial to Duke's founding president Dr. William Preston Few, a graduate of Wofford (1889). The installation of the Brombaugh organ at Duke Chapel marked a transition back to the sounds and techniques of the early Italian organs before the time of J. S. Bach. The Brombaugh is one of few organs in the United States that can faithfully reproduce the sounds of organ music from over three hundred years ago. Robert Parkins, university organist, supervised its installation and played the dedication recital in 1997.

The Chapel's most important organ, the Flentrop Tracker (or Benjamin N. Duke Memorial Organ), rises above the entrance to the nave, spectacu-

lar in its height and design. It is the last organ designed and built under the direction of Dirk A. Flentrop in Zaandam, Holland, before his retirement from organ building. The organ contains 5,033 pipes with four manual keyboards and a pedal keyboard. It was designed and constructed to have the features of early-eighteenth-century northern European organs from around the time of Johann Sebastian Bach. Installed in 1976, the Flentrop organ is used mainly for processionals, recessionals, hymns, and voluntaries at worship services and university events. It also is heard in a free series of Sunday afternoon recitals by organists from around the world. Fenner Douglas, university organist at the time, played the inaugural recital.

Left to right: James Semans, Mary Semans, Ben Smith, Ella Fountain Pratt, *Seated:* Giorgio Ciompi *(Courtesy of Ella Fountain Pratt)*

The presence of these organs and a series of university organists of great virtuosity, such as Douglas, Peter Williams, the current university organist Robert Parkins, and the current Chapel organist David Arcus, have made Duke a center for organ study and performance. Daily noonday concerts serve the campus and visitors. The chapel also has a fifty-bell Taylor carillon, upon which J. Samuel Hammond, the university carillonneur, plays brief afternoon recitals.

The Duke Chapel music program, led from its inception by J. Foster Barnes and his successors Paul Young and James Young (not related), has commanded the respect of the sacred music community up and down the East Coast. With the arrival in 1968 of J. Benjamin Smith (1931–1989), the role of the Chapel's music expanded in both quantity and community outreach. Smith received a B.M. from the University of Kentucky and an S.M.M. from Union Theological Seminary in New York. When he arrived at Duke he already had much experience in choir direction (in New York, Georgia, Missouri, and Virginia) along with additional studies at the Fontainebleau and Paris conservatories. Wishing to bring Duke and Durham closer together, he successfully recruited townspeople for the Chapel Choir and initiated programs that involved collaboration among a number of Duke, NCCU, and Durham musical groups. He mounted Benjamin Britten's *Noye's Fludde*, which combined the Ciompi Quartet and Duke Symphony along with singers from the Duke University Chorale, the Durham

Boys Choir, the Carolina Friends School choir, and several Durham church choirs. The Duke University String School and the Triangle Recorder Society also contributed musicians. Another effort was Smith's presentation of the *African Sanctus* by David Fanshawe, with the Duke Chorale and the Modern Black Mass Choir. Along with memorable works old and new, Smith staged three operas in the chapel and utilized other musical styles to dramatize the services: liturgical dancing on a Palm Sunday and a jazz program for an All Saints Sunday. He also directed and gave the premières of commissioned works by Iain Hamilton, including *Raleigh's Dream*.

Rodney Wynkoop, who became musical director of the chapel and teacher of choral conducting in the music department in 1989, has continued his predecessor's work along these lines with exceptional artistic achievement. During his directorship the Chapel Choir has toured extensively, performing at Carnegie Hall, the Cathedral of St. John the Divine, and the Washington National Cathedral. Internationally they have sung in Poland, the

Rodney Wynkoop, © 2006 Frank Fournier / Contact Press Images (*Courtesy of Rodney Wynkoop*)

Czech Republic, and England, where they performed Handel's *Messiah* at St. Martin in the Fields with members of the English Festival Orchestra. The choir's annual performances of the *Messiah* with professional soloists and orchestra are a highlight of the holiday season for many Durhamites, and its spring oratorio concert, at which major choral works are performed, has long attracted full houses. In 1996 the Chapel Choir toured China with the Duke University Chorale.

The Duke University Chorale was created by Benjamin Smith in 1970, combining what had been for many years two separate choirs: the Men's Glee Club and the Women's Glee Club. Smith remained the conductor until 1983. He was succeeded after an interim year by Rodney Wynkoop, who remains conductor to the present day. Composed of fifty to seventy-five singers, most of whom are undergraduate or graduate students, the chorale is the primary choral group of the Music Department, performing in concert and on tour. Its annual tours during spring break have taken them from coast to coast and to Europe and China. The chorale's annual Christmas concert fills the chapel and inspires audience members to donate thousands of pounds of food for the hungry. Wynkoop's extraordinary success as leader of the music in Duke Chapel is matched by his achievements in the Durham community. Since 1986 he has conducted the Choral Society of Durham and the Vocal Arts Ensemble, an elite chamber choir that he founded in 1996.

Another campus venue with equally dedicated audiences is the Nelson Music Room, a beautiful old room in East Duke Building. It memorializes Ernest Nelson, a faculty historian and amateur pianist who was instrumental in establishing the Chamber Arts Society in 1945. The society has brought world-renowned ensembles to Durham every season for sixty years. Nelson is credited with doing much to create an environment in the city that allowed this type of programming to flourish. After consulting with a handful of dedicated musicians and music lovers, Nelson scheduled a roster of quartets for the first season. The first was the Carnegie Quartet, an ad hoc group created by members of the Pittsburgh Symphony for the occasion. Nelson handled the publicity and subscription correspondence, often making up from his own pocket any deficit at the end of a

Ernest W. Nelson *(Courtesy of Duke University Archives)*

season. He chauffeured performers from the airport when necessary and gave many well-remembered after-concert dinners for them and his committee. In 1963 Professor Leland Phelps took over the management of the society; during his tenure he wrote the history of this group, which has added much luster to the music community.

Duke University's influence in providing music of the highest quality for both students and community is exemplified by the creation in 1965 of the Ciompi Quartet, a resident group that teaches and performs regularly on campus and on worldwide tours. The conception for a resident musical entity of this sort was that of Allan Bone, who helped make it a reality while he was chairman of the Music Department. Duke's president Douglas Knight, Julia Mueller, and Ernest Nelson, along with the Semanses and the Biddle Foundation, were the other principal players.

The first Ciompi Quartet, 1965, Giorgio Ciompi—violin, Arlene di Cecco—violin, Julia Mueller—viola, Luca di Cecco—cello *(Courtesy of Ciompi Quartet)*

(Right) The present Ciompi Quartet, Eric Pritchard—violin, Hsiao-mei Ku—violin, Jonathan Bagg—viola, Fred Raimi—cello *(Courtesy of Ciompi Quartet)*

Giorgio Ciompi, a well-known violinist at the Cleveland Institute of Music and with the Albineri Trio, was asked to join the music department with the understanding that he would establish a resident quartet. He arrived in 1964 and by the following year he had put together the desired ensemble, which performed its initial concert that year. From the start, the quartet was fully integrated into the university, the players holding faculty positions and teaching regular courses as well as providing studio instruction. Like Ciompi, all the quartet members throughout the years have been enthusiastic teachers, working closely with their colleagues whether performing for music history classes or helping composition students understand the mechanics of musical instruments. They also record works by composition students to contribute to their portfolios. The original quartet comprised Ciompi, first violinist, Arlene di Cecco, second violinist, Julia Mueller, violist, and Luca di Cecco, cellist.

Ciompi loved Mozart, Schubert, and the French composers but did not care for Schoenberg and the other atonal composers. But since Ciompi's death its repertory has expanded to include the work of contemporary composers. Often the quartet commissions one or two new works a year or performs the latest works of composers in the music department. Because of the quartet's stature at the university and the loyalty and sophistication of its audience, the Ciompi Quartet has a certain freedom to be innovative in programming new and experimental music. During the course of many changes in personnel — six violinists, four violists, and two cellists — it has reached new heights in musicianship and mastery. Current members are all exceptional players: Eric Pritchard, first violinist (and newest member, though with over ten years' standing), Hsiao-Mei Ku, second violinist, Jonathan Bagg, violist, and Fred Raimi, cellist.

One other Duke-related program utilizing music in community outreach should be mentioned: the program integrating the arts into medical care and healing. It was the inspiration of Dr. James Semans, who was struck by the positive effect that music had on one patient's attitude. Initially funded by grants from the National Endowment for the Humanities and the Biddle Foundation, the program put paintings on the hospital walls and offered poetry to patients and staff, music for premature infants, and singing workshops for parents, young children, and women in pre-natal classes. Janice Palmer, who had been active in getting the arts into public schools, became the first director of the program.

Janice Palmer
(*Courtesy of Janice Palmer*)

Music for Children

A notable program involving children, now under Duke University's aegis although principally benefiting the community, is the Duke String School for Children, organized by Dorothy Kitchen and Arlene di Cecco in 1967. Paul Bryan conducted the string school orchestra in the early years. Later, when Mrs. Kitchen had difficulty obtaining volunteer conductors for the Saturday rehearsals, she took on the job herself after studying conducting with Allan Bone. While open to all children, the course of study remains rigorous. The school came under the wing of Duke University in 1973 when H. A. Fletcher made a sizable donation to the university's music school on the condition that it establish a string program for the young. Fletcher felt that it was critical to engage young people in classical music. One of the school's successful graduates is Nicholas Kitchen, Dorothy Kitchen's son, who went on to study at the Curtis Institute of Music and has become an internationally recognized soloist and chamber musician.

Another children's program in the city's cultural landscape is the North Carolina Boys Choir, established as the Durham Boys Choir in 1972. Although it has had no formal connection with the university, it has participated in many concerts in Duke Chapel, beginning with *Noye's Fludde* in 1975. After its performance with the North Carolina Symphony in 1983, the governor changed its name to North Carolina Boys Choir, though it remains an organization distinctly tied to Durham. Besides a full schedule of local concerts, it tours the state and nation.

Nicholas Kitchen, Ella Fountain Pratt, Robert Ward *(Courtesy of Ella Fountain Pratt)*

In a discussion of music for children, the music program in the Durham public schools must not be overlooked, particularly that at the historically black Hillside High School. Phillmore Hall, a classical and jazz musician, inaugurated the music and band programs there after his arrival in 1945. Hall rounded up and refurbished old instruments and added new ones to the collection. By 1951 his marching concert band totaled 125 students and had become known as one of the best in the state. Hall helped to establish the North Carolina Negro Bandmasters Association, which inaugurated annual competitions and festivals for black high school bands. Hall's students remembered him as a great instructor who worked under difficult conditions but enabled the bands to perform challenging concert music.

Many of Hillside's students went on to professional careers in music. One of them, Clarke Alston Egerton Jr., became director of music at Hillside from 1968 to 1997 and director of its symphonic, concert, and marching bands. He accomplished much given the limited resources available to him and trained a number of excellent musicians who in turn went on to successful professional careers in music, among them Andre Raphael Smith, who has been an assistant conductor at the New York Philharmonic and the Philadelphia Orchestra as well as a guest conductor with a number of other orchestras.

Other Community Music

Durham has been rich in its number of community-based classical instrumental and vocal groups. One of the oldest, the Choral Society of Durham, was established in 1949 as the Durham Oratorio Society. There had been earlier choral societies, but by this time those who wished to sing in such a group had to look to Raleigh. In 1949 Jane Watkins Sullivan and Marian Wallace Smith decided to establish a choral ensemble in Durham. Through their efforts a group of sixteen singers was formed, and the next winter it performed its first concert with Allan Bone and the Duke Symphony. During Paul Bryan's tenure as director (1957–62) he achieved an integrated chorus by merging the group with the NCCU choral group, made up of students and members of the black community. In 1961 Afrika Hayes, professor of music at NCCU and daughter of the famed singer Roland Hayes, was the first black soloist with the chorus.

Performing under several names, the Choral Society has grown to 150 singers and performed classical choral masterworks, both sacred and secular, as well as a few commissioned modern works. Its sterling performances have been due to high standards of admission to membership and excellent training by its several directors, including Bone, Bryan, Robert Porco, and since 1986 Rodney Wynkoop.

Governor James Martin and Vincent Simonetti, ca. 1990 *(Courtesy of Vincent Simonetti)*

Similar circumstances—lack of a group based in Durham and a long commute to play in an orchestra—resulted in the organization of the Durham Symphony Orchestra in 1977. The North Carolina Symphony's move from Durham to Raleigh increased the sense of need. An enterprising group of musicians remedied the loss and assembled interested musicians with Vincent Simonetti as their conductor. Simonetti, a tuba player, had previously played with the North Carolina Symphony. The organizing group consisted of Alice Smith, oboist, Chris Meyers, bassoonist, Virginia Zehr flautist, and Dan Zehr, double bass player. They put up posters around town to advertise an organizational meeting and within a few months had a full orchestra. Originally all members were amateur musicians with the exception of Earl Sanders, a violinist at NCCU. Impressed with the nascent orchestra, Ciompi appeared as a soloist with the group from time to time. Today the orchestra is made up of about equal numbers of amateurs and professionals. After rehearsing for many years wherever it could find space, in 1990 the orchestra found a permanent base at the Durham Arts Council.

When Simonetti stepped down in 1984, the group found a new conductor in Alan Nielsen, formerly founder and conductor of the Raleigh Symphony and principal flautist with the North Carolina Symphony. Open to all professionally trained musicians by audition, it aims to foster appreciation of music and conducts an active outreach program. It performs at shopping malls, parks, nursing homes, and schools and conducts a Young Artists Competition from which winners are invited to perform with the symphony.

After leaving the Durham orchestra, Vincent Simonetti organized the Durham Community Concert Band with Randy Guptill, the successful leader of the Lowes Grove junior high school band. In 1985 Clark Edgerton became director of the group and the word "community" disappeared from the name. It remains truly a community band, however, and includes fifty-five members of various ages and ethnic backgrounds. Now directed by Tom Shaffer and associated with the Durham Arts Council, the band performs a regular series of concerts in various places including the Forest at Duke and other retirement communities, as well as at fairs, celebrations, hospitals, malls, sporting events, and parades.

For its size, Durham has an exceptionally large pool of talented musicians—enough to support several other instrumental ensembles, including the Chamber Orchestra of the Triangle and the Mallarmé Chamber Players. The Chamber Orchestra was incorporated as a nonprofit group in 1988 under the direction of Lorenzo Muti. Originally it had been a small chamber orchestra, formed in 1982 through the efforts of the director of music at St. Stephen's Episcopal Church, Joseph Kitchen. Later it was conducted by George Taylor, violist of the Ciompi Quartet. Although the group was originally called St. Stephen's Chamber Orchestra, only a few of the original twenty musicians were members of the church. No longer church-sponsored, the orchestra now supports itself through ticket sales, donations, and other funding. Its particular charm is its widely varied repertory of classical music played by equally varied combinations of instrumentalists.

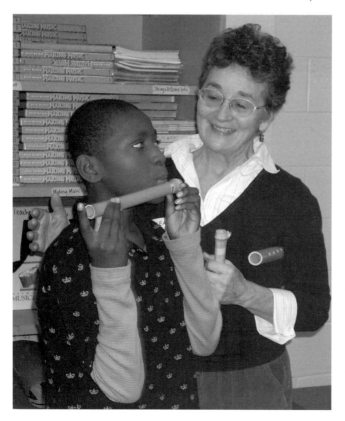

Anna Wilson, making bamboo flutes with an Eastway Elementary 5th grader *(Courtesy of Anna Wilson)*

The Mallarmé Chamber Players grew out of the Tuesday night concert series held by the Durham Arts Council in the lounge of the Carolina Theatre in the 1980s. Anna L. Wilson and Jane Hawkins, along with the artist services director of the council, Margaret DeMott, had founded the group in 1984. Two years later they incorporated it as an independent nonprofit entity. Wilson has served as artistic director and principal administrator since that time. Under her direction the twenty-five regular members have focused on rarely performed works from the classical repertory as well as works of diverse and unusual interest. The ensemble broke new ground by presenting nontraditional participatory and interdisciplinary performances, combining music with dance, poetry, and visual art, sometimes with commentary by the artists. The players have also offered a strong children's education program and taken their music to the schools throughout North Carolina. In 1990 the group moved its performances into the newly renovated theater of the Durham Arts Council.

Musical Theater and Opera

Durham's musical menu has also included musical theater and operatic efforts. The Durham Savoyards, like its sister organizations throughout the world, is devoted to performing the comic operas of William S. Gilbert and Arthur Sullivan. While the establishment of this organization in 1965 gave Durham a firmly based troupe that has mounted annual productions for over forty years, occasional performances of Gilbert and Sullivan had been staged in previous decades. The Durham Conservatory of Music produced *The Mikado* about the beginning of the twentieth century. Under the sponsorship of W. M. Upchurch, selections from Gilbert and Sullivan were sung in the 1930s between showings of feature films at Duke Quadrangle Pictures. J. Foster Barnes directed and Professor Paul Gross and his wife, Estelle ("Peter") Peterson Gross, mounted a *Mikado* for the annual convention of the American Chemical Society (1937), and during the war years they staged *The Pirates of Penzance* and *Iolanthe* as benefits for the British War Relief. Jake Waggoner led the Temple Baptist Church Choir in a production of *Trial By Jury*; Ken Shepherd of St. Joseph's Episcopal Church organized performances of *The Mikado* and in 1944, through the Braggtown Baptist Church, *Ruddigore*. He called his troupe the Durham Light Opera Company. Finally, a group of Gilbert and Sullivan enthusiasts persuaded the Durham Theatre Guild to mount a production at the end of the 1963 season. With unbelievable speed they produced *The Pirates of Penzance* under the direction of Paul Bryan and Bill McIlwinnen in the Durham High School auditorium that May, and the next season they did *H.M.S. Pinafore*; both played to enthusiastic audiences. The Durham Savoyards was formed when the guild persuaded the devotees of the operettas to establish their own group.

Besides the Duke professors Bryan and Bone, musical and artistic directors for the Savoyards have been NCCU's professors Randolph Umberger and Benjamin Keaton. The organization attributes its longevity and suc-

Paul Bryan conducting
in Baldwin Auditorium,
Duke University, pho-
tograph by Jim Wallace
(Courtesy of Paul Bryan)

cess to its high standards of performance. Live orchestra, good soloists, and costumes, lighting, and settings of professional quality have produced top-notch amateur performances to the delight of the community. One of the originators, a fine singer himself and a participant in twenty-five of the operettas, was Dr. Patrick Kenan, who took the whole group to Durham, England, to perform in 1995. Another participant, Michael Best, voice student of John Hanks at Duke who starred in the 1963 production of *The Pirates of Penzance*, went on to a career with the Metropolitan Opera Company, and Brenda Hartill, the set designer for the 1969 production, left to design sets for the National Theatre Company in London.

The success of the Savoyards encouraged Umberger and Keaton to form the Long Leaf Opera in 1999. They hoped to perform significant works originally written in English and inspired by the American experience—works by such composers as Bernstein, Barber, Copland, Joplin, and Marsalis. The company is composed of young singers (chosen by auditions), who perform three major operas a season and one concert performance of operatic arias.

Opera had been tried in Durham's past but without lasting results. An exciting effort in the early 1980s ended after an interesting and rewarding decade. It resulted from the collaboration of several people inspired by the same dream. About the time that Robert Ward's opera *The Crucible* was produced under the auspices of Duke's drama department and the newly created Institute of the Arts, the Semanses, who had financed and accompanied students from the North Carolina School of the Arts on successive study trips abroad, were pondering an idea of their own. They had experienced the success of the German composer Hans Werner Henze's "street opera" technique, which brought opera directly to the people, and engaged the interest of Barrie Wallace, an opera enthusiast and Arts Council leader, in developing the concept. Wallace involved Michael Marsicano, Arts Council director, who in turn consulted Ward. Ward believed that Durham's picturesque renovated tobacco warehouses in Brightleaf Square would be an excellent location for such an experiment, and he immediately hit on Bizet's *Carmen*, the story of a cigarette girl, as an appropriate first production. The street opera came to life

Michael Best *(Courtesy of Ella Fountain Pratt)*

under the auspices of the Arts Council with Ward as the artistic director, John Clum, English professor and member of the Duke drama program, as stage director, and Ella Fountain Pratt, a former director of the Duke Office of Cultural Affairs, as producer and general manager. Clum was able to bring in the vital support of Duke's drama production staff, which provided access to costumes and scenery. The group drew on local talent, enlisting the Durham Symphony, a chorus made up of singers from the Savoyards and the Choral Society, and professional soloists from the local and national arenas. Hilda Harris, a Durham native, NCCU graduate, and Metropolitan Opera star, sang the title role.

The resounding success of the opera, which drew coverage in the *New York Times*, inspired Ward to continue. In 1985, with the help of Duke's director of cultural affairs Susan Coon, the new director of the Institute of the Arts, Michael Cerveris, Clum, and Pratt, who again undertook the fund-raising and practical details of the production, Ward formed the Triangle Music Theater Association. TMTA obtained financial support from a number of generous donors as well as the Durham Arts Council, Duke University, and the Biddle Foundation. They presented a different opera each summer for almost ten years, but failed to establish a strong development strategy, with the result that the company suffered financially

World premiere of "Strange Fruit," June 2007, Erina Newkirk as Nonnie Anderson, Charles Stanton as Tracy Deen, photograph by the News and Observer *(Courtesy of Long Leaf Opera)*

when the original backers began to withdraw support. The summer of 1994 spelled doom for the outdoor event; five of its ten scheduled performances were canceled because of bad weather, and the company had its first deficit. In spite of measures to retrench, among them producing only tested operatic winners instead of including innovative new works along with the old, TMTA came to an end. The effort continued a further eight years as Triangle Opera under the musical direction of Scott Tilley, a former student of Ward in composition and conducting, but it folded after the 2001–2 season.

Church Music

Music has been part of virtually all religious establishments in the South. Most Durham churches have clung to the traditional Protestant hymns and European sacred classics, performed until the 1920s primarily by amateurs under the direction of other amateurs. Gradually, as professional organists and choir directors became the norm in the wealthier churches, the quality and sophistication of church music rose. A change in the repertory also occurred with the introduction of gospel music in some evangelical and black churches.

Along with the improvement in performance came a demand for better organs, the instrument with a central role in church music. In addition to the organs in the Duke Chapel, several town churches invested in superior instruments. St. Stephen's Episcopal Church, like Duke Chapel, has a Flentrop organ, the gift of the philanthropist Frank Kenan, installed in a sanctuary especially designed for musical performances. Besides having incubated what became the Chamber Orchestra of the Triangle, St. Stephen's continues to present varied musical concerts of exemplary quality, thus fulfilling the wish of the Duke mathematics professor Joseph Kitchen, music director there until 1988 and current organist, that such a marvelous environment be used to full capacity and shared with the wider Durham community.

St. Philip's Episcopal Church has also offered memorable concerts under its choir directors, currently Kent Otto and his predecessor David Pizarro, a professor of organ at NCCU. Both have conducted active music programs outside the regular worship services. Pizarro played an important role in establishing Sunday afternoon concerts at Duke, NCCU, and the community churches under the auspices of the local American Guild of Organists (AGO). While Pizarro was music director, he discovered that funds were available from the musicians' union to pay professional musicians when they performed for nonprofit organizations. This enabled him to present top-notch musical performances. Pizarro was also known for his playful and maverick approach to liturgical music. Madrigal dinners and Early Music have become yearly Christmas features in recent years at St. Philip's.

Duke Memorial Methodist Church had Jane Sullivan as its organist and choir director in the late 1950s and 1960s. She drew on her students' talents to embellish the church music. She was succeeded in 1961 by the accomplished organist and choir director Ruth Seifert Phelps. About the same time the church acquired a fine new Holtkamp organ, enabling Phelps to add organ concerts to the musical fare of the church. She also presented other performers, choral and instrumental, with professional soloists and ensembles. For almost seventy-five years the church has also contributed to the town a daily noonday peal from its ten-bell carillon, a gift in 1908 from the Stagg family. Albert Buehler has rung the bells since 1980, currently sharing the responsibility with Fuller Sasser and J. Stuart McCracken.

The two oldest and most influential churches in the black community, White Rock Baptist Church and St. Joseph's A.M.E., also have active music programs for community enjoyment. Charles Gilchrist was the music director of St. Joseph's for a number of years, and John Henry Gattis was director of the senior choir and organist at White Rock for over forty-four years; both were trained musicians. The musical repertory in these churches has expanded to include Negro spirituals and gospel music, both musical forms embraced by mainstream black society. It was the Reverend Miles Mark Fisher (1899–1970), pastor from 1933 until 1965, who reintro-

Miles Mark Fisher
(Courtesy of White Rock Baptist Church)

duced the Negro spiritual to his parishioners in a series of annual fall lectures. His love and understanding of the Negro spiritual and "its place in old-time religion" were learned from his father, a Baptist preacher in Chicago who had been a slave. He won the American Historical Association's prize for the best historical study in 1953 for his book *Negro Slave Songs in the United States*, which traced the evolution of the Negro spiritual.

While the larger churches were improving the quality and variety of their musical offerings, a uniquely American sacred music—gospel—was emerging in the community's smaller churches and religious gatherings. Gospel drew on the Negro spiritual form along with other forms of folk music, including Tin Pan Alley songs and secular ballads, reworked with religious lyrics. Shape-note singing schools and non-denominational camp meetings, in which both blacks and whites took part, were significant contributors to gospel's origins. Gospel music was originally thought of as antithetical to the secular blues and jazz, which were becoming popular in the same period. The Pentecostal and Holiness Churches that emerged in the 1910s, and their emotional and participatory style of worship, contributed to the further development of gospel music. Later the Free Will Baptists took up the form. The congregations of these churches were made up primarily of rural residents and of mill and factory workers. Music publishers soon latched on to the trend. National companies such as James D. Vaughan, Stamps-Baxter, Thomas Dorsey, Martin & Morris, and Roberta Martin Music, the latter two started by black women, not only published sheet music but were prominent in establishing singing conventions that became popular with members of Pentecostal and Holiness churches. Durham had its own camp meetings and singing conventions as early as the 1890s, and these lasted until about 1960. In the tobacco factories, where the black workers commonly sang as they worked, quartets developed that also competed with each other in public competitions.

While the white and black congregations each developed their own form of gospel music—now known as southern gospel and black gospel—the two genres developed from the same roots and with much sharing of material and ideas. Southern gospel could be found in the churches of West Durham's mill village, where the workers held monthly Sunday hymn "sings" at each church in turn. Often professional quartets would perform there—such as the Porter Sisters or the Friendly Four. "Sings" were commonly held at the Durham Athletic Park during the 1960s and later, until 1993, at Durham High School. In that year J. D. Sumner and the Stamps Quartet per-

Friendly City Gospel Singers, ca. 1940 (*Courtesy of North Carolina Collection, Durham County Library*)

formed along with the local group the Spokesmen, formed in 1967 by Linwood Wilson of the West Durham Church of God and J. L. Jack of the First Wesleyan Church. In 1971 this group went on the road; it has since toured extensively on the southern gospel circuit. Now based in Bahama, North Carolina, it has issued several recordings.

In 1941 the minister of West Durham Pentecostal Church, D. D. Freeman, started a Sunday morning radio program on WDNC, which broadcast the Porter Sisters as well as the church choir and lasted until 1954. About the same time WDNC began to broadcast a black gospel program originated by Norfley Whitted, who had been a janitor at the station before his golden voice earned him a promotion to announcer. Whitted featured his own group, the Swanees, as well as other local groups such as Just Come Four, the Patriotic Four, Bright Moon Quartet, and the Four Internes. The Four Internes were Duke Hospital workers (Eugene Mumford, Theodore Freeland, Raymond David, and Mac Farrell) who would sing during their breaks, much to the appreciation of the doctors and nurses. Encouraged by the medical staff, they held their first public performance in 1941 at East End school. By 1950 the Internes was the first Durham gospel group to have a regularly broadcast television program—on WTVD.

With time there was a crossover of the southern and black gospel circuits. The Landis Family gospel group, a black group now known as Landis and Company and based in Creedmoor, sings both black and southern gospel music on the southern gospel circuit. Charles Johnson, a resident of Durham and former member of the Sensational Nightingales, consciously

Norfley Whitted announces radio broadcast, ca.1940 *(Courtesy of North Carolina Collection, Durham County Library)*

Shirley Caesar
(Courtesy of Eno River Association)

mixes the two styles in an effort to bridge the separation, as he says, and to celebrate the music that speaks to all Americans' religious needs.

Although some gospel singers may record professionally and take their music on tour, for most the music is a form of evangelism, a way to bring their ministry to the people. This is certainly true for the most widely known of Durham's gospel singers, the "first lady of gospel" Shirley Caesar, for the Spokesmen, and for many others.

Popular Music

Gospel is not the only uniquely American music to which Durhamites have contributed. Innovative musicians and their devotees living in the area have played important roles in the development of blues, jazz, string band, and country music, to mention a few. Perhaps best known because it has been extensively researched is the active blues scene in Durham. The association of blues with slavery and the black underclass delayed its acceptance into the musical mainstream. Its musical patterns and verse forms, with lyrics expressing melancholy or cynicism about life's problems, distinguish it from other forms of black music. Piedmont blues, the Durham variety, is distinguished from Delta blues by its upbeat, dancelike rhythms and picking style of guitar playing. The music evolved out of rags and reels—country dance tunes—originally played on banjos with fiddle and percussion accompaniment. The Piedmont musicians also picked up elements of jazz and Delta blues—music that they would have heard from touring musicians and available recordings.

The most famous and influential blues artists to emerge in the 1930s and 1940s included Blind Boy Fuller, the Reverend Gary Davis, Sonny Terry, and Brownie McGhee. Fuller, the most often recorded, was famous for his syncopated rhythms, while Davis, a prominent guitar teacher, was known for making the guitar "talk," a feature of Piedmont blues. Terry and McGhee won national recognition after they moved to New York in 1941, and they were the first blues musicians to tour in Europe in the 1950s. The fame of these players is due to their discovery by J. B. Long, the manager of the Dollar Store in Durham, and his determination to record and profit from the sale of their work. The records were commercial successes.

Some blues singers took up street performing as a livelihood. During the Depression, they were drawn to Durham by the still-thriving tobacco markets. They haunted the warehouses and picked up tips, which they supplemented by playing at "house parties" (unadvertised meeting places where liquor could be illegally obtained with other entertainment) and in other informal social settings. Their instruments were cheap, readily available, and easy for self-taught musicians to learn to play—guitar, washboard, and harmonica. An occasional blues pianist would be hired by a legitimate venue. The Wonderland Theatre in Hayti employed Duncan Garner, known as one of the best jazz pianists.

As some musicians moved north and as popular taste changed, the blues scene in Durham faded away until its rediscovery in the 1970s. In 1974 the state established the Office of Folklife in the Department of Cultural Resources, which helped to rekindle interest in all aspects of folk culture. But the revival was also spurred in part by the "British Invasion" and the popularity of rock-and-roll bands that were performing blues classics. Mick Jagger of the Rolling Stones and Eric Clapton had both heard, as children, the music of Terry and McGhee on British television. Bob Dylan, Jerry Garcia of the Grateful Dead, and Jorma Kaukonen of Jefferson Airplane also heard the bluesmen and sought out and were influenced by the original recordings. The Grateful Dead, who had played in Durham in 1971 and 1973, performed Davis's *Samson and Delilah* at Duke in 1976. White youths who embraced this rock music then went on to rediscover its sources for themselves. Those in Durham found the musicians in their own backyard.

A number of musicians from Durham participated in the early blues scene and saw their careers rejuvenated during the 1970s. John Snipes, John Dee Holeman, and Fris Holloway were tracked down and persuaded to perform for the first time at schools and public functions. Some performed at the North Carolina Folklife Festival in 1976, their first time before a large and ethnically diverse audience. McGhee and Terry also came back to Durham to perform at that time. Glenn Hinson, then a student at UNC and now a professor of folklore there, did much to bring back the blues tradition to Durham. Specializing in the study of black vernacular music, he lent his enthusiasm to the revitalization efforts, and in 1987 he was the master of ceremonies for the original Bull City Blues Festival. It recurs annually as the Bull Durham Blues Festival, sponsored by Hayti Heritage Center.

Holeman (1929–), a native of Orange County, is one of the last musicians to have heard the first Durham bluesmen and carries on the tradition in his own playing. He heard the music when he went with his father, Willy Holeman, to the warehouses for the fall tobacco auctions. At fourteen, Holeman taught himself to play the guitar by observing the musicians at country get-togethers and listening to their recordings. He began to perform himself at corn shuckings, wood choppings, pig pickings, and other social gatherings. Discovered in the 1980s and asked to perform at the Eno River

John Dee Holeman & Fris Holloway *(Courtesy of the Eno River Association)*

festivals, he has continued to play across the country and in Europe and Africa. He has received the North Carolina Folk Heritage Award and a National Folk Heritage Award Fellowship.

Music historians have not given jazz in Durham the same attention as the blues. Failure to recognize its importance has been due perhaps to lack of a friendly environment. For many decades, liquor laws discouraged bars and similar establishments from offering live entertainment; the area also lacked radio stations that programmed jazz or a J. B. Long interested in recording local jazz musicians. These factors have combined to obscure the presence of a rich local jazz scene.

Yet North Carolina has produced many noteworthy jazz musicians who have influenced jazz nationally, including Thelonious Monk of Rocky Mount and John Coltrane of Hamlet. Even Dizzy Gillespie, though born in South Carolina, received his musical training in North Carolina at the Laurinburg Institute from Phillmore Hall (later music director at Hillside High School in Durham). These artists shared deep roots and drew inspiration from their spiritual base as church musicians. After leaving the state to pursue their careers, they met in the North to perform, share ideas, and create the foundation of modern jazz, their Carolina sensibilities infusing the whole. Later Durham musicians had parallel experiences: Grady Tate, Mickey Tucker, and John Malachi, all of Durham, performed in their churches and played with Monk, Coltrane, and Gillespie when they too moved north.

In the 1930s and 1940s, while the bluesmen were working the crowds on the streets and at house parties, strains of jazz were heard elsewhere. It was the big band era, and nationally known groups visited Durham to play in the empty warehouses downtown and at the Wonderland Theatre and the Biltmore Hotel in Hayti. There were stars such as Duke Ellington, Count Basie, and Fletcher Henderson. Duke University itself had a number of notable swing bands. In 1926 the university recruited George "Jelly" Leftwich as both an undergraduate and leader of the student bands. The Blue Devils Band was born. After Leftwich's graduation the band was directed by Les Brown. Both men went on with professional careers as bandleaders with their own bands, and Les Brown Jr., still carries on with his father's "band of renown." Johnny Long established the Collegians and di-

Wonderland Theatre, 1923
(Courtesy of North Carolina Collection, Durham County Library)

The Duke Ambassadors, left to right: Norm Nelson, Dick Gable, Forrest Cox, John Ziolkowski, Farris Anderson *(Courtesy of Charles Register)*

rected them from 1931 to 1934. In the mid-1930s Sonny (Joe) Burke extended the tradition with the Duke Ambassadors. While at Duke these bands performed during the students' dinner time and at weekend dances. Off campus they played on the local radio station and at honky-tonks. One such place was on Chapel Hill Road not far from Hope Valley's gates. It was a favorite haunt of Duke students, frequented by whites and rumored to have been visited by Thomas Wolfe and William Faulkner.

During the Second World War, because of the nearby Camp Butner, Durham developed a busy nightlife that lasted well into the 1960s. After the war all kinds of people were moving to town and black music was "jumping in Durham," as the UNC folklorist Glenn Hinson relates. Most significant was the arrival of Phillmore "Shorty" Hall, a trained musician from the Laurinburg Institute, to teach at Hillside High School. Hall, an orphan by the age of nine and always short, was adopted and raised by a white family in Indianapolis. At Tuskegee Institute in Georgia, where he earned his undergraduate degree, the bandmaster, Captain Frank Drye, recognized Hall's musical talent and trained him with the exacting discipline of a soldier in European styles and techniques. Hall was adept at playing difficult variations and "tonguing." From 1925 until 1931 he played trumpet with the Black Birds of Paradise, a black jazz band in Montgomery, Alabama, and recorded short pieces on an album released under the Black Patti label by the Gennett Company.

Hall became a teacher and established his first band at Laurinburg Institute in 1934. He also toured with Speed Webb's band, based in Cincinnati, and played cornet at the 1939 New York World's Fair. In the 1940s he played with Tony Pastor's and Fletcher Henderson's bands. Having received an advanced degree, he moved to Hillside High in 1945. Not only did he produce musicians there who went on to careers in jazz, such as Grady Tate, the well-known trumpeter, drummer, and vocalist, but he also had his own swing band, the Bull City Night Hawks, who performed at the warehouses and other places around town, including the Carolina Theatre. The band consisted of Hall, trumpet, William ("Lanky") Cole, piano, and Frank Wright, alto sax, as well as a bass player and a drummer. This group continued to play for dances and at a number of town venues into the 1950s. Later Hall moved to Fairfax, Virginia, where he taught in the Fairfax County schools until his retirement in 1973.

One place that drew these local musicians as well as visiting performers was the nightclub the City News Stand, whose owner, Ike Linsey, was a drummer and xylophone player. The News Stand survived for some time, unlike most nightclubs that have come and gone. In the 1960s there were not many places where a band could play. The Triangle Coffee House on Duke University Road, however, was a hangout for one musician who had played guitar with the Duke Ambassadors in his student days—Harrison Register. A native of Durham, Register performed in a number of later bands, for example the Harlequins, for whom he arranged and composed. He also arranged and composed for radio and television stations and worked as an audio engineer in the recording business.

The 1970s brought Brother Yusef Salim, jazz pianist, and Carole Sloane, jazz vocalist, to Durham. Salim's restaurant and nightclub on West Chapel Hill Street provided a place for jazz and is credited with creating an upsurge of interest in jazz and with fostering young local jazz artists such as Nnenna Freelon, Eve Cornelious, Lois Deloatch, and Bus Brown. More recently Salim has performed with Adia Ledbetter, vocalist, and her father Freeman Ledbetter, bass player, in a group called Generations.

Carole Sloane, a Rhode Islander who lived and performed mostly in Durham from 1977 to the mid-1980s, lured nationally known jazz musicians to perform in Durham and the surrounding areas. Her introduction to one Durham resident, Lee Wing, proved mutually productive. The two were brought together by Connie and

The Harlequins
(Courtesy of Charles Register)

The original Journeymen: Harrison Register, guitar; Paul Montgomery, piano; J. Paul Scott, bass; Dave Moffett, drums *(Courtesy of Charles Register)*

Billy Banks, Yusef Salim, and Chuck Owen *(Courtesy of Yusef Salim)* Thanks to Jeff Ensminger and Elissa Brown

Montrose Moses, untiring supporters of both drama and jazz in Durham. Sloane found Wing to be an unheralded jazz composer and aficionado and began to perform many of Wing's vocal compositions. She played a role in Wing's musical "The Scandalous Mrs. Jack" for which Harrison Register wrote the musical arrangements. It was performed in Raleigh, the music supplied by the Jazz Journeymen, in which Register played the guitar and Paul Montgomery the piano.

Born Lee Abrahmson in New Orleans, Wing had little formal musical training but a great deal of natural talent. She got her first break when Pearl Bailey sang her song "Pushin' Forty" in 1965, the year Wing moved with her husband to Durham. As a neighbor of the Moses family, she was quickly drawn into their jazz circle, which included Paul Montgomery and the Jazz Journeymen. Wing's son, now a professional musician and faculty member at UNC, carries on the jazz tradition in his spare time after a start at venues such as Brother Yusef's and the Stallion Club on Alston Avenue. For a time the lounge of the Carolina Theatre was a focal point for jazz in Durham when Stephen Barefoot, the theatre booker, ran the nightclub Stephen's After All there.

The Triangle now also supports the North Carolina Jazz Repertory Orchestra, founded in 1993, which includes eighteen musicians, of whom many are local university educators.

Rhythm and blues, or R&B, which evolved from the blues, emerged in Durham in the 1960s as the popularity of the blues waned with the younger generations. R&B could be heard on the "chitlin' circuit," the name for a collection of bars, theaters, and nightclubs available to black performers in the 1950s and 1960s. In Durham touring R&B artists would play at the Regal Theatre and at the Stallion Club on Alston Avenue, which catered to an ethnically mixed audience. Native R&B artists in the 1950s included Eugene Mumford (originally a gospel singer with the Internes) and Clyde McPhatter. During the 1960s the local group Modulations performed at the Stallion Club; their member Willie Hill runs a recording studio and has performed at the Talk of the Town on East Main Street. Two nationally known artists and NCCU graduates, Sunshine Anderson and Yasirah, launched their R&B careers there. Over time R&B evolved nationally to soul and funk but has retained its popularity in Durham.

Since the 1970s Durham has provided an increasingly strong audience for other forms of popular music: rock-and-roll, beach music, hip-hop, reggae, and zydeco. Radio stations that play these kinds of music have had an important influence in sustaining their popularity and in determining which varieties thrive. During the 1980s Durham was home to a number of rock bands, such as the Flying Pigs, led by Pat O'Connell, who performed at Halby's in Forest Hills and the Hideaway Lounge on Duke's campus. Billy Stevens organized two bands: the Red Herring and the Boney Maroney Band. Today Little Brother, a hip-hop group, reaches a national audience through its recordings. Hip-hop and its international influences were the subject of a conference at Duke in 2003.

String band, country, and folk music also developed in Durham, this time within its mill communities. In the 1950s, when television came on the scene with the local station WDNC, country and old-time string band music, which had been kept alive in mill villages and rural communities, now came to prominence. The sources of these genres were many: vaudeville, which blended older folk music and Tin Pan Alley hits, gospel, and blues. In addition to the fiddle, one of the principal instruments was the banjo, of African origin. While both blacks and whites commonly played the music, in Durham County it tended to be identified with the white working class. Dance halls on the edges of town provided the venue. The West Durham mill village had its own performance place, Erwin Auditorium, which survived into the 1960s. All kinds of community activities took place there, from "stew" dinners to concerts, picnics, and square dances, always with live music. Cocky Bennett, manager of the auditorium and a square dance caller, in the 1950s started a tradition of Saturday night square dances with music by the Tobacco Land Playboys. Players included Faison Perry, fiddle, Ike Browning, bass, Calvin Blake, guitar, and the callers Cocky Bennett and Norwood Tew, "the singing blacksmith." Later Tew had a live radio program on which he and other mill musicians performed.

Nashville, known as the center of "hillbilly" music after the Grand Ole Opry was established there, attracted many of Durham's mill-village musicians, some of whom settled there permanently. John D. Loudermilk, now in the Nashville Songwriters' Hall of Fame, grew up in West Durham's mill village. When he was only twelve he had a radio show on WTIK called the "Little Johnny Dee Show." Later his song "A Rose and a Baby Ruth" was picked up there and recorded by George Hamilton IV, who sold more than a million copies. In 1958 Loudermilk moved to Nashville, where he plunged into the country music industry, working for Chet Atkins and writing and performing songs. Loudermilk's hit "Tobacco Road" (1962), based on a notorious Durham alley, was taken up in 1964 by nationally known performers.

Other Durham songwriters who moved to Nashville were Tom House, Phil Lee, and Don Schlitz. Another product of the West Durham mill village, Schlitz got his break in Nashville in 1978 when Kenny Rogers recorded his song "The Gambler." Of his dozens of songs the one called "Oscar the Angel" has particular meaning for Durhamites, who remember the lovable street person who is its subject. In 2001 the Broadway musical *The Adventures of Tom Sawyer* brought Schlitz fame for its music and lyrics.

A Durham cousin and collaborator of Schlitz, Tom House has had similar success in Nashville. Poetry has also been of primary importance to him, and he continues to publish poems as well as perform and record music. He has collaborated on several operas based on stories by Southern authors, including Faulkner and Lee Smith.

While native Durhamites were busy in Nashville pushing their way into

the country and folk music industry, a number of others were participating in the long tradition of hillbilly music at home. The 1930s saw the emergence of one of the earliest string bands in Durham—the Swingbillies, whose member James "Dunk" Poole was the son of Charlie Poole, leader of the North Carolina Ramblers. Dunk teamed up with Starvin' Sam Pridgin and Hash House Harvey Ellington to play live on WPTF in Raleigh six days a week; the name Swingbillies was suggested by the station manager. Unable to support themselves as a combo, the members eventually disbanded after recording their music. Pridgin and Ellington continued to perform and record with a group called the Tobacco Tags, cutting over a hundred sides before disbanding in the 1940s. During the next decades Pridgin and Ellington performed both separately and together; the 1980s found them playing at several of the Eno River festivals.

Since the 1950s string band and country music have been heard in northern Durham at Clover Hill Dance Hall on Roxboro Road and the Pick and Bow on Guess Road, both built by the Terry family. The Terrys played at dances every other Saturday night from the mid-1950s into the 1960s. Other members of the family formed the Doc Branch Band in the late 1970s. The Terry family, which settled in the area that became Durham County in the eighteenth century, has had a very long tradition of music making: a photograph from about 1900 shows the present generation's great-grandfather, W. S. Terry, on horseback in front of the family house surrounded by his descendants, most of them holding musical instruments. In the 1930s the family was playing for square dances and other local affairs. In the 1950s and 1960s the band included John Roland Terry, accordion, Edsel, fiddle, Mike, banjo, Sam, bass, and Ike Brown, guitar. They often invited other musicians and dance callers to join them.

After a lull in the early 1970s, family members started up the square dances again. While some of the older players like Edsel Terry were still involved, the new band grew to include John Roland's sons and their cousin Wayne Walker, as well as several friends. They were still playing locally and at fiddlers' conventions as recently as 2004. In 2005 the family was recognized with an award by the North Carolina Folklore Society for its perpetuation of the country music tradition and service to the community in playing and fostering traditional music.

Hollow Rock String Band *(Courtesy of Jessie Eustice)*

In the mid-1960s, farther south in the county at the Hollow Rock grocery store on Erwin Road, another string band scene was developing. The store owner, John Brown, held musical gatherings on Friday nights, the music supplied by his neighbor Tom Turner, the Crabtree boys, and a UNC graduate student from West Virginia, Tommy Thompson, and his wife Bobby. Turner had a large repertory of bluegrass and country music, and to it they added songs by the Carter family and Charlie Poole. By 1966 as many as 150 people would show up on Friday nights at the Thompsons' house, where the growing audience could be better accommodated, a different group performing in almost every room of the house. The Thompsons also played at the Null and Void Coffee Shop in Chapel Hill, where they came into contact with Alan Jabbour.

Jabbour was a graduate student in folklore at Duke whose deep interest in folk music led him to discover and record string bands in the area. A classical musician since childhood, he learned to play the fiddle tunes he recorded as well as those taught by his fiddle teacher, the master fiddler and octogenarian from Glen Lyn, Virginia, Henry Reed. Jabbour brought a host of traditional fiddle tunes to the Thompsons, adding to the mix when he became a member of a new band formed in 1966. The Hollow Rock String Band was made up of Tommy and Bobby Thompson, Jabbour, and Bertram Levy, another Duke student. They played together for two years at square dances, the Duke Folk Festival, and numerous string band contests and conventions. They also recorded an album on the Kanawha label before Levy and Jabbour left the area, Levy to become a doctor and Jabbour to become director of the American Folk Life Institute at the Library of Congress.

Other regulars at the Thompsons' jam sessions in 1968 were James Watson and William deTurk, both sons of Duke professors, and Bill Hicks, a native of Raleigh drawn to the music scene at Hollow Rock. In 1970 Hicks joined the Thompsons as a fiddler in the Fuzzy Mountain String Band, which they had created in 1967. By then the band was playing all the tunes

Red Clay Ramblers, *left to right:* Mike Craver, Jim Watson, Bill Hicks, Tommy Thompson *(Courtesy of Jessie Eustice)*

that Jabbour had collected from Reed as well as those from the local tradition. All the Hollow Rock players were studying the music and learning about it in a way that had not been done in this area before, their sessions developing into a local old-time string band revival.

In the fall of 1972 Tommy Thompson, whose wife had recently been killed in an automobile accident, joined Hicks and Watson to form the Red Clay Ramblers, a group which became nationally known, and which, with a change of personnel over the years, is still performing today. At first the band played in local clubs, adding music from a wider range of sources to its stock of folk tunes. It also toured the Midwest, made a number of recordings, and performed off Broadway, beginning with *Diamond Studs* and *A Lie of the Mind*. Thompson also composed a solo musical play, *The Last Story of John Profitt*, which tells the tale of Daniel Decatur Emmit and the first blackface group, the Virginia Minstrels.

The 1980s were an especially fertile time for groups interested in traditional music of all kinds. Chris Turner and Rachel Maloney, traveling from Maryland on their way farther south, had a chance meeting with Robert Van Veld and ended up staying in Durham to form the Nee Ningy Band. They also became part of the Banished Fools, which included Jane Peppler, Judy Allen, and others. This group produced musical plays best described as "old hippie operas." They played in May Day celebrations, Eno River festivals, and the Hillsborough Christmas parades. Later, Peppler and Van Veld joined with Bob Vasile and Peter Cunningham to form the Pratie Heads, which played music from the British Isles and colonial America.

Pratie Heads, Bob Vasile and Jane Peppler *(Courtesy of the Herald-Sun)*

(Above, top) Mappa-mundi, 1995 (Courtesy of the Eno River Association)

(Above, bottom) Hi Tones, 1980s (Courtesy of the Eno River Association)

Peppler also formed Mappamundi, a group that played early colonial North Carolina music. In the same decade came Rebecca and the Hi-Tones, who played swing, blues, and boogie, and continues to perform to the present day.

In the new century some of these musicians are still going strong, continuing the traditional music, infusing it with new influences, and passing it on to newer players.

Music Today

From symphonic works to jazz, from gospel to country, music has been the single most pervasive art form in all parts of the Durham community. Every segment of the population has participated in the making of music. Today newly expanding ethnic communities are already contributing their musical styles to the mix. Whether it is the Ciompi Quartet performing avant-garde chamber music or gospel ministers embracing the newest form of "holy hip-hop," Durham has reason to be proud of its musical past and hopeful of its future.

The optimism is warranted even as every kind of live music—classical and popular—seems to be declining nationwide. Small cities that used to enjoy regular visits from top artists no longer attract them; recordings are replacing live performances everywhere. Radio broadcasts that used to bring live concerts and operas into the home now broadcast mainly recordings. Only the largest cities provide a rich variety of live music. Yet Durham, despite its modest size, has a vibrant musical life and a host of live performances—a number that continues to increase as the population grows and as the Research Triangle Park and educational institutions expand. Because of the commitment of its musicians and their audiences, Durham can consider itself doubly fortunate.

7. Theater

RANDOLPH UMBERGER

Theater is, by its very nature, the most collaborative of the performing arts. Even a cursory glance at a theater program reveals the large forces necessary to produce one single play of any size. Over the span of a year, hundreds of people may have given of their time and talent, both on stage and off, to make an organization's entire season a success. What then is to be said about the scores of individuals and groups in a single community who over many decades have contributed to this art form as actors, directors, designers, writers, technicians, stage hands, business managers, and teachers? Durham theater has had many talented and visionary people in its ranks whose unique vision and enduring service have altered the course of local theater, both at the universities and in the community at large.

Durham has community, educational, and professional theater. The theaters of two universities, the high school and community theaters for young people, and the little theaters and professional companies that have flourished for varying amounts of time within the city's borders have all created a rich tapestry of theatrical art for a wide range of ages, races, and tastes. This variety is part of the city's heritage.

At the beginning, however, Durham was a tobacco town that did not possess a ready-made audience for theater, nor did a single state-of-the art theater facility exist in the area for many years. Before the mid-1980s the population of the city was not considered by most to be large or cosmopolitan enough to support a major professional company. The presence of better community facilities in Raleigh and more advanced academic programs in Chapel Hill also made a duplication of such programs a low priority for Durham itself. Moreover, Durham's theaters and movie houses were racially segregated until the 1970s, and the effects of this separation lingered for many years. Despite these challenges, a dedicated and determined nucleus of individuals persevered at both the community and university levels, laboring to keep theater alive during indifferent times and managing to see it flourish in what was often barren soil.

Theater at Trinity College, the forerunner of Duke University, found

Taurian Players *(Courtesy of Duke University Archives)*

Alford T. West, photograph by Blank and Stoller *(Courtesy of Duke University Archives)*

early champions in the students. The Trinity College Dramatic Club, all female, put on two one-act plays in the fall of 1920. By December 1922 men were members of the club, which by 1923 had a new name, the Taurian Players. Directed by "Peter" Gross (Mrs. Paul M. Gross) and supported entirely by box-office receipts, these students put on three to four plays annually in the poorly equipped Craven Hall until Page Auditorium opened in 1927. Indeed, Durham lacked adequate space for theater anywhere until the Carolina Theatre opened its doors in 1926 as a venue for touring productions. Unfortunately these productions were not as profitable as the new art form, motion pictures, which were added in 1929 and quickly became the staple of the house.

Upon Mrs. Gross's retirement from her volunteer position in 1930, Professor Alford T. West came from the North Carolina College for Women (later UNC-Greensboro) to join the English faculty at Duke and direct the Taurian Players. West introduced four theater courses to the curriculum of the English Department (on play production, the history of theater, playwriting, and the speaking voice) and reorganized students into the Duke Players.

West's most supportive ally was the chairman of the English Department, Frank C. Brown, who was also university comptroller. He not only budgeted stage lights, a sound system, and set-construction equipment but also agreed to West's suggestion that the rear wall of Page Auditorium, then under construction, be torn down and moved farther upstage, thus allowing a stage deep enough for theater. Although West's involvement in facilities met with immediate success, his quest to develop a drama department independent of the English Department came to naught; it was not to be realized for over half a century. Nevertheless, he guided the Duke Players for the next seventeen years, selecting its plays and designing its sets and lighting, and directing three to four plays each year. He reinvigorated Theta Alpha Phi, the honorary Thespian society, and its members participated in lighting, costuming, and set building as well as acting.

Duke Players in "Key Largo," *left to right:* Bill Thomas, Joe Gutstadt, Dacky Johnson, Garvey Fink, Cil Glassman *(Courtesy of Duke University Archives)*

Across town on the campus of North Carolina College for Negroes (later North Carolina Central University), a different picture emerged. Marjorie E. Bright was appointed an instructor in English and dramatic art in the English Department in 1935. In 1937 B. N. Duke Auditorium was constructed as yet another multipurpose university assembly space in Durham, but without fly space and virtually without wing space. Like Page Auditorium and the Carolina Theatre, B. N. Duke Auditorium lacked production support facilities for making scenery and costumes. Nonetheless, by at least March 1938 the Bri-Dra-So Stagers were mounting their productions there; by the fall of 1939, theater courses were listed separately from English courses in the NCC catalogue, although the faculty was still listed under English. Also in 1939, Dr. James Shepard invited the famed Harlem Renaissance folklorist Zora Neale Hurston to the campus to teach drama. Her appointment lasted only one year and there is no evidence that she directed a play, but from 1940, three or four plays were mounted each academic year under the auspices of the North Carolina College Thespians. These productions of European and American classics were directed by noted faculty, including Dr. Helen Edmonds and Val Dora Turner. During this time the university increased its course offerings in drama to twelve.

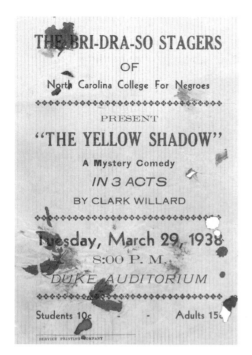

THE BRI-DRA-SO STAGERS

OF

North Carolina College For Negroes

PRESENT

"THE YELLOW SHADOW"

A Mystery Comedy

IN 3 ACTS

BY CLARK WILLARD

Tuesday, March 29, 1938

8:00 P. M.

DUKE AUDITORIUM

Students 10c   -   -   Adults 15c

SERVICE PRINTING COMPANY

The 1940s were a busy decade for theater groups throughout the city. In 1941 another student organization began to produce one student-written show a year on the Duke University campus. Hoof 'n' Horn was established for the production of musical comedies, to be supervised by a faculty director but produced entirely by undergraduates. Although Professor West opposed this idea on the grounds that young directors should serve an apprenticeship under a more experienced faculty member, the group succeeded. From 1952 it produced Broadway musicals, a tradition which continues today with the presentation of three to four musicals each academic year. Hoof 'n' Horn is the oldest student-run musical organization in the South.

In the 1940s three other theater efforts began in Durham. In 1943, after five years of sponsoring professional entertainment for children, the Children's Theatre committee was formed by the Junior League as a project to be run entirely by the League itself, and in the next quarter-century

(Above, top) Bri-Dra-So Stagers program *(Courtesy of the Department of Theatre, NCCU)*

(Above, bottom) "CanCan," Hoof 'n' Horn *(Courtesy of Duke University Archives)*

(Right, top) "Foamin Over," Hoof 'n' Horn *(Courtesy of Duke University Archives)*

(Right, bottom) Junior League Children's Theater, "3 Billy Goats Gruff," 1962–63, photograph by Larry Marlin *(Courtesy of the Herald-Sun)*

its productions were trouped each year to an estimated ten thousand children in the city and county schools. Also, under the busy Professor West, the Durham Little Theatre (later the Durham Theatre Guild) was organized in May 1946 and began producing two or three community plays annually, drawing talent from the local citizenry and from nearby Chapel Hill. Initial performances were held in Carr Junior High School.

In 1949 Mary Bohanon was appointed the first official chairwoman of the Department of Dramatic Art at North Carolina College, finally separating from the English Department both in curriculum and in faculty. Under Bohanon's leadership (1949–1964) course offerings increased and two major productions, as well as bills of one-acts, were mounted annually.

The third theater group formed during the 1940s was the Wesleyan Players, an organization of Duke students sponsored by the university's Methodist Student Center. The group produced two major plays and several

one-act plays, many of them American classics, every year until the mid-1970s.

During 1953 the Theatre Guild was inactive, but a meeting called by West and the guild president at the end of the year resulted in the formation of Allied Arts of Durham. A home was found for the alliance in the old Watts home on Proctor Street and a new theater space was improvised. There, on a stage the size of a postage stamp in what had been the stairwell of the mansion, the Durham Theatre Guild produced plays and musicals, for the next quarter-century, relying on directors from Duke, UNC-Chapel Hill, and NCC along with a variety of Durham residents to work as volunteer designers, carpenters, seamstresses, and performers. Nancy Clark was the costumer and archivist for the Theatre Guild for most of its existence.

The years following the Second World War saw a steady growth of interest in the theater, and occasional plays were still performed at the downtown Carolina. Two stars in particular—Katharine Hepburn and Tallulah Bankhead—drew large crowds. Dr. West died suddenly in 1947, and Kenneth Reardon was hired as the second director of the Duke Players, a position that he held until he resigned at the end of the 1967–68 season. His tenure was marked by an impressive array of performances and readings. During his first three years, three productions each season were given in Page Auditorium. The facility was too large for most of these shows, and in 1949 the group was given the Branson building on East Campus. It was renovated as an arena stage, furnished with army surplus chairs, and soon became popular with students and community alike. Its first production was in 1950, the same year Victor Michalak joined the English Department to become technical director and later associate director of the Players. Because of his arrival a summer offering was added, the result of a summer play-production class, and a fourth play was added to the regular season, with Michalak directing one play each year.

For the next ten years, activities in Durham's theater world remained relatively stable. One important change was made in the operations of Duke Players. The funding was moved from the budget of the English department to that of the University Student Union, thus bringing it into the realm of student affairs rather than academics. The debate over the appropriateness of theater as an undergraduate major however continued, and the creation of a separate speech and drama department would ultimately prove the weak link in the construction of a proposed fine arts complex for music, art, and drama. Because of the enormous cost of a drama department and the urgency of the Music Department's and Art Department's needs, the university scrapped plans for a complex. Instead it ended up with a new music building, a new art museum (first in a renovated building and later in the Nasher Art Museum), and a promise to drama to renovate Baldwin Auditorium, a promise never kept.

Kenneth Reardon *(Courtesy of Duke University Archives)*

In the summer of 1963 a community-based summer stock company, the Triangle Repertory Theater, was founded by Wesley Van Tassel and Charles "Buck" Roberts. The company employed professional actors for its 1964 season, and in 1965 it produced a sixteen-week summer season. Unfortunately the community was unable to sustain such an ambitious schedule, and the company was forced to close in the following year. Also in 1965, Mary Bohanon returned to the English Department at North Carolina College and her position in the Department of Dramatic Art was filled by a number of faculty members, Dr. Helen Adams most notable among them. After Adams, the award-winning Shubert Foundation playwright Randolph Umberger was appointed chairman in 1970. During his tenure the faculty was increased to five and the number of course offerings to thirty, and six concentrations were developed, including one leading to certification in theater education, the first such program in the area. Also at

Ranny Umberger
(Courtesy of Ranny Umberger)

John Clum, founding Director of the Duke University Program in Drama *(Courtesy of Duke University Photography)*

NCC, construction began on the Farrison-Newton Communications Building, with an intimate, up-to-date theater, support space for classes, and construction space for sets and costumes, all under one roof.

After Professor Reardon's resignation from Duke Players in 1968, the dean of student affairs, William Griffith (later vice president) hired professional directors to stage Duke drama, one play per director. Among these directors were two former Duke Players: Richard Parks, who did a full season and part of a second, and Earl McCarroll. This solution was generally unsatisfactory, however. In 1971 Scott J. Parker joined the staff as resident managing director of Duke Players. And in 1968 the void of professional theater in Durham was filled to a large extent when the Duke Union began its Broadway at Duke series, bringing tours of high quality to the Durham community.

Summer theater was tried once again when Professor John Clum of the Duke English Department and the technical director Scott Parker inaugurated Summer Theater at Duke, designed to bring theater to the area as well as to give students more experience in play production. In 1972 they put on three shows, all directed by Clum, thereafter using guest directors for one or two shows per season. Summer Theater at Duke mounted five to seven offerings each summer through 1984. During this time Clum became the founding director of the program in drama and chairman of the Committee on Drama. Though still technically a part of the English Department, courses were now offered under the rubric of drama, and by 1975 the university approved drama as a major. Together with Parker (later director of the Institute of Outdoor Drama in Chapel Hill), Clum forged a dynamic new era in the history of Duke, producing six student shows during the academic year and from five to seven during the summer. In the meantime, at NCCU Umberger returned to full-time teaching in 1975, and the department continued to grow under the leadership of Dr. Linda Kerr Norflett, with increasing emphasis on African and African-American scripts.

Linda Kerr (Norflett) *(Courtesy of the Department of Theatre, NCCU)*

Lisa Harris Hampton in "Purlie" *(Courtesy of the Department of Theatre, NCCU)*

Faculty of NCCU Department of Theatre, early 1980s. *Left to right:* K. Sullivan, R. Umberger, L. Norflett, K. Dacons-Brock, D. Schneider, J. Alston *(Courtesy of the Department of Theatre, NCCU)*

"Dream Girls" *(Courtesy of the Department of Theatre, NCCU)*

In 1978 Allied Arts of Durham changed its name to the Durham Arts Council, its old home was closed, and it moved into the former City Hall on Morris Street. A new theater was temporarily constructed in the old council chambers on a budget of $50, some donated lumber, and a roll of burlap. This facility was used until the mid-1980s, when the space was converted into the People's Security Theatre, once again a presenting space without construction or storage facilities, although it did provide an office for the Durham Theatre Guild. Despite this disadvantage the guild struggled on for several more years, but it was never to regain its former vitality after the move from Proctor Street. It finally disbanded after the 1992–93 season.

The People's Security Theatre, a pleasant and intimate facility seating two hundred without backstage or fly space, is currently the venue for local dance groups, musical recitals, and small theatrical events. The Durham Arts Council building also contains the WTVD Theatre, a small performance space where Jeffryn Stevens's popular Young People's Theatre has operated successfully since the renovations, offering performance classes and plays of all types, performed by children and young teens.

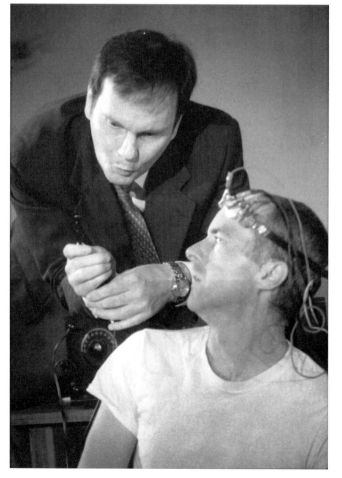

Manbites Dog Theater's 2007 production of "The Pillowman," *left:* Gregor McElvogue as Tupolski, *right:* Jay O'Berski as Katurian, photograph by Alan Dehmer *(Courtesy of Manbites Dog Theater)*

In 1985, as Clum returned to the English Department at Duke, David Ball became the director of the drama program. Shortly thereafter the university instituted Broadway Previews at Duke, not only a tryout for new scripts by nationally known authors but also a chance for internships for students on their way to a professional career. In the following year the Bryan University Center was constructed, providing the Reynolds Industries Theater, a modern seven-hundred-seat theater well-equipped for this exciting new repertory. The Bryan Center also included the smaller Shaefer Theater, a black box space for more experimental staging. Off campus, under the founding guidance of Jeff Storer and Edward Hunt in 1987, Manbites Dog Theater opened as a professional venue for experimental new scripts in a storefront on West Main Street. Providing alternative theater with a "bite," the offerings proved popu-

"Mules and Men"
(Courtesy of the Department of Theatre, NCCU)

lar enough over the coming decade to justify a larger, permanent location downtown on Foster Street. As the original Manbites Dog was opening, however, the Carolina Theatre was closing for a complete renovation and restoration and did not reopen until March 1994, when the Durham Savoyards presented *Patience*. The facility proved too large and expensive for most community theater use, and today it is a presenting house only, with additional film theaters attached.

At NCCU, both African-American and standard American classics held the stage, growing in quality and numbers. Two additional part-time faculty were added to the five already employed, with numerous professional guest directors and performers. In 1991 Randolph Umberger produced *Mules and Men*, which won the national American College Theatre Festival award over 850 other entries. Adapted by Umberger from the book of the same title by Zora Neale Hurston, *Of Mules and Men* was performed that year at the John F. Kennedy Center for the Performing Arts in Washington. John Alston became chairman of the department in 1996, which in 1997 was fully accredited by the National Association of Schools of Theatre, becoming the only nationally accredited theater school in the Triangle. A new concentration in musical theater was approved in 2001, and since 1999 the department has collaborated with Long Leaf Opera in mounting three professional, English-language opera productions.

After David Ball's resignation at Duke University, Dale B. J. Randall was appointed interim director of the drama program and chairman of the search committee for a new person distinguished enough to be not only head of the department but also the Mary D. B. T. and James H. Semans Professor of the Practice of Theater Studies. In 1992 the lighting designer Richard Riddell, winner of a Tony Award for his work, became head of the drama program, charged with turning it into a department. In 2002 he became the first chairman of the Department of Theater Studies. The curriculum was expanded, the faculty enlarged, and Broadway Previews, which had been renamed Theater Previews at Duke in 1993, became the professional producing arm of the Department of Theater Studies. Summer study in London is now also offered by the department. While retaining its space on East Campus, the department added a Theater Studies Building adjacent to the Bryan Center in the fall of 2003. Major upgrades to the lighting systems for both Reynolds and Shaefer Theaters are under way, and plans have been made to renovate Branson Theater into the Brody Theater.

The Durham public schools have also made progress over the last decade, with a number of active programs in the high schools and several new facilities. Both Hillside and Riverside High Schools have been winners in state drama competitions, and Hillside has made a number of international trips with its program. There is of course much theater activity at the Durham School of the Arts, as well as a strong extracurricular program at the North Carolina School of Science and Mathematics. Durham Academy has had an active theater program for a number of years.

Altogether Durham can boast a wide spectrum of theater offerings each season, with enough theater of high quality throughout the year to satisfy any number of tastes. Triangle residents enjoy both professional touring companies and pre-Broadway presentations at Duke, and standard European, American, and African-American classics on its more traditional academic stages. They can venture to Manbites Dog and its repertory of alternative works, or to small community groups that surface from time to time. Though Durham may lack a resident professional company and facilities for serious community or professional theater, it has been blessed with talented people in its ranks, and those who are mentioned here are but the barest representation of the many whose vision and service have altered the course of local theater, for both town and gown.

8. Visual Arts

KATE DOBBS ARIAIL

The visual arts have burgeoned in Durham in the last two decades, although historically they have not had the same cultural force that music and theater have had in the Piedmont town that tobacco built. While auditoriums and theaters were erected and filled with enthusiastic audiences, galleries and museums—not to mention individual artists—struggled for recognition and survival. Matters have improved significantly since 1945, but the visual arts still lag behind their artistic cousins. Nonetheless, Durham has some rich visual history, and the visual arts are poised for growth.

To appreciate the advances made by art in Durham, you must imagine Durham as it was in the mid-1940s. Thanks mostly to tobacco, business was good. The town was jumping. Downtown had half a dozen movie theaters to choose from—but most of the other visual riches took the form of architecture. You could look at the grand houses of the tobacco kings and the acres of handsome brick factories and warehouses where their money was made, or you could go to the movies. At the county fair you might have visited a display of colorful quilts, but unless you were connected with Duke University or the North Carolina College for Negroes (now North Carolina Central University), you were unlikely to see much, if any, artwork. If you wanted to look at a painting or a sculpture in 1945, your choices were severely limited.

There were no museums or galleries, other than a display area in the Woman's College Library (now Lilly Library on the Duke East Campus). NCCU did not have dedicated gallery space until 1958, shortly after the campus installation of the handsome statue of the founder of North Carolina College, James E. Shepard, in 1957, although it had begun its art program in 1942. There was no arts council. Oddly, although several murals were painted in the state under the Federal Art Project of the WPA, none were in Durham.[1]

Your best bet for color and imagery—and all of that religious—was the stained glass in a few churches. Many churches clung to their austere, unornamented beauty, but some of the larger congregations in town

Statue of James E. Shepard
by William A. Zorach
*(Courtesy of Amanda van
Scoyoc)*

had put up brilliantly hued stained glass in their dignified brick and stone buildings late in the nineteenth century and early in the twentieth, after the iconoclastic tradition of the Protestant church began to relax. Notable among these pictorial windows were those at St. Joseph's A.M.E. Church, the First Presbyterian Church, the Watts Street Baptist Church, Duke Memorial Methodist Church, and the splendid series in the more recently erected Duke Chapel.[2]

Public sculpture in town was limited to a few memorials whose interest was, and remains, more historical than aesthetic: in front of the county courthouse stand two rolls of honored dead from the two World Wars (a monument to the soldiers of Korea and Vietnam was added in 1994); a bronze bust of Malbourne Angier looks down on those entering the courthouse; and a three-quarter-scale bronze figure of a Confederate soldier elevated on a tall granite base stands guard over all, his rifle at the ready. This last was purportedly given by "the people of Durham," but that surely is an overly inclusive phrase, as it was actually erected by the United Daughters of the Confederacy.[3]

A more conciliatory monument designed by W. H. Dacy towers over the modest cabin at Bennett Place, marking the spot where South and North officially rejoined after Johnston's surrender to Sherman at the end of the Civil War. "UNITY," proclaims the stone slab resting atop two Corinthian columns. Although the ludicrous conjunction of fancy columns and plain yeoman farm buildings hardly presents a unified or harmonious image, and the monument functions less as a sculpture than as a sign, it does perfectly convey the complicated mixture of old regional pride and the forward-thinking conviction of the white historians and civic leaders who erected it.[4]

Should you have had business on the Duke University campus in the years following the Second World War, you might have paused a long moment to admire the bronze monument to the memory of Washington Duke, unveiled in 1908 on the original campus of Trinity College (now East Campus). Even in today's crowded visual environment, this unusual larger-than-life-size figurative bronze by the sculptor Edward Valentine of Richmond, Virginia, remains a compelling sight and one of the most in-

(Left) Bust of Malbourne A. Angier *(Courtesy of Amanda van Scoyoc and Eli Van Zoeren)*

(Above) J. B. Duke statue by Charles Keck *(Courtesy of Amanda van Scoyoc)*

triguing pieces of sculpture in Durham. Unlike most monuments to men of achievement (including many from Valentine's own hand), in which the subject stands or perhaps sits astride a stallion, Washington Duke was modeled reposing in a throne-like easy chair, his strong, blunt hands resting on its lion-headed arms as he gazes out over his domain. He may be seated, but he nonetheless emanates power.[5]

In 1945 the bronze statue of another Duke dominated the center of the university's West Campus, as it does now. Sculpted by Charles Keck to honor the university benefactor James Buchanan Duke, the figure has a stance that cunningly mimics the forms of the Gothic Duke Chapel soaring behind him. The man stands with legs apart, and the space between them mirrors the chapel's portal and lancet windows, while the legs themselves appear as sturdy as its towering pilasters. Duke grasps a cane, pressing it to the ground at an angle like that of the building's buttresses. And while there is nothing on the building directly analogous to Duke's cigar, that roll of tobacco leaves serves a visual role similar to that of the carved details ornamenting the building—while also reminding viewers of the humble source of all this glory. Both sculpture and chapel were dedicated in 1935, and both remain central to the self-image of Duke University and the town of Durham.[6] Visitors in the chapel would have been struck by the three beautifully rendered sarcophagi of Washington, James, and Benjamin Duke, also by Keck.

To jump forward a few decades and complete a survey of campus sculpture, in quite recent years the university added a standing statue of Benjamin Duke (1999). Its creator was Stephen H. Smith, who also made a dramatic medical triage scene honoring the university's 65th General Hospital during the Second World War (2002) and two bas-reliefs of the composer Iain Hamilton (2002) and President William P. Few (2004).

Since 1986 a plethora of busts have joined the collection. The Athletic Department, wishing to commemorate its own heroes—coaches and administrators—commissioned the North Carolina artist Franklin V. Creech Jr., a former football player, to make more-than-life-size busts of Wallace Wade, Edmund Cameron, William D. Murray, John Wesley Coombs, Vic-

Camel statue on Duke campus by Jonathan Kingdon *(Courtesy of Amanda van Scoyoc and Eli Van Zoeren)*

tor A. Bubas, and Tom Butters. Creech also made a bust of Terry Sanford—governor, senator, and Duke president—for the new Terry Sanford Institute of Public Policy. Frances G. Woodall, wife of the provost Barnes Woodall, made a bust of the surgeon and Duke president Julian Deryl Hart and donated it to the university.

In a quite different vein, the most recent acquisition, placed outside the biology building, is the sculpture of a life-size camel viewed by the standing figure of the retired zoology professor Knut Schmidt-Nielsen, who studied how animals survive in harsh environments. It was a gift to the university from another retired zoology professor, Stephen A. Wainwright, and the work of Jonathan Kingdon.

Another artwork likely to have been noticed by Durham residents in 1945 was "The Sower," a bronze figure on the lawn of what is now East Campus. Before the oak trees dotting the grounds grew so large, this representation of a sturdy seventeenth-century peasant sowing his grain would have been much more visible from Main Street than it is today, and would have been understood as a symbol not only of agrarian life but of intellectual and moral life as well by both townspeople and academ-

"Sower," on Duke's East Campus by Stephan Walter *(Courtesy of Amanda van Scoyoc and Eli Van Zoeren)*

ics. The seeds of artistic culture sown by these scattered artworks would however be long in sprouting further growth. That they did grow was due in large part to the energetic care supplied by Ella Fountain Pratt beginning in the 1950s. She became Duke's first director of cultural affairs, and created—along with exhibitions, programs, and student art committees—the expectation that one would find all the arts at Duke. By the time of her retirement in 1984, that was the case.[7]

A key event in the development of the visual arts in Durham took place in 1947, when a small band of working artists formed the Creative Art Group (later the Durham Art Guild) as a spur to their improvement as painters. The group met regularly to critique each other's work, and soon enlisted Gregory D. Ivy, head of the art department at Women's College of the University of North Carolina in Greensboro (now UNCG) as their regular visiting critic and mentor. Ivy, himself a painter, had built a strong department, the best in the state, and at the time the only one to offer both B.F.A. and M.F.A. degrees. Through his work with the Creative Art Group, Ivy brought the influence of the "Greensboro School" to Durham, where its precepts flourished in the work of such "Ivy League" painters as Ola Mae Foushee, Lib Lyon (a Women's College alumna), and many others.

The Creative Art Group re-formed in 1948 with a broader mission, now intent on an expanded membership, which notably soon included two Modernists born and trained in Europe, Marianne Manasse and Edith London. The first meeting of the Durham Art Guild was held in July 1949, and since then the DAG has been crucial to the health of the visual arts in Durham. From the beginning the DAG had an educational mission, but its primary purposes remain to provide a community for artists, to encourage high standards in the practice of art, and to furnish opportunities and locations for local artists to show their work. Whereas early on the guild focused more on education and criticism for its members, since 1988 the DAG has expended most of its energies in mounting exhibitions in the CCB Gallery, a 52,000-square-foot facility in the Royall Center for the Arts (Durham Arts Council building). Artists compete to exhibit in the gallery, which can accommodate four individual shows simultaneously. The guild also organizes a juried exhibition annually, bringing in a nationally known curator to choose the works. There is an annual unjuried members' exhibition as well. Over the decades all of the area's most significant artists in early to mid-career have shown in the Art Guild exhibitions, and many have served on the DAG board of directors.[8]

Visual artists were not alone in starting organizations during the cultural upswell at mid-century, and by 1953 these several groups were sufficiently strong and numerous to create an umbrella organization to share and streamline administrative efforts. The DAG, the Durham Theatre Guild, the Camera Club, and the Durham chapter of the North Carolina Symphony first grouped together as United Arts; shortly thereafter the group's name was changed to Allied Arts and it was joined by the Chamber Arts Society, the Durham Civic Choral Society, the Durham Children's Museum, and the Duke University Arts Council. Housed in its early years in grand houses on Morehead Hill,[9] Allied Arts quickly became a cultural force, instituting an array of programs, classes, and events over two decades.

Among the most important efforts were the Triangle Festivals of Crafts. These festivals—the first was held in 1967—coincided with the burgeoning interest in folk music nationwide and the simultaneous craft revival, during which the new craftspeople brought a heightened aesthetic sensibility to traditional functional crafts, and in the process began to dismantle the

Durham Art Guild Auction committee, *left to right:* George Pyne, Frank DePasquale, Joan Condoret, A.M. Tidd, 1965 *(Courtesy of Milo Pyne)*

wall between the crafts and the fine arts. The crafts are well covered elsewhere in this book, but a key point to remember in relation to the "fine arts" is that for many people the crafts provided a point of entry into visual culture. This greater visual awareness helped pave the way for commercial art galleries, without which an artistic community cannot thrive. In 1972 Joe Rowand opened Durham's first art gallery, Somerhill, in the Straw Valley building on Chapel Hill Boulevard. Somerhill was soon joined by Craft House, which sold the type of fine crafts juried in the Festival of Crafts.[10]

Allied Arts had become more than the sum of its components by the early 1970s, and in 1975 it altered its structure and identity to become the Durham Arts Council, with the remaining member organizations of Allied Arts becoming "funded affiliates" of the new DAC. The Arts Council grew rapidly and moved into the former City Hall in the heart of downtown in 1978. The building housed some artists' studios and exhibition space, as well as offices and facilities for other arts disciplines. In 1982 the

DAC hired as its executive director a newly minted Duke Ph.D., Michael Marsicano, who led the organization through a period of dizzying growth. In 1984 Marsicano recruited Ella Fountain Pratt to volunteer at the DAC (where she remained twenty years later) and soon the Emerging Artists grants program was begun.[11] The DAC's annual street festival (now called CenterFest) attracted many artists and craftspeople to show their work — and drew the crowds who would buy it. The DAC also undertook a thorough renovation of its building, to which it returned with a huge gala in September 1988.

The renovated DAC no longer offered individual studio spaces, but it did include a much better exhibition space than had previously been available in the community. One of the high points of the gala reopening was the first exhibition in this building's new gallery, the creation of which was funded by Central Carolina Bank, long a supporter of the arts in Durham. "Partners in Patronage" highlighted the crucial role that corporate collecting was already playing in the development of what might be called "art consciousness" and of viable markets for visual art in the area. Lacking a social heritage of individual art patronage such as exists in major cities, corporations had become leaders in collecting, providing in their workplaces richer visual environments and encouraging by example the buying of art. Because there were buyers, it became possible for more galleries to open, which in turn encouraged more people to purchase artwork — which made it possible for artists to create more work.[12]

Many critical building blocks for a strong visual culture were firmly in place in Durham by the late 1980s, and the visual arts blossomed over the next dozen years. The Arts Council was now highly visible in the community, thanks to its building, its educational programs, and a high-profile national conference on public art. The funded affiliates (though, unknown to themselves, soon to be defunded) thrived in their new home: Durham Art Guild could now mount dozens of solo and group shows annually. Corporate collecting continued apace, and individual collecting surged. Mr. and Mrs. Allen Aldridge Sr. donated Durham's first piece of non-memorial public sculpture: in 1988 Be Gardiner's carved white marble *Laocoön '87* was installed at the intersection of University Drive and Old Chapel Hill Road. It remained there until 1999, when a DOT road-widening project required its removal.[13]

No other outdoor art appeared in the city during the 1980s and 1990s, but art did begin to show up in other public places like City Hall and the county's libraries. Notable pieces include Andrew Preiss's large hanging sculpture in City Hall; tapestries by Silvia Heyden there and in the Main Library; and an elaborate pictorial quilt by Hollis Chatelain and a ceramic sculpture by Ursula Goebbels-Ellis in the same building. Mural artists re-

Frega railing at Pea-
body Place *(Courtesy of
Amanda van Scoyoc and
Eli Van Zoeren)*

ceived commissions for large projects in and around downtown. In a move
unprecedented in Durham, two downtown business owners, Richard and
Jacqueline Morgan, hired the sculptor Al Frega to integrate art into architecture in their Peabody Place redevelopment near Brightleaf Square. Local criticism and reportage on the visual arts had a robust decade, further
increasing interest in and understanding of art and artists.[14]

As art's profile grew, so did the urge toward censorship; arguments that
raged throughout the country did not bypass Durham. What was obscene,
what was "appropriate," and what the public could and should expect for its
public arts funding or in its public buildings—and who got to decide—were
questions consuming artists, community leaders, and especially politicians
and funders from the late 1980s through the mid-1990s. The National Endowment for the Arts at that time still made grants to individuals, and two
in particular of the NEA's grantees (Andres Serrano and Robert Mapplethorpe, both photographers) set off a brushfire of disgust and condemnation. Nearby the flames were fanned by the Southeastern Center for Contemporary Art in Winston-Salem, and soon the culture wars were being
fought in nearly every possible venue, carried on by artists with a penchant
for the "transgressive." A small exhibition of Mapplethorpe's beautiful, disturbing photographs was shown in Durham under guarded conditions and

caused only a small ripple, but the local "process" artists Max Below Toledo and Kim Irwin created more of a fuss when they submitted large-scale
nude photographs of themselves and their same-sex companions for an exhibition in the Durham Art Guild in 1994. A rose by any other name may
smell as sweet, but a penis in an art nude is still a penis is still a problem.
The artists were eventually pressured into "self-censoring," and in the en-
suing years art in Durham has been quite "well behaved."[15]

On the campuses, great strides had been made by the 1980s. Art had been
shown for decades at NCCU, but only in makeshift spaces. The school's
first art instructor, Marion C. Parham, organized the first student show in
the Fine Arts Building, and the first chairman of the art department, Edward Wilson, asked for a room to be set aside there, and it was used as an
exhibition space from 1958 to 1964. When Lynn Igoe became the art gallery director, a gallery proper was created in a portion of the old cafeteria, in 1972. Her successor, Nancy C. Gillespie, pressed for a building designed for mounting exhibitions and for housing the university's forming
art collection.

The NCCU Art Museum was designed and constructed under Nancy
C. Gillespie's directorate. Nancy left the university in December 1975, just
before the museum was completed. Norman Pendergraft became director
in January 1976 and began preparations for the move to the new building.
The NCCU Art Museum was formally dedicated and opened to the public
by Governor Hunt on November 4, 1977.

Designed to house the growing collection, mainly of works by African-
American artists, the new museum building also made it possible to mount
temporary exhibitions for an audience beyond the university. In 1986 an
endowment was established through a gift from Irwin Belk, and the museum's gallery was subsequently named in honor of Carol Grotnes Belk. Pendergraft established an active exhibition schedule and continued his stew-
ardship and collection development. The NCCU Art Museum now holds
a remarkably broad collection of works by African-American artists of the
nineteenth and twentieth centuries—without peer in the state except perhaps for the Hewitt Collection at the Afro-American Cultural Center in
Charlotte—as well as a small collection of African art.

After thirty years of service Pendergraft retired, and the painter and
art historian Kenneth Rodgers assumed the directorship. During Rodgers's tenure numerous ambitious exhibitions have been mounted. Notable among them are one of Rodgers's first shows, a beautiful exhibition of
works by the nineteenth-century landscape painter Edward M. Bannister;
the nationally-circulating "To Conserve a Legacy" exhibition, a portion of
which was shown at NCCU in 2000; a survey of Elizabeth Catlett's prints

which Rodgers organized in 2001; and a retrospective in 2004 of paintings by Allan Freelon, grandfather of the Durham architect Philip Freelon.[16]

In the mid-1980s Duke University declared that it would build a real art museum to replace the minimal facilities created in 1969 by the remodeling of a former chemistry building on East Campus. From 1969 through 1986 the museum organized few temporary exhibitions, mainly displaying objects from its collections, which included disparate groupings ranging from ancient Chinese jades to pre-Columbian ceramics and textiles to Middle Eastern carpets to medieval stone sculpture and stained glass, but relatively little painting. In early 1987 Michael Mezzatesta arrived to head the Duke University Museum of Art, and to spearhead fundraising for a new museum building to serve both the university and the public. Mezzatesta professionalized the museum, built a staff and an ambitious exhibition schedule, and began collecting, notably contemporary Russian art. But although he had brought with him the interest and promised financial support of the Texas developer, art collector, and Duke alumnus Raymond Nasher, internal university politics and slow fundraising delayed construction of the new building, eventually called the Nasher Museum of Art in honor of the Nasher Foundation's donation of $10 million to the project's total cost of $23 million. Mezzatesta was ousted as director in May 2003, even before the steel was erected for the complex. Designed by Rafael Viñoly, the Nasher opened in October 2005 with considerable fanfare, and with a new director, Dr. Kimerly Rorschach, who had led the Smart Museum at the University of Chicago.[17]

Meanwhile, strong students were emerging from the art departments of both universities. Although Duke does not offer a studio art degree, some particularly motivated young artists complete the certificate program that it does offer. The most impressive of these in recent years have been Andrew Preiss and Jonathan Hexner, both of whom studied under the sculptor and photographer Bill Noland.[18] Hexner left Durham a few years after graduation, but Preiss established himself as a sculptor and metalworker in Durham. After several years of working within the Vega Metals artist-blacksmithing studio, he opened his own ARP studio in the Liberty Warehouse and became one of the anchors of what would soon become the Foster Street arts corridor.

Beverly McIver, a painter, is the star student to have come out of the NCCU art department. A native of Greensboro, McIver studied with Elizabeth Lentz at Central before receiving her M.F.A. at Penn State. The Greensboro School—or Ivy—traditions in painting were thus continued, as Lentz had received her M.F.A. at UNC-Greensboro. McIver, who is black, has put her own twist on European styles of painting still lifes and portraits through her use of black subjects and her rich use of patterning in her pictures. McIver herself taught at NCCU and at Duke before taking a teaching position at Arizona State University.[19]

In 1972 a group of parents led by Pauline Silberman, Dorothy Borden, Alice Alston, and Janice Palmer initiated a program to introduce the arts into the public schools. The success of their pilot project, funded by the First Presbyterian Church, led to the adoption by the schools system—city and county—of what was called the CCAPS program: Council for the Creative Arts in the Public Schools. By the 1980s CCAPS was assimilated by the Durham Arts Council (DAC) and today exists as a partnership of the DAC and area school systems. It places artists in public and private classrooms throughout Durham and Orange counties. The art instruction they provide is integrated into the core subjects, so that all children can transmute into dance, visual arts, film, and writing aspects of their regular course of study. Further evidence of the Durham public school system's commitment to the arts is the arts magnet school, opened in 1996 in the center of town in the old Durham High School.[20] Now called the Durham School of the Arts, it provides broader and deeper training in the various art disciplines than is available in most schools, and thus acts as a feeder for the university programs—as well as raising expectations among its graduates that the city's cultural life will include the visual arts.

New institutions and alliances of varying degrees of formality arose during the 1990s as well. Hayti Heritage Center, a new cultural center attached to the former sanctuary of the old St. Joseph's A.M.E. Church, was opened by the St. Joseph's Historic Foundation in 1992. Although it focuses on performance and cultural activities, it does have a regular exhibition schedule in the Lyda Moore Merrick Gallery, generally showing work by African-American artists or work about African-American culture that does not have a venue elsewhere in town. Lyda Moore Merrick, for whom the gallery was named, was an accomplished artist, trained at Fisk and Columbia universities. She painted several portraits for building dedications; one of her mother is in the Hayti Heritage Center. The Duke Center for Documentary Studies, with a focus on the best of documentary photography, opened downtown in 1989. After its move to Lyndhurst House on Pettigrew Street, the center quickly became a mecca for everyone around the Triangle interested in photography.

Increasingly during the 1990s, artists took action to create their own places. The Venable building, a former warehouse recast as a small business incubator, filled up with artists appreciative of its cheap space and excellent light. In 1995, when the photographer and arts lawyer Dan Ellison created Artsplace in the long-vacant Palms restaurant building downtown, not only did the studio spaces fill immediately, but fledgling galleries appeared. Several artists attempted Durham's first (though short-lived) co-op gallery, Artomatic, and the artist Jimmy Kellough opened his inimitable Modern Museum downstairs. Kellough, without any backing, briefly operated this tiny space as a gallery for noncommercial artwork, particularly installations by local artists like Bryant Holsenbeck, David Solow, Laura Ames Riley, and June Merlino, and as a salon where conversations about contemporary art could occur, the transcriptions of interviews that Kellough conducted with each artist being starting points. This was a true "alternative space," and during the short years of its existence it drew viewers from throughout the Triangle and as far away as Winston-Salem and Wilmington.

More artists took up unutilized spaces scattered around the downtown core, and still others created studios in nearby warehouse space. By 1999 there was a sufficient concentration of artists and gallery spaces within walking distance of each other downtown that a group of the artists, along with the downtown improvement organization Downtown Durham Inc., started the Durham Artwalk, a downtown studio tour and sale. Further east, between Elizabeth Street and Alston Avenue, South East Efforts Developing Sustainable Spaces (SEEDS), the brainchild of Brenda Brodie, made a beautiful garden by its office on Gilbert Street and began holding regular community art days called Art Grows in Durham. The east end of that block is now anchored by Al Frega's studio compound in the long-disused former city livery stable (more recently part of Southern States), where he and several other professional artists work.[21]

Many of the same artists who were developing Durham into an artistic center during the late 1980s and throughout the 1990s were also representing Durham to great acclaim throughout the state by being involved with residency programs and by winning fellowships and grants. Durham's artists were commissioned to do pieces for the Artworks in State Buildings program administered by the North Carolina Arts Council, and were consistently well represented in the North Carolina Artists Exhibitions organized by the North Carolina Museum of Art.[22]

After the heady days of the 1990s, arts institutions and individual artists suffered during the downturn following the bursting of the technology and dot com bubble shortly after 2000. As government funding, grant money, corporate sponsorships, and individual patronage all dwindled or disappeared, it began to feel as if Durham was in danger of losing all that it had worked so hard to gain during the second half of the twentieth century. But a few years of slow spending cannot unmake communities of artists or established arts institutions, and a fresh upsurge of activity promises to make the first half of the twenty-first century as productive as the second half of the twentieth.

Liberty Arts Pavilion, designed by Frank DePasquale *(Courtesy of Liberty Arts)*

Detail of metal work at Liberty Pavilion *(Courtesy of Amanda van Scoyoc and Eli Van Zoeren)*

Downtown and the Foster Street corridor just to the north have continued to attract artists and designers of all kinds, many of whom show the same kind of civic spirit that inspired the formation of Allied Arts more than fifty years ago. These artists are a key component of the Artist Business Coalition for Downtown (ABCD), which is fast becoming a powerful influence on the way Durham develops culturally in the twenty-first century. One leader in ABCD is the Scrap Exchange, a nonprofit on Foster Street founded to promote the creative use of industrial and consumer scrap that would otherwise go to waste. Under the leadership of its executive director, the artist Ann May Woodward, the Scrap Exchange and its gallery have become a hub for "green" art in the Triangle.[23] At Duke, where art exhibitions in Durham began, the Nasher Museum's pale walls have risen among the trees of Central Campus. Other exhibition venues on campus now include the John Hope Franklin Center, the Institute of the Arts, the Freeman Center for Jewish Life, and the Center for Documentary Studies.

Government agencies too are increasingly aware of the importance of art in society. In 2003 Durham County began the process of researching and defining the county's cultural needs, including visual art. The completed Cultural Master Plan was accepted by the County Commissioners in August 2004. The City of Durham is working to make downtown an arts and entertainment district by design and with incentives, and a staff member in the Office of Economic and Employment Development will help to implement the Cultural Master Plan.[24]

Large strokes of corporate philanthropy again enable new projects. Central Carolina Bank (now SunTrust), outdoing even its own record of support for the visual arts, funded the construction by the nonprofit Liberty Arts, Inc., of a new art-producing facility, the George Watts Hill Pavilion for the Arts, dedicated in October 2003. Located downtown in Durham Central Park, along the Foster Street arts corridor, the pavilion houses an art bronze casting studio run by Liberty Arts. The group's double mission is to provide a place where artists can make (or have made) their cast work at a reasonable cost, while also encouraging the commissioning and siting of large-scale artworks throughout the region.

As part of its gift, CCB commissioned Liberty Arts to create the first large-scale bronze sculpture to be publicly sited since the Daughters of the Confederacy put up their monument in 1924. This one really is for the people of Durham: the artists, Michael Waller and Leah Foushee, have sculpted a bronze sculpture of a bull ten feet long and weighing a ton and a half, the symbol of this Piedmont town since tobacco made it famous the world around. The iconic sculpture dominates the corner of Corcoran and Parrish streets in the center of town; it serves both as a visual representation of

"The Major" by Leah Foushee and Mike Waller *(Courtesy of Amanda van Scoyoc and Eli Van Zoeren)*

Durham's character—dignified, powerful, dangerous if provoked—and as a symbol of our transition from a railroad depot on the rural fringe to a city of art.[25]

Notes

1. Marlene Park and Gerald E. Markowitz, *Democratic Vistas: Post Offices and Public Art in the New Deal* (Philadelphia: Temple University Press, 1984), 222. For more on the development of a gallery and the beginnings of an art department at Duke, see Robert F. Durden, *The Launching of Duke University, 1924-1949* (Durham: Duke University Press, 1993), 153–54, 266–71. Also see *Objects of Art in the Library of the Woman's College, Duke University* (Durham: Duke University Woman's College Library, [19—]) and Betty Irene Young, *The Library of the Woman's College, Duke University, 1930-1972* (Durham: Regulator Press, 1978). For more on the Shepard statue see the Profiles.

2. Claudia P. Roberts and Diane E. Lea, *The Durham Architectural and Historic Inventory* (Durham: City of Durham, 1982), 36, 120, 138, 182, 213. For a complete discussion of Duke Chapel's windows see William Blackburn, *The Architecture of Duke University* (Durham: Duke University Press, 1937).

3. The Confederate memorial was put up in 1924. See Jean Bradley Anderson, *Durham County* (Durham: Duke University Press, 1990), 327. Contemporary newspaper accounts are cited in her notes. For more discussion of public art and its role in a town see Kate Dobbs Ariail, "Beyond Beige," *Independent Weekly*, April 16, 1997, 25.

4. The Unity Monument was dedicated in October 1923. Anderson, *Durham County*, 326–27. For further details see her endnotes.

5. "Exercises at the Unveiling of the Washington Duke Memorial Statue and Biographical Sketch, Trinity Park, Durham, N.C., June 10, 1908" ([Durham: Trinity College,] 1908). See also William E. King, *If Gargoyles Could Talk: Sketches of Duke University* (Durham: Carolina Academic Press, 1997), 179.

6. King, *If Gargoyles Could Talk*, 179–80. Keck was an assistant to the great American sculptor Augustus Saint-Gaudens for five years in the 1890s, and Saint-Gaudens's influence can be seen in Keck's combination of forceful spatial design with detailed surfaces and inspired portraiture.

7. "The Sower" is the work of the German artist Stephan Walter and dates from about 1899. It was donated to Trinity College by James B. Duke in 1914. For more information on this gift see William E. King's article in *Duke Dialogue*, June 14, 1991. Alicia J. Rouverol, interviewer and editor, *I Am Ella Fountain Keesler Pratt* (Durham: Durham Arts Council and Mary Duke Biddle Foundation, 1999), 51–56, 80, provides lively stories about the early years of the arts at Duke. Particularly wonderful are Pratt's memories of giving Edith London her first Durham exhibition, in the Book Lovers Room of East Campus Li-

brary, and a nearly incredible story about the unexpected arrival of van loads of great paintings borrowed from the Phillips Collection by Gil Ravenel, then a student and later head of design at the National Gallery in Washington. The Phillips Collection's founder was still living; Ravenel's father was the gallery's attorney—and the young Ravenel asked. Pratt took the vans to the library, and Ravenel hung what must be one of the most ravishing exhibitions seen in Durham to this day. For another interview with Pratt see Selaine Benaim Niedel, "The Voices of Durham, a Shared Tradition: An Oral History of the Arts in Durham" (typescript and cassette tapes, Duke University honors paper, 1989).

8. Ola Maie Foushee, *Art in North Carolina: Episodes and Developments, 1585–1970* (Chapel Hill: Self-published, 1972), 56–59, 153–56. A particularly useful source for visualizing the many-stranded development of Durham's artists in the second half of the twentieth century is *DAG 50 Years: A Retrospective Exhibition of the Durham Art Guild, 1948–1998* (Durham: Durham Art Guild, 1998). This catalogue includes a complete checklist and good-quality black-and-white reproductions of most of the works included in the exhibition, as well as a short essay by the curator, Daniel R. Robinson, placing Durham's artists in a broader context. Useful for understanding the impact of European-trained Modernists on the local scene is *Edith London: A Retrospective* (Durham: Durham Art Guild and Durham Arts Council, 1992). In addition to beautiful color plates, this catalogue includes an extensive and wide-ranging interview with London.

9. Foushee, *Art in North Carolina*, 155–56.

10. Joe Rowand, along with many other Durham arts leaders, was interviewed by Selaine Benaim Niedel for her 1989 Duke Master of Arts in Liberal Studies thesis. Niedel, "The Voices of Durham."

11. Michael Marsicano, "The Relationship between Artists and Institutions of Higher Education in North Carolina" (Ph.D. diss., Duke University Department of Education, 1982).

12. Charles Millard, *Partners in Patronage: Selections from Corporate Art Collections in North Carolina* (Durham: Durham Art Guild, 1988).

13. The DAC and the North Carolina Arts Council sponsored the very successful "Public Art Dialogue," held in June 1989 at the DAC and the Civic Center and attended by artists and arts professionals from around the state and the country. It was accompanied by an infamous project for which a pair of artists wrote a great deal of text on a broken sidewalk, which was then taken up and used as riprap. See Kate Dobbs Ariail, "Not a Grand Gesture: Interview with Kate Ericson and Mel Ziegler," *Artvu* 3, no. 2, 12–15. For more on "Laocoön '87" see Kate Dobbs Ariail, "Slithering toward Durham," *Independent Weekly*, June 16, 1999, 44. The DOT offered to move the sculpture, but the artist insisted that it was site-specific and that to move it would destroy it. The DOT

then provided a sum of money to the DAC to pay for the compensatory commissioning of another public artwork for the city. As of this writing, no work has been commissioned.

14. The main critics in local publications were Kate Dobbs Ariail in the *Independent Weekly*; Linda Johnson Dougherty in the *Spectator*; Norman Pendergraft in the *Durham Sun*; Blue Greenberg in the Durham *Herald-Sun*; Max Halperen in the *Spectator* and the *News and Observer*; Stephen Litt, art and architecture critic for the *News and Observer*; Michelle Richards Natale, first in the *Chapel Hill News* and later in the *Spectator*; and Chuck Twardy, who replaced Litt at the *News and Observer*. Critical coverage of visual arts subsequently fell off sharply: of the above, only Greenberg still regularly covered the visual arts in 2003. The *News and Observer* dropped criticism in favor of previews and features, but began running short reviews by Michelle Natale in mid-2004.

15. Interview by the author with Tom Russo, then president of the Durham Art Guild, February 25, 1994. According to Russo, the DAC executive director, E'Vonne Coleman, had been upset by Irwin's and Toledo's works, and had said to them that the penises were the problem, and further that one-third of her board members favored removing the artworks from the Art Guild's gallery. See also letter from Kim Irwin and Max Below Toledo to E'Vonne Coleman and the DAC board members, Susan Hickman and the DAG board members, and DAC staff, February 24, 1994 (copy in the author's possession).

16. Kenneth Rodgers, *Re-connecting Roots: The Silver Anniversary Alumni Invitational* (Durham: North Carolina Central University Art Museum, 1997), 2–4. Rodgers gives a succinct history of the art department and the museum at NCCU, and the exhibition catalogue gives a visual overview of the range of art made by NCCU graduates.

17. See Fiona Morgan, "Monument in the Making," *Independent Weekly*, August 6, 2003, 20–25, for the story of the founding of the Duke University Museum of Art and its subsequent evolution into the Nasher Museum. For an earlier overview focused on the planned new museum's major donor, Raymond Nasher, and Michael Mezzatesta, then DUMA's director, see Geoff Edgers, "The Sum of His Arts," *News and Observer*, February 14, 1999, § G, pp. 1, 3. For things as they appeared slightly earlier, see Kate Dobbs Ariail, "Let's Hear It for Duke," *Independent Weekly*, November 18, 1998, 25. For a more thorough examination of the beginning of the museum see Foushee, *Art in North Carolina*, 86–87; Durden, *Launching Duke*, 153–54; and Anderson, *Durham County*, 466–67. For background on the Brummer Collection, which formed the nucleus of DUMA's holdings, see Carolina Bruzelius with Jill Meredith, *The Brummer Collection of Medieval Art* (Durham: Duke University Press in association with the Duke University Museum of Art, 1991), 7–10. Louise Tharaud Brasher, in *Selections from the Bequest of Nancy Hanks* (Dur-

ham: Duke University Museum of Art, 1986), outlines the significance of the gift from Hanks, a Duke alumna, of her varied personal collection of nineteenth- and twentieth-century artworks and her role in the founding of the museum as well as the Duke Institute of the Arts. Many of DUMA's finest pre-Columbian ceramics are illustrated and put in context in the catalogue of the important exhibition organized by Dorie Reents-Budet, then curator of pre-Columbian art, *Painting the Maya Universe: Royal Ceramics of the Classic Period* (Durham: Duke University Press in association with the Duke University Museum of Art, 1994). On Rorschach's hiring see Joanna Kakissis, "Duke Museum Has Chief," *News and Observer*, April 13, 2004, § B, p. 1.

18. Kate Dobbs Ariail, "Men of Steel: Metal Urges," *Duke Magazine*, May–June 1994, 38–40.

19. Kate Dobbs Ariail, "Radical Grace," *Independent Weekly*, October 12, 1994, 21–22. Yonat Shimron, "Black Palette: Portrait Artist Beverly McIver Illuminates the African-American Experience," *News and Observer*, October 17, 1994, § C, p. 1.

20. Kate Dobbs Ariail, "Attracting Excellence," *Independent Weekly*, December 11, 1996, 29–33.

21. For more on individual and group efforts by artists in the urban core see Kate Dobbs Ariail, "O Pioneers," *Independent Weekly*, May 24, 2000, 21–23.

22. For more on the Artworks in State Buildings program see Jeffrey York and Linda Johnson Dougherty, *Creating Place* (Raleigh: North Carolina Arts Council, 2002). For the NC Artists Exhibitions see the catalogues produced by the North Carolina Museum of Art to accompany the exhibitions in 1990, 1993, 1996, and 1999.

23. For more on the Scrap Exchange's art philosophy, Kostelnik, and ABCD, see Orla Swift, "Turn Scrap into Artwork," *News and Observer*, July 30, 2004, § E, p. 1; Orla Swift, "He Sees Gems, Not Junk," *News and Observer*, August 8, 2004, § B, p. 1, and Fiona Morgan, "Downtown Renaissance," *Independent Weekly*, August 18, 2004, 21.

24. The Cultural Master Plan was commissioned by the County of Durham and its sixty-two-member project steering committee and managed by the Durham Arts Council. The consultant was Wolf, Keens & Co. The two-volume plan is available in hard copy at the DAC and in the offices of the city and county clerks.

25. Liberty Arts and the bronze casting facility were founded by Jack Preiss, Walker Stone, Kate Dobbs Ariail, Frank A. DePasquale, and Frances Vega in the spring of 2000 to complement the increasing growth of metal artwork in the Triangle area. In the summer of 2000 the original board members added three new members: Robert Bell, Nick Tennyson, and Mary D. Jacobs. For background see Liberty Arts minutes in the offices of DTW Architects. For background see Jim Wise, "Hill Arts Pavilion Is Dedicated," *Herald-Sun*, Oc-

tober 25, 2003, § B, p. 1. Fiona Morgan puts Liberty Arts in the context of the Foster Street arts corridor in "Central Casting," *Independent Weekly*, November 5, 2003, 32. For the creation of the Bull see Jim Wise, "Creating Some Bully Art," *Herald-Sun*, April 12, 2004, § A, p. 1; Cynthia Greenlee-Donnell, "Sculptor Pours Life into Center," *Herald-Sun*, May 8, 2004, § B, pp. 1, 4; and Harry Lynch, "That's a Lot of Bull," *News and Observer* (Durham edition, captioned photo), June 12, 2004, § B, p. 6.

In Closing

Through many decades of increasing diversity and excellence, the arts in Durham have now reached a point of rooted maturation. Hearts and pocket books are open to them. While the bright leaf that once earned Durham fame and fortune no longer prevails here, Durham enjoys greater and more lasting riches from brighter leaves—its arts.

Profiles

AADE	African American Dance Ensemble
ADF	American Dance Festival
AIA	American Institute of Architects
CAPPS	Creative Arts in the Public/Private Schools
CCB	Central Carolina Bank
CDCG	Carolina Designer Craftsmen Guild
DAC	Durham Arts Council
DSA	Durham School of the Arts
DU	Duke University
ECU	East Carolina University
NCCU	North Carolina Central University
NCSU	North Carolina State University
NEA	National Endowment of the Arts
NPDC	New Performing Dance Company
UNC	University of North Carolina
UNC-Chapel Hill	University of North Carolina at Chapel Hill

African American Quilt Circle

Four women—Bertie Howard, Jereann King, Helen Sanders, and Candace Thomas—founded the African American Quilt Circle in 1998. Their purposes were to enjoy the craft of quilting, pass on the tradition of African-American quilting, and keep history alive through depictions in quilts. At first focusing on the tradition of making bed quilts for warmth and comfort, the circle later pushed the boundaries of quilting in new directions. Service projects undertaken by the circle have included making quilts for premature babies at UNC Hospital. Circle members have also made quilts for high school graduates at the Oxford Manor Achievement School and for residents of Durham public housing. Members stitched a wall hanging to accompany the photo exhibit "The Mule Train," a display of pictures from the Poor People's Campaign of the late 1960s, and donated a quilt to the Amistad Friendship Quilt Project, a nationwide effort to provide quilts for the bunks of the schooner *Amistad*.

American Dance Festival (ADF)

The mission of the American Dance Festival (ADF) is to present dance, train dancers, support new work, build audiences, enhance public understanding, and preserve the history of modern dance. ADF offers a six-and-a-half-week season of modern dance performance and a school for dance each year. It began at Bennington College, Vermont, in 1934 as the Bennington Festival. When Charles Reinhart became director in 1968 he changed the name to American Dance Festival, and in 1977 he moved ADF to Durham. Before and during Reinhart's tenure, ADF commissioned and gave the première of numerous dance works. Some recent commissioned works have included *River* by Eiko and Koma, *Wings at Tea* by Tatiana Baganova, *Promethean Fire* by Paul Taylor, *The Rite of Spring* (parts one and two), and *Connect Transfer* by Shen Wei.

The organization has a permanent staff of fifteen, which explodes to over one hundred during the summer dance season, when more than five hundred dance students and professionals from around the world present performances of some of the most famous world dance groups. ADF is a leader in modern dance teaching and performance and attracts national and international attention.

Archipelago Theatre

The Archipelago Theatre was founded by Ellen Hemphill and Rafael Lopez-Barrantes in 1990. An outgrowth of the Roy Hart Theatre of France, Archipelago stresses the emotional content of sound and its passage into words, and strives to have the body and gestures manifest that content on stage, all in a harmonious relationship. Now under the direction of Hemphill, Archipelago produces one or two plays a year in various locales in the area, almost all with music, and most of them original. Its repertory includes a movement piece for six actor-singer-musicians, *Outraged and on the Wire* (1993); a cabaret, *Another Time . . . Another Place . . . Someone Else* (1997); a work based on one-act plays by Harold Pinter, *Landscape, Silence, and Night* (1995); and a piece based on Calamity Jane's letters to her daughter, *She Didn't Like the Moon without Clouds* (1991), which was later produced at the Sun Valley Performance Arts Center (1997) as well as at Duke University (1998). Recent productions include *Eulogy for a Warrior* (1998), *Snow* (2002), and *And Mary Wept* (2002), all produced at Duke.

Arrocena, Catalina (1956–)

A Uruguayan painter and fabric artist, Catalina Arrocena was unable to study art at her university under her country's military dictatorship. Consequently, she took a degree in psychology and studied painting privately. In 1985, when she arrived in Durham with her husband, the Duke art professor William Noland, Arrocena began painting in her home studio. She received a fellowship from the North Carolina Arts Council in 1992, taught at the Durham Arts Council, and had exhibits at the Asheville Museum and the Duke Art Museum.

When Arrocena discovered a group of old kimonos in her mother-in-law's basement, she began to work with the materials, creating kimono-inspired pillows, scarves, and shawls. Her work was shown at the Durham Arts Council's series of Art in Translation dinners in 2005.

Art and Art History Department, Duke University

Art history courses were first offered at Duke with the founding of the Woman's College in 1931. These were little more than a few modest courses taught through the Department of Philosophy by one of the first female architectural historians in the United States, Louise Hall (1905–1990). Hall lectured on art and architectural history alone until a new Department of Aesthetics, Art, and Music was established in 1942 under Katherine E. Gilbert. With Hall still teaching the bulk of the courses, a department solely for art and art history was established in 1962. Among the many important hires during these early years were the Renaissance scholar John R. Spencer (1923–1994) and the Dutch baroque scholar William S. Heckscher (1904–1999). A reorganized Department of Art and Art History was founded in 1986 with a broadened curriculum that included methodology and criticism, and faculty who covered the areas of African, East Asian, and Latin American art history. A Ph.D. program was instituted in 1992.

The current Department of Art and Art History comprises both a studio art program in the arts warehouses and a nationally ranked art history program housed in the East Duke building on East Campus. The department is noted for its strengths in nineteenth- and twentieth-century art, French, Dutch baroque, Chinese, modern Japanese, and African-American art, and art economics, with an emphasis on interdisciplinary study. The faculty comprises four named professorships, currently filled by Richard J. Powell, Annabel Wharton, Caroline Bruzelius, and Neil McWilliam, a score of other permanent appointments, and adjunct faculty. Certificates in architecture and museology are available to undergraduates, as well as art history study abroad programs in Italy, the Netherlands, and Belgium. A graduate symposium each spring attracts students and scholars from around the country. The department also hosts annually the Edward H. Benenson Lectures, generally a weeklong lectureship by a single scholar on a focused theme. The Department supports a visual research collection of 300,000 images.

Art and Art History Department, NCCU

The NCCU Department of Art was established in 1939 when Dr. James E. Shepard, president and founder of North Carolina College, hired Marion Parham Cordice to be director of art studies. In addition to guiding studies and mounting the first student art exhibition, she also laid the foundation for the NCCU Art Museum by purchasing a number of artworks. Cordice hired Ed Wilson, sculptor, and he became the chairman of the Art Department. Wilson hired William Zorach in 1956, also a leading sculptor, who was commissioned to create the statue of Dr. Shepard which stands in the center of the university's entrance circle.

Initially the Art Department shared space with the music, dramatic art, and dance programs, but since 1978 it has occupied the entire Fine Arts Building. Robert Kennedy was chairman for a short period from 1964 to 1965. Lynn Igoe, who was hired during that time, pushed for the establishment of a museum and became its first director in 1971. Igoe expanded the collection but eventually left the museum to work on a two-volume bibliography of African-American art, which has become a standard reference in the field. Igoe also hired Norman Pendergraft, later the director of the museum, and Dr. Lana Henderson, an art educator, who later became chairwoman. In 1973 Charles Joyner added luster to the department with his fine prints and established a program in visual communications, which became very popular. When Joyner left in 1977, Melvin Carver, a specialist in graphic and product design who would much later become chairman, replaced him. During her tenure as chairwoman, Dr. Henderson hired Isabel Levitt in ceramics and photography, Acha Debela in computer graphics, Michele Patterson in art history, and Carlyle Johnson in printmaking. She also worked to improve the physical facilities. Henderson held the chair for thirteen years and was succeeded in 1990 by Melvin Carver, who has held the position since then.

Visual communications and digital design are the strengths of the department, supported by advanced computer labs. Carver has started a study-abroad program with the University of Science and Technology in Kumasi, Ghana. He has also established a four-year scholarship in art study with the aid of the Red Hat Corporation.

The future of the department is bright, and enrollment is increasing. The department's nationally recognized graduates include Ernie Barnes, Willie Nash, and Beverly McIver. The Art Museum is recognized for the quality of its collection of African-American art.

Art galleries

Durham's art galleries comprise galleries affiliated with universities and nonprofit organizations, as well as private establishments. Universities became dominant early on, with the opening of the gallery in the Woman's College library, now Lilly Library of Duke University, East Campus. With the appointment of Ella Fountain Pratt as Duke's first director of cultural affairs in the 1950s, arts and exhibitions played prominent roles at Duke, and her influence continued until her retirement in 1984. Duke now has a new art museum, the Nasher Museum of Art, which opened in the fall of 2005. The Duke Center for Documentary Studies, opened in 1989, shows works by local photographers. NCCU opened a gallery in 1958 and began the construction of its Art Museum in 1977, a building devoted to works by African-American artists.

Nonprofit arts organizations have also played an important role in offering gallery space. The Durham Art Guild has historically shown the works of local artists and since 1988 has mounted exhibitions in the CCB Gallery of the Durham Arts Council. The Hayti Heritage Center exhibits work by African-American artists in the Lyda Moore Merrick Gallery. Festivals organized by both Allied Arts (the Triangle Festival of Crafts) and the Durham Arts Council (CenterFest) have exhibited and sold the work of local artists.

Somerhill, opened by Joe Rowand in 1972, was the first private art gallery in Durham. Artsplace, a co-op gallery named Artomatic, and the artist Jimmy Kellough's Modern Museum provided exhibit space to artists in the 1990s. The George Watts Hill Pavilion for the Arts, a bronze casting studio operated by Liberty Arts in Central Park, was dedicated in 2003.

Nonprofit efforts to encourage appreciation and participation in the arts downtown have included Durham Artwalk, which began in 1999 to give the public an opportunity to tour artists'

studios and art galleries. The "Art Grows in Durham" events sponsored by South East Efforts Developing Sustainable Spaces (SEEDS) have shown how art can be incorporated into community and urban gardens.

Azenberg, Emanuel (1934–)

A noted Broadway producer of over fifty plays and winner of numerous Tonys, Drama Desk Awards, and Drama Critics Circle Awards, Emanuel Azenberg has been associated with the Duke University Drama Program (now the Department of Theater Studies) since 1986. Besides teaching, through the program Broadway Previews (later Theater Previews) he has staged performances at Duke of *Long Day's Journey into Night* (1986), *Broadway Bound* (1986), *A Month of Sundays* (1987), *An Evening with Waylon Jennings* (1987), *Moonlight and Valentino* (1989), and *Laughter on the 23rd Floor* (1993).

Baird, Stanley (1943–)

Stanley Baird first played saxophone in junior high school and organized a band at the age of fourteen. After serving in the U.S. Continental Army Band he received an M.A. in music from NCCU. A music educator, he has taught at Durham's Shepard Middle School, where he cofounded the summer Shepard Jazz Camp and established a scholarship program, the Stanley Baird Youth Jazz Foundation, funded by the National Heritage Foundation. Baird is also a performer: his latest ensemble, the Stanley Baird Group, was formed in 1991 and has released over four albums on the Saxony Records label.

Ball, David (1942–)

David Ball came to Duke University in 1985 to head the program in drama. He hired professional faculty, enlarged the curriculum, and made plans for an equity theater. In the first season there were two productions in Reynolds Theater, *Hot*

L Baltimore (Lanford Wilson) and *Romeo and Juliet*, as well as three others in Branson Theater: Douglas Ward's *Day of Absence*, Scott McCrea's *Past Grand Night*, and Sam Shepard's *Suicide in B Flat*. Ball instituted a program called World Premières (later known as New Works Festival), which presented short pieces by students, faculty, and staff which he produced using students as actors, directors, and technicians. In 1986 the Broadway producer Emmanuel Azenberg began bringing shows that he was working on for out-of-town rehearsals and productions at Duke. These constituted what was at first known as Broadway Previews, later as Theater Previews. In 1991 Ball, who was interested in the theater of the courtroom, left Duke to become a full-time legal consultant.

Bamberger, Bill (1956–)

A documentary photographer, Bill Bamberger earned his B.A. in American studies from UNC-Chapel Hill in 1979. From 1981 to 1982 he was a fellow at the Duke Center for Documentary Studies, which published a companion book of portraits, *Durham County Photographs*, for an exhibition at the Southeastern Center for Contemporary Art. His best-known work is *Closing: The Life and Death of An American Factory*, with text by the Duke English professor Cathy Davidson, a book that documents the closing of White Furniture Company in Mebane, North Carolina. Bamberger had a solo exhibition of these photographs at the North Carolina Museum of Art in 1998 and at the Smithsonian in 2000. His exhibition "Boys Will Be Men," at the Flint Institute of Art in 2002, showed boys coming of age. As a visiting fellow at the Center for the Study of the American South at UNC, Bamberger co-directed a public arts initiative on affordable housing, "This House Is Home," from 2001 to 2003, and he has lectured at UNC and Duke. His work has appeared in the *New York Times Magazine*, *Harper's*, and

Doubletake. Bamberger won a grant from the National Endowment of the Arts/Mid-Atlantic Arts Foundation (2000), the Mayflower Prize in Non-Fiction (1999), a grant from the North Carolina Humanities Council (1994), and the Lyndhurst Prize (1986–88).

Barnes, Ernie (1938–)

Born and raised in Durham, Ernie Barnes is an internationally known African-American artist. He committed to art in elementary school; later he became an accomplished football player at Hillside High School and North Carolina Central University, where he majored in art. After graduation he played professionally for the Baltimore Colts, San Diego Chargers, and Denver Broncos.

He was retired from football by New York Jets team owner David Werblin, who became his patron and hosted his first solo exhibition in New York in 1966. His defining moment came when he moved into the Fairfax area of Los Angeles where he discovered the spiritual intelligence of the Jewish culture. The experience led to the signature feature in his work—the "closed eyes" of his subjects—to suggest "how blind we are to one another's humanity," says Barnes. It also resulted in him reinvesting African-American lives with meaning and potency through his exhibition "The Beauty of the Ghetto," which featured paintings that became a way to raise consciousness and have an organic function within the community. In 1973, the High Museum in Atlanta, Georgia, presented this exhibition and in 1978 it was hosted by Governor James Hunt at the North Carolina Museum of Art.

In 1984, his paintings of sports yielded him the top cultural spot of the XXIII Olympiad at Los Angeles, the Official Olympic Artist. Credited with reviving 16th century Mannerism and presenting it in 21st century form, Barnes is a synthesizer of all cultures. He has received numerous awards, including the prestigious University Award from the University of North Carolina Board of Governors. His civil rights painting *The Advocate*, hangs in the law school at NCCU, which honored him with a doctorate in 1990. Barnes has written about his life in "From Pads to Palette."

Barnes, J. Foster (1894–1956)
Born into a musical family, J. Foster Barnes sang in the church choir as a child. After earning B.A. and M.A. degrees in other areas of study, he ultimately chose a career in music and became a professionally trained baritone. In 1924 he recorded with organ accompaniment for the Victor Talking Machine Company.

In 1927 Barnes joined the faculty of Duke Divinity School, where he directed the men's glee club and the choir at Trinity Methodist Church in Durham. He was affectionately known as "the Bishop" among the glee club members. Upon completion of the university chapel in 1932, Barnes founded the chapel choir and became the university director of social and religious activities. He established the annual traditions of a performance of the *Messiah* at Christmas and of an oratorio at Easter.

Belans, Linda (1946–)
Linda Belans is a radio broadcaster and director of the Health Arts Network at Duke who has been an influential figure in Durham's dance scene. A native of Pennsylvania with a B.A. from Goddard College in Vermont, she has studied dance all her life. She joined the New Performing Dance Company, formed from Dance Associates of Allied Arts (now the Durham Arts Council), shortly after her arrival in Durham in 1974. Belans has written about dance since 1976 for the *North Carolina Anvil*, the *Spectator*, and the *News and Observer*. She taught dance and theater at Carolina Friends School from 1978 to 1985 and dance appreciation at Meredith College in Raleigh. She

directs and has written libretti for Carolina Ballet, including "The Kreutzer Sonata" and "Stravinsky's Clown," has lectured nationally on dance, directed international conferences of dance critics, and developed the post-performance discussion series "Talk About Dance!" She was the creator and original host of "The State of Things" on local public radio and a co-creator and host of "Do No Harm," a series on medical ethics, which won a Gracie Allen Award for Women in Broadcasting and a Silver Reel for National Public Affairs Programming. Belans's mission has been to bring awareness, understanding, and enjoyment of the art of dance to the community.

Black, Robert (Bob) Keith (1939–)
Bob Black is a stoneware potter and painter. A native of North Carolina, he has a B.S. from Wake Forest University and an M.F.A. from the University of Georgia. He pursued additional studies at Parsons School of Design and North Carolina State University. He and his partner Ormond Sanderson left their teaching jobs at Atlantic Christian College in Wilson in 1958 to open a crafts studio and gallery on property that Sanderson's uncle owned in Durham. In the old farmhouse, they promoted good design through shows of work by local, regional, and national artists. They worked with the potter Vivian Dai and became involved through her in Allied Arts (now Durham Arts Council). Black has won prizes at the North Carolina Museum of Art Craft Show, the American Craftsmen Council show, the Mint Museum in Charlotte, and the Gallery of Art and Design at NCSU. His commissions include works for a residence designed by Frank Lloyd Wright, the Gallery of Art and Design at NCSU, various churches in North Carolina, and private clients. In the 1970s Black and Sanderson expanded their facilities for commercial space, which they called Straw Valley, and housed the Somerhill Gallery

and the Craft House of Durham. Straw Valley has had a stimulating and lasting effect on the arts in Durham.

Blair, Elizabeth (1961–)

A dancer, choreographer, and visual artist, Betsy Blair holds degrees in creative writing, design, and dance and has studied art throughout her life. Blair, who calls her solo dances "color-speaking-poems," formed the children's dance troupe Rainbow Dancers. Her awards include the Raleigh Medal of Arts, the Hitchings Award for Service to the Art of Dance, and an Emerging Artist grant from Durham Arts Council, as well as other local and state grants. Very much aware of the need for instructional materials, she has produced a teacher workbook, *Dance-Songs for Young Children*, and an audio and video presentation, "The Dance of the Sunshine Children." Recently she has divided her time between the design and production of teachers' workbooks for leading educational dance activities and the creation of watercolors. She also works with young people as a dancer, choreographer, and visual artist and plays the Sprite on the Frog Hollow program on WRAL-TV.

Blake, Robert L. (1917–)

Robert Blake had a long career as a medical illustrator at Duke University from 1942 until 1983. Born in Pleasantville, New Jersey, and raised in Medford, he finished secondary school in Philadelphia and then went to work, at the same time attending art classes at night at the Philadelphia Sketch Club. Primarily self-taught, he gained experience in his job as an illustrator of men's clothing for tailors' catalogues. A medical illustrator's position attracted him to Duke Medical School, where he was trained on the job. Since living in North Carolina he has become a master of its landscape, particularly the Piedmont and coastal areas. His hundreds of watercolor paintings capture the character of every aspect of rural life and architecture.

For a number of years Blake painted backgrounds for early planetarium shows in Chapel Hill, where he was allowed to exhibit his work. He also exhibited at Duke Hospital, CenterFest, and West Point on the Eno. He was a founding member of the Durham Art Guild and has won prizes for his watercolors in guild exhibits at the Woman's College Library at Duke and elsewhere.

Bohanon, Mary L. (1913–1989)

Mary Bohanon was chairwoman of the Department of Dramatic Art at NCCU from 1949 to 1964. During her tenure she increased the offerings from twelve to fifteen courses, including dramatic literature, play production, acting, directing, oral interpretation, voice, stagecraft, and lighting. She also increased the faculty from one to three members and staged two major productions annually. Bohanon devoted her directing energies to American and European classics, and the quality of her productions is discussed today with great respect and admiration. Her productions included Sophocles' *Antigone*, Euripides' *Medea*, *King Lear*, Williams's *The Glass Menagerie*, Shaw's *Don Juan in Hell*, Eliot's *Murder in the Cathedral*, Michael V. Gazzo's *A Hatful of Rain*, and *The Medium*. Several of her students became successful theater professionals, most notably Jacqueline Bames, who performed Off Broadway with William Marshall and with the film actor, director, and producer Ivan Dixon.

Bone, Allan (1917–1992)

A musician and teacher, Allan Bone played as his first instrument a clarinet bought for $14 from Sears, Roebuck. He received a B.A. from the University of Wisconsin and an M.A. from the Eastman College of Music, earning his way through college by playing in the school jazz band. Bone taught music for several years before coming to Duke in 1944, where he taught until his retirement in 1989. He was involved in many initiatives both within and outside of the university. He was the conductor of the Duke Symphony, first conductor of the Durham Civic Choral Society, and conductor of the Durham Savoyards. He was also director of music at St. Philip's Episcopal Church.

Bone, Dorothy (1916–2006)

Dorothy Biersach Bone worked primarily in the business side of Craft House of Durham along with Dorothy Davis, Florentina McKinney, Jan Gregg, and Pepper Fluke. She developed a technique for creating handwoven lampshades for Dorothy Davis's ceramic lamps. She was born in Wisconsin, earned a B.M. from the University of Wisconsin, and pursued graduate studies at the Eastman School of Music. In 1944 she and her husband settled in Durham, where she became active in the city's and Duke University's music community.

Broadway at Duke

Broadway at Duke is a subscription series at Duke University that presents four to seven shows a season. Initiated by the officers of the Student Union in 1968 under the guidance of Ella Fountain Pratt, then program director of the Student Union, it has presented notables in concert, including Barbara Cook (1981), Ben Vereen (1982), and Patti LuPone (2001). Among its presentations have been the musicals *Side by Side by Sondheim* with Hermione Gingold (1978), *Sugar Babies* with Eddie Bracken (1981), and *Ragtime* (2002); the plays *The Belle of Amherst* with Julie Harris (1979), *Tru* with Robert Morse (1993), and *Master Class* with Charlotte Cornwell (1999); and several hard-to-classify shows like *William Win-*

dom Plays Thurber (1978), *Penn and Teller* (1997), and *Evocations*, an evening of poetry readings by Princess Grace (1980).

Broadway Previews. See Theater Previews

Broderson, Robert (1920–1992)

A native of Connecticut, Robert Broderson was a painter and art teacher at Duke University from 1952 until 1964. He developed an interest in art as a sophomore at Duke after service in the Second World War enabled him to earn a college degree in his late twenties. He then went on for an M.F.A. at the University of Iowa before starting his teaching career. He later taught at NCSU and the Skowhegan School of Painting and Sculpture in Maine. Broderson was the recipient of both Ford and Guggenheim fellowships. In the late 1960s he gave up teaching and he devoted the rest of his life to painting, primarily oils, concentrating on imagined human figures and animal forms. His paintings are in the Whitney Museum of American Art, the North Carolina Museum of Art, the Smithsonian Institution, the Carnegie Institute, Princeton University, and many other art collections.

Brown, Les, Sr. (1912–2001)

Les Brown was one of the notables of the "big band" era. Born in Pennsylvania, he learned trumpet and saxophone at an early age. During his high school years he studied at the Ithaca Conservatory of Music, where he learned to play the clarinet. Brown was touring with his band the Rainbow Men when members of the Duke Blue Devils heard him and suggested that he enroll at Duke so that he might play with their band. The prospect of free room and board in exchange for performing on weeknights at the Student Union persuaded him to make the move in 1932. The Duke band was so successful under his leadership that during his senior year it obtained a record deal with Decca.

After graduating from Duke, Brown directed a professional band in New York and went on to become Bob Hope's music director in the 1950s. During his long career he performed with almost all the major popular stars of the day, including Frank Sinatra, Ella Fitzgerald, and Nat "King" Cole. Brown returned to Duke in 1985 as a guest conductor of the jazz ensemble and again in 1987 when he established the Les Brown Endowment and his band played a benefit performance.

Bryan, Paul (1920–)

Paul Bryan received a B.A. in music education, an M.A. in music theory, and a Ph.D. from the University of Michigan in musicology. He studied counterpoint and composition privately with Vittorio Giannini and conducting with Thor Johnson. Besides learning the trombone and euphonium with Simone Mantia, Gardell Simons, Donald Reinhardt, and Wayne Lewis, he studied the violoncello with Oliver Edel, William Klenz, and Raphael Kramer and piano with Selma Kramer. He taught at the University of Michigan and in 1951 joined the music faculty at Duke University, where he taught music theory, music history, and brass instruments. He also conducted the concert and marching bands until 1988 and spent several semesters as conductor of the Duke Symphony. Bryan was also active in the Durham Civic Choral Society and the Savoyards. In 1961 he founded the Triangle Little Symphony, a chamber ensemble that performed works from the classical period. The ensemble toured the Triangle and beyond during the summer season and accompanied the Savoyards for their performances until it was disbanded in the 1980s.

Bryan received the Vincent H. Duckles Award from the Music Library Association for his manuscript *Johann Wanhal, Viennese Symphonist:* *His Life and His Musical Environment.* He was also recognized as an Outstanding Conductor by the magazine *School Musician* and the honorary music fraternity Phi Beta Mu.

Burchfield, Donna Faye (1958–)

Donna Burchfield, a dancer and choreographer, has been dean and associate director of the American Dance Festival (ADF) since 1984. With B.F.A. and M.F.A. degrees from Texas Christian University, she is also associate professor of dance and chairwoman of the dance program at Hollins University, Roanoke, Virginia, where she directs a Master of Fine Arts program jointly sponsored by the university and ADF, as well as the university's Repertory Dance Company. Burchfield teaches dance internationally as well, most recently with ADF in Moscow and Seoul. Since 1979 she has been choreographing and performing her own work, for which she has received commissions from Center Stage at NCSU and Contemporary Dance in Fort Worth, among others. For her choreography she was the recipient in 1992–93 and 1993–94 of an Artist Project Grant in Dance, given by the North Carolina Arts Council.

Burt, Thomas (1900–)

Thomas Burt was a talented blues guitarist in Durham from the 1920s to the 1940s. His parents, who worked as sharecroppers, were both musical: his father played accordion for local dances and his mother sang hymns as she worked. Burt first learned to play the banjo in his early teens but subsequently took up the guitar. He worked full time in a variety of places including tobacco factories, but with his wife Pauline he performed weeknights on the porch of his sister's house on Corporation Street as well as in Raleigh, Winston-Salem, and other towns. After the Second World War the Burts withdrew from the music scene, but Thomas picked up his guitar again in the

1970s, when new fans of blues music rediscovered him in Creedmoor. He then appeared at a number of folk festivals and in several television documentaries, and recorded two albums. In 1987 he was awarded the Brown-Hudson Award from the North Carolina Folklore Society.

Caesar, Shirley (1938–)

An award-winning and nationally known gospel singer, Shirley Caesar has recorded a number of albums and today is considered the "first lady of gospel." She was born into a musical family: her father, a worker at Liggett & Myers, was the lead in a gospel quartet, the Just Come Four, and her brother Leroy performed with the Royal Jubilee Singers. Caesar credits her father with instilling in her the love of music. When her father died she began singing professionally at the age of seven to help support the family. At ten she began to sing as "Baby Shirley" with the Charity Sisters of Durham, and as a teenager, she traveled with the Reverend Jesse Jackson on the gospel circuit. In 1958 she joined the Caravans, and in 1966 she formed her own Gospel group, the Shirley Caesar Singers. She is now pastor of the Pentecostal Mount Calvary Word of Faith Church in Durham and continues with an active outreach ministry. With over forty recordings of her music, Caesar has received many awards, including almost a dozen Grammy, Stellar, and Dove awards. She was inducted into the Gospel Music Hall of Fame.

Catlett, Elizabeth (1915–)

Elizabeth Catlett is an African-American master sculptor and printmaker whose widely acclaimed works combine themes of protest and justice. A native of Washington, D.C., she received a B.A. from Howard University in 1935. That same year she moved to Durham to work as a teacher at Hillside High School and also served as supervisor of school art programs in Durham's black elementary schools. She left teaching in Durham in 1938 to enter graduate study at the University of Iowa, and in 1940 she was awarded the university's first M.F.A. degree. She then went to the Art Institute of Chicago to study ceramics. As her work received significant recognition in the art world, a fellowship grant in 1941 from the Julius Rosenwald Fund gained her international attention. She used the Rosenwald fellowship to study in Mexico with the Taller de Grafica Popular, an art community that protested social injustice. She headed the sculpture section of the National School of Fine Arts in Mexico City and later married the Mexican artist Francisco Mora and became a Mexican citizen.

Catlett's works range from commissioned linocuts in the 1940s, such as those in the series "Negro Woman," to well-known prints like *Sharecroppers* and *Malcolm Speaks*, along with pieces influenced by her life in Mexico. Exhibitions of her works include a seventy-piece retrospective in 2001 at the NCCU Museum of Art funded by the North Carolina Arts Council and the Duke-Semans Fine Arts Foundation. While the exhibition was in Durham, NCCU awarded Catlett an honorary doctorate of humanities in recognition of her many artistic contributions and advocacy efforts for racial equality. Catlett's early life and move to Mexico are presented in *An American Artist in Mexico*, by Elizabeth Herzog (University of Washington Press, 2000).

Cedar Creek Gallery

A gallery in northern Durham County, Cedar Creek Gallery was opened in 1968 as Strawberry Fields by Sid and Pat Oakley, who both grew up in nearby rural Granville County. Pat studied at the Penland School of Crafts and UNC-Chapel Hill. Sid received his B.A. and M.A. from UNC-Chapel Hill. The Oakleys' promotion of North Carolina crafts and their mentoring of numerous craftspeople through their gallery earned Cedar Creek the North Carolina Governor's Award for

Excellence in Arts. Sid, who became recognized for his signature crystalline-glazed pottery and his painting, received the North Carolina Living Treasure award from UNC-Wilmington.

The gallery began as a potters' studio with a few simple shelves for exhibits. A wider array of crafts, including glassblowing and jewelry making, are now practiced by local artists in several studios at the site. Cedar Creek hosts special exhibits throughout the year, holds kiln-opening events twice a year, and is home to the triennial National Teapot Show.

Center for Documentary Studies, Duke University

Since the Center for Documentary Studies (CDS) opened its doors at Duke University in 1990, it has been a gathering place—a campus and community crossroads for people interested in the creativity and power of the documentary arts. Set in a historic house in the heart of Durham, the center is home to photographers and writers, historians and filmmakers, musicians and folklorists, and many others who understand how documentary stories can wake us up, change perspectives, and move us to action.

The center was established through an endowment from the Lyndhurst Foundation and has focused since its early days on cultivating new talent in the documentary field. It has published award-winning books, mounted exhibitions of new and established artists, and offered nationally recognized training for community youth fieldwork projects in the United States for documentary fellows abroad, undergraduate courses, and popular summer institutes that attract students from across the country. The center is committed to sharing documentary work with a broad audience and educating students of all ages and levels of expertise.

Every year more than five thousand students and visitors to CDS take classes, view exhibitions, work on fieldwork projects, use the darkrooms and digital editing labs, participate in public discussions, produce radio shows, complete certificates in documentary studies, screen their work, and engage in lively conversation.

Ciompi, Adriana (1921–)

A dancer and teacher, Adriana Ciompi was already well-known in her native Italy for her participation on Olympic swimming and skiing teams when she came to Durham in 1964. She had also studied ballet with the lead dancer of the Vienna Opera Company. In the United States she continued her dance training with José Martinez in Cleveland and Anya Holm and Norman Corrick in Colorado Springs. In Durham she initiated ballet classes for Allied Arts (now the Durham Arts Council), which created a studio for her with mirrors and bars. When she taught one year at North Carolina College (NCCU), the football coach sent eight of his players to study ballet with her. She also taught ballet at Duke's dance studio, the Ark. She retired from teaching in 1977.

Ciompi, Giorgio (1918–1983)

Giorgio Ciompi was born in Italy; his father was a Florentine jewelry designer and his mother a professional pianist. He learned to play the violin early and performed at the age of nine with his brother, a cellist, accompanied by their mother. During his youth he was befriended by American benefactors, who sponsored his attendance at the Paris Conservatory, where George Ionescu was his coach. After graduation he made his professional début in a solo concert at La Scala, and subsequently went on an American tour with the New York Philharmonic under the direction of Toscanini. Ciompi made his home in the United States from 1947, living first in New York City and then in Cleveland, where he joined the faculty of the Institute of Music and was a member of the Albineri Trio. In 1964 Ciompi accepted an offer from Duke University to teach in the music department and establish a resident string quartet.

Cipriano, Krista (1950–)

Krista Cipriano, a native of Massachusetts, was assistant dean and director of the Union Craft Center at Duke University for over twenty-five years. Having received a B.F.A. from East Carolina University, she taught pottery at the Durham Arts Council and volunteered at the Durham Art Guild before being named director of the Craft Center in 1975. There she taught pottery, silk-screening, and weaving and was also the advisor of Freewater Productions, the student filmmaking organization, and of the student radio station, WXDU-FM. In time she expanded the craft program by hiring additional artists to teach jewelry making, woodworking, photography, and other crafts. Among the artists were Conrad Weiser, Barbara Yoder, Robert Stone, Bill Wallace, Nancy Ford, and Emily Wexler. Duke supplied studio space in Southgate Residence Hall, the basement of the Bryan Center, and the Ark Annex. The center, which was eventually named in Cipriano's honor, was closed in 2004.

Clum, John (1941–)

John Clum came to Duke University as a member of the English Department in 1966 and immediately became involved in drama through the Office of Student Affairs, which handled all dramatic activity at that time. In 1972 he founded the Summer Theater at Duke to give drama students a chance to learn all aspects of play production and to provide the community with more theater. He produced three to eight plays a season, mostly contemporary, and directed many of them. In 1975 the Program in Drama was created, independent of the Office of Student Affairs, and Clum became the founding director, a position he held until 1985. He directed the first production in the new Reynolds Theater, *Shaw's Misalliance*, in 1982 as well as over ten main stage productions between 1975 and 1985. In total he has directed over sixty plays. He became chairman of the Department of Theater Studies in 2003. Clum turned to playwriting in the 1990s. Many of his plays have received their première at Duke in the New Plays Festival, but there have also been numerous productions of his plays elsewhere, including in Atlanta, Baltimore, Indianapolis, Carmel (California), San Francisco, and New York.

Cohn, Edie (1948–)

The portrait artist Edie Cohn was born in New Holstein, Wisconsin, and grew up in a family of artists. She earned her associate degree in art from Foothills Junior College in California in 1969, studied further at Hayworth State College, and in 1973 moved to Durham, where she began with studio space and two grants from the Durham Arts Council. Cohn has helped youths to create murals along with executing her own mural work, including a piece on the building that houses the Durham Food Co-op. Her main focus is portraiture. She began drawing newborn infants at Durham Regional Hospital around 1989, a practice now continued in her studio. In 1991, funded by a grant from the North Carolina Humanities Council, she began to draw and interview residents of the Community Shelter for H.O.P.E. This work has been shown in a traveling exhibit, "No Call for Pity," displayed at the Durham Public Library and the Eno River Unitarian Universalist Fellowship. Cohn has also produced a short documentary about a disabled child, "Sophie's Promise," which was shown at the Fresh Docs series of the Center for Documentary Studies in 2002.

Coleman, Leonora (1941–2008)

A potter and the founder of Claymakers Studio, Leonora Coleman was born in Wadesboro, North

Carolina. She took an interest in pottery only after moving in 1983 to Durham, where she took her first pottery class at the Edison Johnson Recreation Center. She also studied pottery at Haywood Community College from 1988 to 1990, and then began to earn a living as a potter, supplemented by teaching. She established Claymakers Studio in the old Durham Awning Company building in 2000. Her mission is to provide resources to help the clay community develop skills and creativity. Claymakers offers classes, workshops, juried exhibitions, and studio space and sells ceramic supplies and books. Tiles created by patients and their families and fired at Claymakers were placed in Duke's Pediatric Intensive Care Unit in 2002.

Condoret, Jon André (1934–)

An architect, Jon Contoret was born and raised in Algiers. After completing his basic education he graduated from the École Spéciale d'Architecture in Paris in 1957. He was then placed in the French army and served for twenty-seven months with the corps of engineers in Algeria. During his studies in Paris he met Joan Earle, from Durham, who became his wife, and upon his army discharge moved to New York City and then to Durham to join Archie Royal Davis Architects. He designed the Nello Teer residences in Hope Valley and worked on the design of Croasdaile Country Club and Carteret High School in Morehead City.

In 1974 Contoret open his own office in Chapel Hill. Most of his professional work is still done in Durham, including many residences. In 1997 he decided to work with only one client, Fitch Creations of Fearrington Village. For them he completed many residences, the Fearrington House Inn, and the Park Building, and made plans for future growth.

Cooley, Jacob (1968–)

Jacob Cooley, a painter, was born in Sydney, Australia, but spent his childhood in Durham, learning his craft early through classes at the Durham Arts Council. He received a B.F.A. in painting from the University of Georgia in 1990 and an M.F.A. in painting from UNC-Chapel Hill in 1993. His smooth-surfaced landscape paintings are shown in galleries across the country. His work hangs in the SunTrust Building, at Durham Regional Hospital, at the Duke Museum of Art, and at the Ackland Art Museum. Cooley owns the Allen Sheppard Gallery in New York and keeps a studio at his home in Durham.

Cornelious, Eve

The jazz singer Eve Cornelious was raised in Newport News, Virginia. She has a B.A. in music, and in addition to her work as a vocalist she studied piano with Mary Lou Williams. She has toured extensively around the world and performed at many jazz festivals. She has also made a number of recordings, some with her husband, Chip Crawford. Cornelious has taught jazz singing at East Carolina University. She and her husband divide their time between Durham and New York City.

Council for the Creative Arts in the Public Schools (CCAPS)

In 1972 a group of several parents led by Pauline Silberman, Dorothy Borden, Alice Alston, and Janice Palmer initiated a program to introduce arts into the public schools. The success of their pilot project, funded by the First Presbyterian Church, led to the adoption by the city and county school systems of what was called the CCAPS program.

By the 1980s CCAPS was assimilated by the Durham Arts Council (DAC). Now a partnership of the DAC and the local school systems, it places artists in public and private classrooms throughout Durham and Orange counties. The art instruction provided is integrated with the core subjects, so that all children can translate aspects of their regular course of study into dance, the visual arts, film, and writing.

Crawford, Chip

The jazz pianist Chip Crawford grew up in Raleigh and started piano lessons at the age of eight. Growing up on a diet of beach music and rock-and-roll, he had no exposure to jazz until a club opened in Raleigh, where as a teenager he saw jazz greats such as Bill Evans and Freddie Hubbard. He attended the Berklee School of Music in Boston in the early 1970s and was soon touring and recording with the Four Tops and Isaac Hayes. Over the next twenty years he worked with a number of jazz artists, including Donald Byrd, Jimmy Heath, and Herbie Hancock, and did arrangements for Teo Macero, Miles Davis's producer. Byrd was influential in sparking Crawford's interest in music education, which led to a master's degree in music performance from NCCU in 1991. Since then Crawford has taught music at Duke, UNC, and NCCU as well as at Shepard Middle School. He also performs and records with his wife, the jazz singer Eve Cornelious.

Dai, Vivian Millicent Chin (1913–2006)

Vivian Dai, an artist and teacher, was an influential force for the arts in Durham from 1943 until 1969. A Chinese-American, she graduated from the Newark School of Fine and Industrial Arts in New Jersey, where she studied painting. When she moved to Durham in 1943 she became aware of a number of women interested in painting, principally faculty wives at Duke University with extra time and no resources for art instruction. Dai brought them together at her house and formed the group known first as the Creative Art group and from 1949 as the Durham Art Guild. The guild was one of the four organizations that in 1954 formed the umbrella organization Allied Arts.

By then Dai was teaching pottery and copper enameling privately as well. She pursued her own study of pottery at Alfred University in New York and at Haystack School of Crafts in Maine. She also studied weaving, which subsequently became her primary focus, with additional study in Sweden and at Mills College in California.

Dai continued to teach pottery at Allied Arts and in 1966 helped to organize the first Triangle Festival of Crafts—a forerunner of CenterFest—to raise community awareness of crafts as art. She was instrumental in creating the Carolina Designer Craftsman Guild in 1970.

One of her first woven works was purchased by the Museum of Contemporary Crafts in New York, and many others are in collections throughout North Carolina. During the last thirty years of her life, when she and her husband had retired to the North Carolina mountains, she exhibited widely and won many awards.

Danser, George (1948–)

George Danser, a native New Yorker, is an artist who works in warm-fused, stained, and etched glass. He studied stained glass with Patrick Reyntiens in England and Dan Fenton in Davidson, North Carolina, and settled in Durham in 1972. Through his Stained Glass Studio, a commercial enterprise that he sold in 2000, he employed numerous craftspersons. He taught classes at his studio and at the Durham Arts Council. His commissions include fourteen stained-glass sections in the entry doors of First Presbyterian Church, and a seventeen-foot-high design for Holy Family Episcopal Church in Chapel Hill. The North Carolina Museum of Art commissioned a piece of his art glass for its collection, and a large wall of glass, thirty by eighteen feet, was commissioned by Caldwell County, North Carolina, for its Performing Arts Center. Danser's glass works also appear in the former Record Bar building on Franklin Street in Chapel Hill and in Record Bar stores throughout the United States.

Davis, Archie Royal (1907–1980)

A native of Morehead City, Archie Davis received his architectural degree from NCSU in 1930 and joined the George Watts Carr firm just at the time it had been commissioned by George Watts Hill to work on the CCB building, originally designed by the firm of Shreve, Lamb and Harmon, at 111 Corcoran Street. In 1939 he opened his own office in the new Hill Building, and he continued in his profession until his death. Davis's firm worked on such projects as the Carolina Inn in Chapel Hill, the Blue Cross Blue Shield building in Durham, the Morehead Planetarium at UNC-Chapel Hill, and the Durham County Courthouse and its offices. Many young architects passed through Davis's office, gaining experience and contributing to the area's architecture. Two in particular have made significant contributions to local residential building: Jon Condoret and Sumner Winn.

Davis, Chuck (1937–)

Charles ("Chuck") Davis, dancer and choreographer, is the founder and artistic director of the African American Dance Ensemble (AADE), which he established in Durham in 1983. An invitation to his previous troupe brought Davis to Durham. The Chuck Davis Dance Company, established in New York in 1964, was invited to perform at the American Dance Festival and participate in its Community Services Program. A native of Raleigh and trained at the theater and dance program at Howard University, he also studied African dance with Babatunde Olatunji, Eleo Pomare, and the Bernice Johnson Dance Company. His mentors have also included Thelma Hill, Jean Leon Destine, Katherine Dunham, and Pearl Primus. Currently he is artist-in-

residence with ADF, working in the outreach program.

Davis has been the recipient of many awards, including the AARP Certificate of Excellence, the North Carolina Dance Alliance Award, the North Carolina Artist Award, the North Carolina Order of the Long Leaf Pine, the North Carolina Award in Fine Arts, the Bessie Award, the Brooklyn Academy of Music Award for distinguished service to the arts world and beyond, the National Governors Association Award for Distinguished Service to the Arts, an Artist of the Year award from DanceUSA, and an honorary doctor of fine arts degree from Medgar Evers College in New York. He has also been recognized by the Dance Heritage Coalition as one of the first one hundred Irreplaceable Dance Treasures in the United States. The City of Durham declared August 5, 2002, Chuck Davis Day.

Davis, Dorothy (1924–)

Dorothy Davis, a potter, was one of the women who helped shape the crafts scene in Durham in the late 1960s and 1970s. She is admired nationally for her ability to create oil spot glazing in the manner of the Chinese Song Dynasty. Born in Illinois, she grew up in Michigan and received her B.S. from Temple University and her M.A.Ed. from Southern Connecticut State University. In addition, she has pursued studies in workshops, including a workshop in oil spot glazing techniques at the Smithsonian Institution. She has helped to establish several craft organizations, including Carolina Designer Craftsmen Guild, Raleigh, and Craft House of Durham. Davis taught art at the Durham School of Design at Lowe's Grove Elementary School from 1967 to 1970.

Davis, Reverend Gary (1896–1972)

Davis, a self-taught musician, was blind from infancy, but started making music at the age of seven with a guitar that he made out of a pie pan and a stick. He settled in Durham in the late 1920s or early 1930s and became an ordained minister. A broken wrist that healed in a distorted position forced Davis to develop unusual chord patterns on the guitar. Davis befriended Blind Boy Fuller in Durham, but they eventually had a falling out over matters of style.

Like Blind Boy Fuller, Davis first recorded for J. B. Long, in 1935. Davis, full of evangelical zeal, at first would perform only spirituals, but later in life he played traditional blues tunes. After moving to New York City and until his death in 1972, however, he performed and recorded chiefly spirituals. While he lived in New York white teenagers sought him out for guitar lessons, and one of them, Stefan Grossman, immortalized Davis's finger picking-technique and teaching style in a set of instructional publications.

Deloatch, Lois (1959–)

Deloatch grew up as Lois Dawson in the farming community of Margarettsville, North Carolina, with nine brothers and sisters. She played piano and sang in the Mount Zion Baptist Church choir in Margarettsville and in the Rising Star Baptist Church in Branchville, Virginia, from the time she was eight. She entered into vocal competitions on the recommendation of her high school chorus teacher and achieved much success. At UNC-Chapel Hill she earned a degree in speech and hearing science, and while there she became a lead vocalist with the BSM (Black Student Movement) Gospel Choir. She soon fell in love with jazz and became primarily a jazz musician, although she also performs blues and spirituals. Early in her career she worked with Ira Wiggins, who recorded several original compositions with her in 1988 and 1989. Deloatch has been on national tours, and since 1998 she has produced a number of recordings, including a collection of Negro spirituals arranged by the Durham pianist Barbara Cooke. She has continued to work with

Wiggins as well as with the pianists Gabe Evens and Tyson Rogers.

Deneen, Doug (1959–)

Doug Deneen, a native of Ohio, is a photographer who shoots large-format transparency film, produces large cibachrome prints depicting abstract nature and still lifes, and explores computerized images. He received his B.A. from Duke University in 1982 and lived in Durham from 1978 to 1997. His commissioned works are in private collections and at the Duke Medical Center. The recipient of several grants from the National Endowment for the Arts, the North Carolina Arts Council, and the Durham Arts Council, Deneen has won over a dozen top prizes in juried competitions. He now lives in New York, where in addition to pursuing his photography he is a freelance television producer and creative services consultant for various stations and networks.

DePasquale, Frank (1925–)

Frank DePasquale, an architect, artist, and craftsman, was born in Roselle Park, New Jersey. After the Second World War he earned a degree in architecture at NCSU (1951). While a student he worked part time with Piatt and Davis Consulting Engineers in Durham, which offered him a position upon graduation.

For five years DePasquale did designs for all of their engineering buildings, including the Northside Waste Treatment Plant in Durham. From 1956 to 1958 he worked with John D. Latimer on residences, industrial plants, and churches, including the new Immaculate Conception Church, marked by a Greek cross bell tower. After spending four years elsewhere he returned to Durham in 1962 and joined the firm of Carr Harrison Pruden and DePasquale, where he oversaw the master plan, design, and construction of projects including the NCCU Student Union, Duke University's first art museum, the Shepard Middle

School, offices for Duke Power Company, a city bus facility, and the headquarters of the Durham fire and police departments.

DePasquale became a senior partner when the firm of DePasquale, Markham, Thompson and Wilson was established in 1978. Additional landmarks came from this partnership, such as branch facilities for Central Carolina Bank, the Easley, Githens, and Riverside schools, renovation of the Durham Arts Council, the Hayti Heritage Center, Grace Lutheran Church, and the George Watts Hill Pavilion for the Arts.

Along with his architecture career DePasquale has pursued other artistic talents such as painting, furniture design and construction, fused warm glass projects (which he studied with George Danser), and metal work (which he studied with Francis Vega at Vega Metals). His achievements in these areas may be seen in his craft commissions: the warm glass light fixtures for IMAX Theater in Raleigh; and altars, pulpits, and baptismal fonts at St. Luke's Episcopal Church and Grace Lutheran Church.

Numerous awards for DePasquale's work in architecture, the arts, historic preservation, and local service have recognized his contributions and importance.

Dorfman, Ariel (1942–)

The playwright Ariel Dorfman was born in Argentina and moved as a youth to Chile, where he received his education, became a citizen, and began his academic and literary careers. Forced into exile in 1973 during the Pinochet regime, he became affiliated in 1984 with Duke University, where he is now the Walter Hines Page Distinguished Professor of Literature and Latin American Studies. A noted essayist, poet, and novelist, Dorfman is also the author of over a dozen plays. Among these is *Widows* (1988), based on his novel of the same name, later adapted for BBC radio, and still later (1991) rewritten with Tony

Kushner for a production in New York; it has been produced in Japan, Israel, Sri Lanka, Turkey, England, Scotland, and Chile.

In 1991 Dorfman's *Death and the Maiden* had its première in London and received international acclaim; it has since been seen in over one hundred countries, won Best Play awards in England, Korea, and Japan, and in 1995 became a successful film (which Dorfman wrote with the director Roman Polanski). That same year saw the première of *Reader* in Edinburgh, with performances later in Denmark, Germany, England, Croatia, Japan, Mexico, and Spain. Dorfman's works in the following years included the award-winning *Prisoners in Time* (1995), a BBC television play with John Hurt; a short film, *My House on Fire* (1997), written with Rodrigo Dorfman; *Dead Line* (1998), a television play also written with Rodrigo Dorfman and based on poems from Ariel Dorfman's *Last Waltz in Santiago*; the stage play *Mascara* (1998), also written with Rodrigo Dorfman and based on his novel of the same name; *Speak Truth to Power: Voices from Beyond the Dark* (2000) for the Kennedy Center, which was taped and later shown on PBS; *Konfidenz* (2000), a radio play written with Rodrigo Dorfman for BBC; and *Purgatory* (2003).

Dorrance, M'Liss (1951–)

M'Liss Dorrance, dancer, choreographer, and teacher, is an associate professor of the practice of dance and director of undergraduate studies at Duke University, and co-director of the Duke Ballet Repertory Ensemble. She has been associated with Duke since 1975, when dance was part of the physical education department. She was one of the original founders of the New Performing Dance Company, which evolved from Dance Associates of Allied Arts (now Durham Arts Council), and she has taught dance at the company and served on its committees.

After receiving her early training overseas,

Dorrance won scholarships to the National Ballet School in Washington and the Harkness and Joffrey ballets in New York. She has danced professionally as a member of the National Ballet, Eliot Feld's American Ballet Company, and the Arlington Dance Theater in Virginia. She is cofounder and director of the Ballet School of Chapel Hill and has been teaching and performing in the Durham and Chapel Hill area since 1974.

Downing, Larry (1962–)

Larry Downing is a sculptor who works in clay and mixed media. He creates freestanding as well as sculptural wall pieces in addition to combining clay with other materials to form mixed-media sculpture, experimenting in textures and glazes. He was born in Fayetteville, North Carolina, received his B.F.A. from UNC-Chapel Hill in 1985, and also studied at Wake Forest University. He teaches middle school and high school students at the Durham School of the Arts and adults at the Durham Arts Council. His work is shown at the Somerhill Gallery in Chapel Hill, the Contemporary Gallery in Raleigh, and numerous other local venues.

DTW Architects and Planners

DTW Architects and Planners LTD is an architectural firm established in 1978 as DePasquale Markham Thompson and Wilson Architects and Planners by Frank DePasquale, Felix Markham, John F. Thompson, and Warren Wilson. As the firm evolved and personnel changed, it went through various name changes, assuming its present name when DePasquale retired. In the latest reorganization Robert Sotolongo and R. Linsey Bute became principals and part owners of the firm.

The firm's clients have included the Central Carolina Bank of George Watts Hill (now Sun-Trust), for whom the firm built many banking facilities throughout central North Carolina. Edu-cational facilities have also been a major part of the firm's work, with the result that the firm has provided thirty-four new or renovated buildings for the Durham public school system. In addition, the firm has worked on projects at NCCU, Duke University, NCSU, and other educational facilities throughout the state, as well as religious facilities, the Hayti Heritage Center, and the George Watts Pavilion. Over the course of its history the present principals of the firm have won over twenty-seven architectural awards.

Durham School of the Arts

Visual and performing arts flourish at Durham School of the Arts (DSA), a school that provides students in the sixth to twelfth grades with in-depth training in drawing, sculpture, photography, dance, theater, chorus, and instrumental music. DSA opened its doors in 1995, as part of the Durham Public Schools' plan to develop magnet schools, ensure equity, and increase choice. Lee Vrana, director of education at the Durham Arts Council, the Durham public schools' arts coordinators Ronnie Lilly and Karen Hall, and DSA's first principal, Ed Forsythe, worked together to design the school, plan the curriculum, and identify key teachers. DSA's faculty and staff participated in the first A+ summer institute, an initiative of the North Carolina legislature to improve schools by teaching through the arts.

DSA quickly gained a reputation for its excellent arts training, rigorous academics, and outstanding faculty, which includes many practicing artists. It has grown from about three hundred students in its first year to fourteen hundred today. The school emphasizes creativity, higher-order thinking, and multiple intelligence theory as guiding principles for both arts and academic courses. DSA's challenging curriculum encourages all students to maximize their potential, enjoy learning, and develop discipline and focus.

While most students do not choose to become professional artists, all leave the school with substantial arts skills, an appreciation for the importance of art in society, and a well-rounded academic education.

Edwards, Catherine Ruth (Norris) (1889–1972)

Catherine Edwards graduated from Shaw University and was a lecturer in music at Kittrell College. In 1928 she came to Durham, where she organized the music program at NCCU. She became the first chairwoman of the newly established Department of Music in 1931 and held that position until her retirement in 1958. Edwards received a B.A. from NCCU in 1937 and an M.A. from the Teachers College of Columbia University in 1939. She also trained at Juilliard, the New England Conservatory of Music, and the Shepherd Conservatory of Music, among other schools. The NCCU music building, built in 1976, was named in her honor.

Egerton, Clarke Alston, Jr. (1932–)

The son of a machinist at Liggett Myers, Clarke Egerton decided to learn clarinet after he attended a performance at Page Auditorium when he was eight or nine years old: it was "The Flight of the Bumblebee" that caught his fancy and led him into a career in music. William "Lanky" Cole gave him his first clarinet lessons on the front porch of his house on Fayetteville Street. He began piano lessons at the age of twelve with Margaret Shearin. Later Egerton attended Hillside High School and studied clarinet and oboe under Phillmore Hall. He received his B.A. and M.A. from NCCU, where he studied bassoon and clarinet.

In the mid-1950s Egerton taught music in Warren County. He transferred in 1956 to Lincoln High School in Chapel Hill, where he taught music and directed the band. From 1961 to 1967 he held these same positions at Whitted Junior High in Durham. In 1967 Egerton transferred to Hillside, where he taught music, directed the marching bands, for which he designed a new facility, and directed the symphonic and concert bands. Under his direction the Hillside bands garnered many awards and trophies. Egerton was twice awarded the North Carolina Music Educators Association "Award of Excellence." He retired from Hillside in 1997.

Estes, Robert Earle (1927–2006)

Known affectionately as "the music man," Robert Estes was born in Worcester, Massachusetts. He graduated from the New England Conservatory of Music, earned an M.S. from Bridgeport University, and taught music in the public schools for thirty-five years. During his retirement in Durham he founded the Durham Chorale, which he conducted for fifteen years while serving as director of music for Aldersgate Methodist Church. He also composed and published music.

Ewald, Wendy (1951–)

Wendy Ewald has been a serious photographer since high school. Born in Detroit, she studied at Antioch College from 1969 to 1974. While in school she taught photography to children on Indian reservations in Canada; a series of projects led her to Appalshop, where she founded the Mountain Photography Workshop in 1975, then to Colombia on a Fulbright grant in 1982, and later to India, Mexico, South Africa, Saudi Arabia, Morocco, and the Netherlands. She collaborated with students, teaching them how to document their communities. In 1989 she began to work with the Durham public school system, and in 1991 she founded the Literacy Through Photography (LTP) Project at Duke's Center for Documentary Studies, where she is a senior researcher. In the LTP program, children and other community members explore ideas by taking photographs and writing about them. LTP grew into a course for Duke students, a series workshops for teachers, and spinoffs like the American Alphabets project, in which students from Ohio to New York examine stereotypes and identity through photos. Ewald's publications include *American Alphabets*, published by Scalo in 2005, and *Secret Games: Collaborative Works with Children, 1969-1999* and *Dreamed I Had a Girl in My Pocket: The Story of an Indian Village*, both published by the Center for Documentary Studies. Her own photographs have been widely exhibited and published in magazines. One outgrowth of LTP was *I Wanna Take Me a Picture: Teaching Photography and Writing to Children*, published by the Center for Documentary Studies and Beacon Press in 2001.

Floyd, Connie (1955–)

Connie Floyd, a printmaker and graphic designer from South Carolina, received his B.F.A. from the Atlanta College of Art in 1975 and his M.F.A. from Clemson University in 1977. He settled in Durham in 1989 and is a professor of art in printmaking, computer graphics, and advertising design at NCCU. In 1991 he was commissioned to create a triptych mural that hangs in the cinema lobby at the Carolina Theatre. The triptych is an acrylic painting on canvas that celebrates the performing arts—music, drama, and dance. With Charles Joyner, Floyd created the design for the tile floor of the Dudley Building (1931) at North Carolina A&T State University in Greensboro. He was one of four artists who designed the large mural at the Mission Valley Cinema in Raleigh.

Fluke, Margaret Pepper (1929–)

A potter and arts activist, Pepper Fluke received a B.A. from Cornell University in 1951. After coming to Durham in 1958 she became active in Allied Arts, now Durham Arts Council (DAC), where she studied silversmithing and, later, ceramics. As part of her craft studies she undertook work at the Mobach Pottery in the Netherlands. In 1966 she began teaching ceramics at Allied Arts.

Fluke has played a significant role in the formation of a number of crafts organizations. By 1967 she had co-chaired the first Triangle Festival of Crafts, the forerunner of the DAC CenterFest, and in 1968 she was instrumental in forming the Craft House of Durham with seven other craftswomen. It opened in 1970, and in 1974 Bob Black and Ormond Sanderson invited its leaders to join the crafts complex at their studios in Straw Valley. Craft House then enlarged its mission to become a gallery as well as a working space. Fluke was also a founding member of the Carolina Designer Craftsmen Guild (CDCG) in Raleigh in 1970. When Craft House closed in 1987 she played an important role in forming Clayworks Pottery Guild, which continues to hold an annual show and sale in Durham. Fluke is a board member of NCCU Art Museum, where she has been the curator of a ceramics show of African-American clay artists.

Freelon Group

An architectural firm, the Freelon Group was launched in Durham in 1990 by Philip G. Freelon, FAIA, (1953–), a native of Philadelphia. He received his initial architectural experience in Boston, Houston, and then Durham with O'Brien Atkins.

In its first fifteen years the Freelon Group grew to fifty staff members, including twenty architects. Over those years its projects included the Freelon office interiors and the Biomedical/Biotechnology Research Institute at NCCU. The firm recently completed the Museum of the African Diaspora in San Francisco and the Maryland Museum of African American History and Culture in Baltimore. All four projects received awards from the American Institute of Architects.

Philip Freelon is also the founder of the North Carolina Organization of Minority Architects.

Freelon, Chinyere Nnenna (Pierce) (1958–)

The jazz singer Nnenna Freelon grew up in Cambridge, Massachusetts. First exposed to music at the Baptist church that her family attended, she felt "called" to be a singer as a young child. She started performing at the age of seven when she sang "Amazing Grace" as a solo for the church congregation. She then began to sing for shut-ins as her mother took her from home to home. In 1982 she received a degree from Simmons College.

Freelon subsequently moved to Durham to work in health care services and raise her family. She remained active as a singer, first performing with Master Tracks, then with Yusef Salim and Bus Brown. In 1992 she released her first record, on the Columbia label. She has since released eight other albums and been nominated for five Grammy awards. Freelon tours internationally, is a member of the National Association of Partners in Education, and holds a number of singing workshops, including classes for parents who want to sing to their infants and song improvisation classes for teens and adults. She has received the École du Jazz Billie Holiday award and the Eubie Blake award.

Frega, Al (1956–)

Alvin ("Al") Frega is a sculptor who works in industrial metal, creating sculptures primarily for public venues. He received his B.A. from the State University of New York, Buffalo, and his M.F.A. from UNC-Chapel Hill. He has taught art classes at UNC-Wilmington, UNC-Chapel Hill, Cape Fear Community College, and the Penland School of Crafts. His commissioned works may be found at Durham Central Park, the American Tobacco Trail, and Peabody Place (all in Durham), as well as at the North Carolina Museum of Art and Artworks for State Buildings (both in Raleigh), among other sites. Frega has received an Emerging Artists Program Grant and a Regional Artist Development Fellowship from the North Carolina Arts Council.

Film Festivals

The Full Frame Documentary Film Festival

Full Frame, held each April, is the single largest festival of its kind in North America. Hailed by *International Documentary* as "arguably the Cannes of documentary film festivals" (July 2004), Full Frame has experienced tremendous growth since its inception. Begun as the Double-take Documentary Film Festival in 1998 by Nancy Buirski, the CEO and artistic director, it took its current name in 2002.

Full Frame generally screens eighty to a hundred films over a four-day period. Attendance has expanded from approximately 10,000 patrons in 2001 to 27,000 patrons in 2007, among them notable directors and participants from film centers across the country.

Each year the festival receives for consideration over a thousand films, from which a selection committee whittles down the entries to approximately a hundred or fewer. The festival is produced by Doc Arts, Inc., and enjoys major sponsorship from several sources, including Duke University, VH1, HBO, the advertising agency McKinney, and the *New York Times*.

North Carolina Gay and Lesbian Film Festival

In 1995 the NC PRIDE Film Series was held at the Carolina Theatre as one of a series of events with gay and lesbian themes during the local NC PRIDE weekend. This event garnered sufficient interest in the community to warrant launching the first annual North Carolina Gay and Lesbian Film Festival in 1996. What began as a screening of eight films with an attendance of approximately eight hundred people in 1996 exploded a decade later into the second-largest gay and lesbian film festival in the Southeast. The NCGLFF has become a cultural highlight of the summer, showcasing feature films, documentaries, experimental shorts, and animation. Produced by the Carolina Theatre staff and community volunteers, the festival draws approximately ten thousand patrons over a four-day period and typically features anywhere from sixty to one hundred films, including a handful with bisexual and transgendered themes.

The festival features films competing for Emerging Film Awards in a variety of categories, including best men's short, best women's short, best men's feature, and best women's feature. The festival has also offered live performances and appearances by celebrities such as the comedians Margaret Cho and Suzanne Westenhoefer and the actor Tab Hunter.

Retrofantasma Film Series

The Retrofantasma Film Series is a monthly feature dedicated to bringing back classic horror, exploitation, and cult films from the '60s, '70s, and '80s and presenting them as they were meant to be seen: on film, on a big screen with a raucous, appreciative audience. Started as a volunteer initiative by a small group of loyal horror film fans, the series has been cultivated by the Carolina Theatre for nearly a decade, making it the longest-running series of its kind in the Southeast and one of the oldest, most widely recognized in North America. The series uses 35mm film exclusively; video and DVDs are strictly forbidden. The goal of the series is to revitalize repertory horror screenings and shows of the "midnight movie" variety while creating an enjoyable fan experience.

The festival began on November 13, 1998, with a screening of *Friday the 13th Part 2*. In the following year the series began doing double features exclusively, with a twin bill of *Re-Animator* and *Bride of Re-Animator*, both produced by Bryan Yuzna, a native of Carrboro, and in August 2003 the series began the monthly schedule that fans enjoy today. As the series enters its tenth year, it has presented nearly sixty double features, over a hundred films, and several hundred vintage trailers.

Nevermore Horror, Gothic, and Fantasy Film Festival

The Nevermore Horror, Gothic, and Fantasy Film Festival was created in 1999 and began in March 2000; one of three film festivals produced by the staff of the Carolina Theatre, it is now one of the oldest continuously running genre festivals in the country. The festival began as an offshoot of the Carolina Theatre's popular Retrofantasma Film Series. Each year the festival takes place over a three-day weekend in February and is dedicated to screening new horror and genre films (shorts and features) from around the world.

The first two years of the festival (2000 and 2001) featured classic repertory films, 95 percent of them cult favorites from the 1930s to the 1990s. In 2002 the festival changed direction. Now it consists almost entirely of new genre products, all of which have horror, fantasy, or similar elements—potential cult classics in the making. Many of these films, despite their high quality, will never receive a theatrical release in the United States. Suspense movies, hyper-violent cinema from Hong Kong, animation, and everything in between are included, with only an occasional repertory or anniversary screening.

What began as a small, quaint festival drawing a little over seven hundred patrons has steadily grown into an event that frequently draws two thousand or more patrons throughout the weekend.

Escapism Film Festival

The newest film festival in Durham, Escapism is dedicated to action, adventure, and animation films from around the world. This festival made its début in 2003 and featured an eclectic mix of shorts and features, many of which were award winners at other festivals. After drawing approximately a thousand patrons in 2004 and 2005, the festival skipped 2006, but returned in the following year with an innovative mix of new features and shorts, as well as a combination of repertory screenings and interactive special events. Highlights that year were a twenty-fifth-anniversary screening of *Star Trek II: The Wrath of Khan* (perhaps the most popular film in the wildly successful "Star Trek" series) and a twentieth-anniversary screening of the cult favorite "The Monster Squad" (1987), complete with a reunion of the cast (including the director Fed Dekker), a question-and-answer panel, and an autograph session.

North Carolina Jewish Film Festival

Although no longer housed at the Carolina Theatre of Durham, this festival was a major part of Carolina Theatre programming from 1999 to 2004. It featured Jewish-themed shorts and features from around the world, presented over a four-day period in either January or February of each year. This festival always opened on a Thursday with an opening night gala followed by a round of films. After a twenty-four-hour break in observance of Shabbat, the festival would continue Saturday evening and all day on Sunday.

This festival routinely showed anywhere from sixteen to twenty-three films in rotation, often scheduling a live event in conjunction with the festival as well, as when the comedians Sherry Glaser and Elayne Boosler gave a live performance of "I Never Saw Another Butterfly." Festival attendance was routinely between 1,400 and 2,000 patrons, with a high of approximately 2,100 patrons in 2002 (the year that the festival gave an exclusive screening of Tim Blake Nelson's film *The Grey Zone* several months before its national release). The festival often showed premières of some sort, and the work of the world's finest filmmakers (Amos Gitai, Abbas Kiarostami, Werner Herzog, Costa-Gavras). The festival moved to Cary, North Carolina, in 2006.

Hip Hop Film Festival

This festival, put on by the local nonprofit group DADA (Durham Association for Downtown Arts), made one appearance in 2002. Held at the Durham Armory, it was a touring festival comprising six features, all focused on hip hop and urban culture. Highlighted by the documentary *Scratch*, this festival drew nearly three hundred patrons over two days to downtown Durham and another group to the campus of NCCU on its third and final day.

Ms. Films

This festival took place in Durham each February from 2001 to 2006 and focused on shorts and features by well-respected women filmmakers. Housed at the Durham Arts Council, it consisted of three days of screenings, workshops, panels, and projects with women filmmakers and received a large amount of positive press. The sponsoring organization, also called Ms. Films, was a nonprofit dedicated to empowering women and girls through access to the media and media making.

W.A.R.P. Film Festival

W.A.R.P. (an acronym for "War, Art, Relationships and Politics") is a competition festival that took place in 2003 and 2004 at the Durham Arts Council. Presenting a variety of shorts from across the country, the festival offered low-budget and independent filmmakers an opportunity to show their work and receive constructive criticism of their efforts.

All-American Film Festival

A competition festival begun in February 2007 at the Durham Arts Council, the All-American Film Festival focuses on shorts and features by independent filmmakers, especially films and videos made by nonstudents with nonunion actors on shoestring budgets. It accepts films from local and national talent, with a special section known as the NC Spotlight Showcase intended specifically for filmmakers from North Carolina. The festival strives to represent as much as possible of the underrepresented cinematic diversity of the United States.

Fuller, Blind Boy (1907–1941)

Blind Boy Fuller was born Fulton Allen in Wadesboro, North Carolina. When he became blind in the late 1920s he learned to play the blues. In 1929 he moved to Durham, where he earned a living by playing on the streets and in the warehouses. He took the name Blind Boy Fuller and was discovered by James Baxter Long, the manager for the United Dollar Store, who was on the lookout for talent that he could sell. Long prevailed on Fuller and other blues musicians in Durham to go with him in 1935 to New York, where they made recordings for the American Record Company. Fuller continued to cut albums through the 1930s; his last recording session was in 1941, the year he died of syphilis. Some of the recordings were done with Bull City Red and Sonny Terry as well as the Reverend Gary Davis. Fuller perfected the syncopated rhythms that are a hallmark of the Piedmont blues, and was the most recorded and best-selling Piedmont blues artist of his time.

Funaro, Elaine (1952–)

Elaine Funaro, harpsichordist, began her musical career playing a variety of instruments in school. She graduated in 1974 from Oberlin College, where she discovered medieval music and the harpsichord, on which she has concentrated her efforts. Since becoming a judge of the Aliénor Harpsichord Composition Competition, she has added contemporary music to her specialties.

Funaro also studied at the New England Conservatory of Music as well as in Florence and Amsterdam. She has performed throughout Europe and the United States as both a soloist and a chamber player. In 1982 she moved to Durham with her husband, Randall Love, also a notable keyboardist and member of the Duke music faculty. For twelve years she produced the Music in the Museum series of concerts at Duke University. She received an Emerging Artists grant from the Durham Arts Council and is a past president of the Southeastern Historical Keyboard Society.

George Watts Carr Architects

The firm of George Watts Carr Architects was established in 1927, consisting originally of Carr and his partner Roy Marvin; the firm continued over eighty years under the leadership of three generations of Carrs. Over that period the firm made a major impact on the architecture of the city and state.

In the beginning Carr and Marvin were engaged in residential development and home design. Associated with developers, they created the Forest Hills subdivision, designing streets, utilities, and houses for the area. In the 1930s the Hope Valley development brought the firm additional residential commissions. These early projects were responsible for many unique houses, characterized by a high quality of site planning and home design that were notable for their day in North Carolina.

With the coming of the Second World War, Carr secured contracts for massive projects with the U.S. Navy. To fulfill these contracts Carr established a one-hundred-man architectural and engineering firm in association with J. E. Greiner Company of Baltimore and in the next four years completed such major projects as the Marine Hospital at Camp Lejeune (with two thousand beds), the Camp Lejeune Marine Base, the Cherry Point Marine Air Base, the North Carolina Ports Authority Terminal at Morehead City, and several buildings at the U.S. Naval Academy in Annapolis.

After the war Carr reorganized the firm in Durham, bringing with him Joseph Rivers, Vernon Harrison, and Jack McMullen Pruden. Carr's son, Robert Winston Carr, also joined the firm. With its experienced and qualified personnel, the firm became a major contributor to many public and private architectural projects, including the Veterans Hospital in Durham and county hospitals in eastern and western North Carolina. The firm also designed educational facilities at NCCU, UNC-Chapel Hill, and NCSU. After Marvin and Rivers retired in the early 1960s, George Watts Carr, while remaining as a consultant, turned over the firm to his son, and it was renamed Carr Harrison Pruden DePasquale (CHPD Architects).

George Watts Carr died in 1975 and his grandson Edgar Carr joined the firm in 1977. During its new incarnation as CHPD Architects, it continued to work on a variety of projects, including the master plan for Coastal Carolina Community College, a number of facilities for Central Carolina Bank, the Duke University Art Museum on East Campus, the Olympic swimming pool on West Campus, the city government center, and additions to several schools. Frank DePasquale, who joined the firm in 1962, left in 1979 to form his own firm, and two years later Harrison and Pruden retired. Robert W. Carr continued with his son Edgar, renaming the firm Robert W. Carr Inc., Architects. They designed such projects as the North Carolina State Museum of Natural Sci-

ence in Raleigh, the Marine Museum in Beaufort, the renovations to the parish hall at St. Philip's Church, and city government alterations and additions.

Apart from its architectural contributions to the built environment Carr's firms have been significant for having launched the careers of many Durham architects.

Goll, Jeffrey (1953–)

Jeffrey Goll, a sculptor and installation artist, has worked in Durham since 1989. He received a B.A. from the University of Illinois in 1975 and a B.S. from the University of Minnesota in 1978. He has shown his work widely and exhibited throughout Africa with the United States Information Agency (USIA). Goll has been the recipient of a North Carolina Arts Council Fellowship and has taught at the Penland School of Crafts.

Goulson, Jo (1926–1992)

Jo Goulson was a woodcarver who carved animals, birds, and other figures. She was born in Alabama and moved to Chapel Hill with her husband in 1954. After receiving an undergraduate degree from the University of Alabama, Birmingham, and a Master of Public Health from UNC-Chapel Hill, she turned her attention to her art. She was a founding member of Carolina Designer Craftsmen Guild and received numerous commissions and honors for her work during her lifetime.

Gregg, Jan

Jan Gregg was born in Alabama, moved to Durham in 1957, and began her career as a potter in 1965 when she studied with Vivian Dai at Allied Arts. She works with porcelain clay at her home studio, Hollow Rock Pottery, housed in the former Hollow Rock Grocery, which was moved to her property. She has a B.S. from the University of Alabama, Tuscaloosa, and pursued further studies at Columbia University. She studied pottery at Colorado State University and Berea College, where she worked with David Leach. She has had a long career working with other craftspersons to establish crafts organizations. She helped to organize the Triangle Festival of Crafts sponsored by Allied Arts (now CenterFest) in 1967, the Carolina Designer Craftsmen Guild (CDCG), and Clayworks, a pottery guild begun in 1987.

Griffin, Marilyn (1952–)

Born and brought up in Durham, Marilyn Griffin is best known for her Kanike Artiste Doll Collection of one-of-a-kind soft-sculptured dolls. She started making dolls in 1992 after seeing a doll that her roommate had bought in Washington. Griffin sculpts the heads, faces, hands, and bodies of her dolls out of clay, which are outfitted in Afrocentric attire and are fixtures at local craft fairs.

Paul M. Gross Chemistry Building

A classroom, laboratory and office building on Towerview Drive on the Duke West Campus, the Gross Chemistry Building was designed by the architectural firm of J. N. Pease of Charlotte and completed in 1968. Its design, like that of the Edens Quadrangle, is an attempt to adapt Gothic principles to contemporary construction and architectural considerations. The building emphasizes verticality and human scale, and its pre-cast stone exterior panels refer to the signature Gothic style of West Campus. Visual weight is offset by repeated vertical lines in the forms of multistory windows and projecting service towers.

Grossman, Susan E. (1955–)

A sculptor who fabricates objects in clay, stone and resin, steel, and cast glass, Susan Grossman was born in Ohio, where she studied at the Cleveland Institute of Art. She received a B.F.A. in 1979 from Alfred College of Ceramics in New York and pursued additional studies at the Archie Bray Foundation in Montana, the Banff School of Fine Arts, and the Pietrasanta Marble Carving Studio in Italy. She moved to North Carolina shortly after graduating from Alfred, co-founded the Lincoln Art Center in Chapel Hill, and created a clay studio for the Carrboro Arts Center. In 1989 she began to develop sculpture studios for the Durham Arts Council and remained as its sculpture studios director for fourteen years, designing programs and studios for glassblowing and Venetian flame working, glass fusing and slumping, kiln-casting glass, glass mosaic and stained glass, metal fabrication welding and forge, clay sculpture and pottery, and stone sculpture.

In 2000 Grossman helped to create a plan for Liberty Arts, a cooperative bronze foundry and sculpture space next to the Foster Street warehouse. She has been commissioned to create sculpture, architectural tile, and mosaic installations for public and private spaces, including a children's water park for the Durham Department of Parks and Recreation. Her work has been widely exhibited and featured in *I.D. Magazine*, *Southern Magazine*, and several books, including *Handmade Tiles* by Frank Giorgini (Lark Books, 1994) and *Making Mosaics* by Leslie Dierks (Sterling Books, 1997). She has also taught sculpture classes in New York, where she now lives.

Guidry, Charles (1954–)

Charles Guidry is a sculptor and woodcarver in the contemporary folk art tradition. A native of Louisiana, he moved to Durham in 1974. He graduated in 1984 from the UNC-Chapel Hill, with B.A. and B.S. degrees. He has shown his work in the Southeast and Northeast regions of the United States and is represented in private collections. He is also technical director of Durham Savoyards.

Hackney, George F. (1905–1997)

George Hackney, a native of Siler City, graduated from NCSU in 1927 with a bachelor's degree in architectural engineering and joined the Durham firm of George Watts Carr Associates. A year later he left to work for the Duke Construction Company, which was building Duke University's West Campus. In 1933 he formed his own architectural firm. The transformation of Trinity College into Duke University created a demand for faculty and staff housing, which Hackney's firm helped to fill. The houses that he designed include those of C. H. Shipp, J. S. McCurck, O. F. Dowd, and J. F. Wily Jr. During the Second World War, while continuing his own practice, Hackney joined the engineering faculty at Duke to teach structural design.

After the war he asked Charles Knott (1911–1982) to join him in creating the firm of Hackney and Knott Architects. Knott, a native of Durham, had graduated from the NCSU School of Architecture and Engineering in 1933. Hackney and he played a major role in Durham's growth. They designed the Durham County Library (Roxboro and Main streets), the BB&T Building (Duke and Jackson streets), and the eight-story South Bank Building (Five Points) among many others. The firm has been the incubator for many Durham architects, among them William Keener, Sam Hodges, and Wade Williams. Several years after Knott's death George Hackney retired and William Sears reorganized the firm, which continued as Hackney, Sears, Keener, and Williams.

Ham, Marion A. (1898–1971)

Born and raised in Florence, South Carolina, Marion Ham received a bachelor of architecture degree from Clemson University. In 1921 he joined Thomas C. Atwood's firm in Chapel Hill, which had been hired to review plans for a major expansion of the UNC campus. Several years later Duke University announced a major expansion at East Campus, and in 1927 Ham left Atwood's firm to open his own office in Durham. His work included renovations and additions at East Campus and residences throughout Durham. During the Second World War he performed architectural work at Camp Butner in association with Piatt and Davis Engineers. His firm continued to grow throughout the Piedmont, designing churches and schools in Durham and Chapel Hill, Roxboro City Hall, Blue Cross Blue Shield on Duke Street, and fire stations for Durham and Cary.

Ham's office was also an incubator for many young architects, including James A. Ward, William Keener, Wade Williams, Sam Brockwell, Howard Haines, and Roger Davis. Upon his death, the firm continued as Ham Keener Williams Architects.

Hamilton, Iain (1922–2000)

Iain Hamilton, a native of Scotland, abandoned his studies as an engineer's apprentice to major in composition and piano at the Royal Academy of Music in London, where he was awarded the Dove Prize at graduation in 1951. He also received a bachelor's degree in music from London University in 1950. It is thought that his early training in engineering shaped Hamilton and informed his compositional style: he reportedly did not compose at the piano as many others did. Instead his method was akin to that of an architect or engineer drafting a plan for a building. Hamilton was on the faculty of Duke University from 1961 to 1977. Among the many works he wrote during those years was *Raleigh's Dream* (1983), an opera celebrating the English landing in America in 1584. He returned to London in 1981.

Hanks, John Kennedy (1917–2002)

A native of Oklahoma, John Hanks received his undergraduate training at Oklahoma City University and then won a fellowship to the Juilliard School of Music in New York, where he also received an M.A. from Columbia University in 1950. He taught at Smith College from 1950 to 1954 and then joined the department of music at Duke University, where he remained until his retirement in 1987. He was a founder of the Duke Opera workshop and also directed the Divinity School Choir.

One of the foremost interpreters and performers of the American art song, Hanks recorded two anthologies issued by Duke University Press, both entitled *The Art Song in America*. Many of his students went on to illustrious careers in opera. Hanks performed at Carnegie Hall, at Tanglewood, and with the National Symphony in Washington, as well as regularly with the Duke Chapel Choir. In 1999 the university established the John K. Hanks Fund for Voice Studies and dedicated a voice studio in his name.

Harris, Alex (1949–)

Alex Harris, a documentary photographer, author, and editor, received his B.A. in 1971 from Yale University. He photographed North Carolina as part of a Duke University research project. In 1972 he began to collaborate with Robert Coles, working with him for six years in New Mexico and Alaska. The collaboration resulted in the publication of two books, *The Old Ones of New Mexico* (1973) and *The Last and First Eskimos* (1978). While commuting from New Mexico to Duke University to teach documentary photography, in 1980 he founded the Center for Documentary Studies at Duke, which he subsequently directed for eight years. Harris is the author of *Red White Blue and God Bless You* (1992), a co-author with William DeBuys of *River of Traps: A Village Life* (1990), the editor of *A World Unsuspected: Portraits of Southern Childhood* (1987), and a co-editor with Lee Friedlander of *Arrivals and Departures: The Airport Pictures of Garry Winogrand* (2003). He also co-edited *DoubleTake* magazine with Coles from 1995 to 1998. Harris is currently professor of

the practice of public policy studies at Duke and teaches in the Hart Leadership Program. His photographs are in the collections of the Museum of Modern Art, the Metropolitan Museum of Art, the J. Paul Getty Museum in Los Angeles, the Addison Gallery of Contemporary Art in Andover, Massachusetts, and the High Museum of Art in Atlanta. His awards include a Guggenheim Fellowship in photography, a Visual Artist Fellowship from the National Endowment for the Arts, and a Lyndhurst Award.

Harris, Hilda (1930–)

A mezzo-soprano from Warrenton, North Carolina, Hilda Harris graduated in the early 1960s from NCCU. She sang with the Durham Choral Society and performed in Durham's street opera *Carmen* before going on to become one of the lead performers with the Metropolitan Opera in New York. She has sung leading roles for several other major opera companies, performed with notable ensembles, and toured internationally, establishing her reputation as a singing actress of critical acclaim. Harris taught voice at Howard University from 1991 to 1994. Later she joined the faculty at Sarah Lawrence College and the Manhattan School of Music. Her albums include *Hilda Harris*; *The Valley Wind*; *Art Songs by Black American Composers*; *X: The Life and Times of Malcolm X*; *From the South Land*; *Songs and Spirituals by Harry T. Burleigh*; and *Witness*, volume II (compositions by William Grant Still). Hilda Harris currently lives in New York.

Harris, Jan

Jan Harris, a potter, was born in Durham and graduated with a B.S. from East Carolina University and an M.A.T. from UNC-Chapel Hill. She obtained a degree in applied physics from ECU, pursued further studies in architecture at the University of Edinburgh and the University of London, and studied weaving at Old Dominion University in Virginia. Harris worked in several positions at the Durham Arts Council (DAC), designed theater sets, and taught in the Durham public schools and at Flora MacDonald Academy in Red Springs, North Carolina. She was also director of the Festival for the Eno and the DAC CenterFest. She has taught art and craft classes at Durham Technical Community College, DAC, the Durham County Department of Parks and Recreation, and the Orange County Department of Parks and Recreation. She won the Freddy Award for sculpture from the Durham Ceramic Guild in 1962.

Hayti Heritage Center

Hayti Heritage Center occupies the former site of St. Joseph African Methodist Episcopal Church at 804 Old Fayetteville Street. The building had remained unused for many years after the congregation moved to a new location on Fayetteville Street in 1975. Concerned about the building's vacancy and deteriorating state, a group of citizens led by J. J. Henderson, Connie Watts, Benjamin Speller, and Lionel Parker and supported by the Historic Preservation Society of Durham started a movement to turn the former church into an arts center for the African-American community. After discussions with the Durham County Board of Commissioners $2 million of a bond issue were allocated to renovate Old St. Joseph's, and in 1987 the architects DePasquale, Thompson, and Wilson were commissioned to create a master plan for present and future space needs. When the bond money became available in 1988, a portion of the funds was immediately used to restore all stained glass windows in the sanctuary area. Construction began on the first phase of the Hayti Heritage Arts Center in 1988 with Walter Norflett as director of the center and Alvin Stevens as project coordinator. The architects created a new entrance facing the relocated Fayetteville Street, overlooking downtown Durham.

A glass-enclosed main entrance lobby and art display area separated the existing sanctuary (the future performance theater) from the renovated office area, classrooms, dance studio, reception area, and lower-level archives and storage area. The existing red-brick church buttresses and the original stained glass window of Washington Duke became striking features of the lobby area. A new red-brick colonnade continues beyond the glass entrance, repeating the buttress design. The first phase of the complex was complete in 1991, celebrating one hundred years of the building's life.

In 1999 funds from another bond issue were allocated for complete renovation of the theater and replacement of the roof. Renovation to the sanctuary involved refinishing the existing semicircular pews on the main floor and rebuilding the existing balcony into a U-shaped design with seating for 156 people, creating a total seating capacity of 450 for the theater. The multicolored, pressed-metal ceiling was completely refinished in its original colors, and the one-hundred-year-old gas chandeliers were refinished and electrified. Finally, to create a larger stage, the large, multicolored organ was dismantled and placed in storage. Completed and dedicated in 2001, this space now functions as a successful theater and meeting facility.

Hayti Mural

This 28 by 177 foot mural, on the side of a Winn Dixie grocery store in Heritage Square shopping center, at the intersection of Fayetteville Street and Lakewood Avenue, commemorates the community of Hayti, which fell victim to urban renewal and declined sharply in the 1960s and 1970s. Emily Weinstein, a painter, muralist, and past recipient of an Emerging Artists Grant from the Durham Art Council, was commissioned as the project's lead artist. Children from W. G. Pearson Elementary and Shepard Middle Schools, the Arts Quest summer camp of the Hayti Heritage Center, Durham's PROUD youth program, and neighborhoods near the site studied drawing and painting two afternoons a week, and helped the volunteer artists portray Hayti's past. It depicts citizens gathered in the streets and playing music, as bright houses and flowers are mingled with the prosperous businesses (such as Associated Cab, Garrett's Pharmacy, and the Regal Theatre). Support for the mural project came from the Mary Duke Biddle Foundation, Heritage Square Associates, the Winn Dixie Association, and the Durham Arts Council, which provided a City Arts Grant. Other artists on the project were M. E. Ackerman, Stikcarlo Darby, Brian Franks, David Wilson, Sharon Barksdale, and Worth and Willie Bigelow.

Hemphill, Ellen (1952–)

Ellen Hemphill is a founder of Archipelago Theatre and now its artistic and managing director. She produces, directs, writes, and performs in many of its productions. She is the creator or co-creator of *Outraged and on the Wire* (1993), *Cassandra's Lullaby* (1994), *Binky Kite and the Oxymorons* (1994), and *Another Time. Another Place . . . Someone Else* (1997), and the sole author of *If My Boundary Stops Here* (1993), *Those Women* (1996), *Eulogy for a Warrior* (1998), *Amor Fortuna* (1999), *Snow* (2000), and *And Mary Wept* (2002). In addition, she has directed twelve of Archipelago's shows as well as *The Crucible* for Duke University (2000), where she has been a member of the theater studies department since 1993. She also has taught voice and gesture with the American Dance Festival, and while a member of the Roy Hart Theatre of France (until 1990) toured and performed for thirteen years throughout Europe, Japan, Mexico, and the United States. In 2000 Hemphill won a North Carolina Arts Fellowship for choreography.

Heyden, Silvia (1927–)

Silvia Heyden is a textile artist who was born in Switzerland and studied at the School of Design in Zurich with the Bauhaus master Johannes Itten. After six years at the school she married Dr. Siegfried Heyden in 1954, and for the next ten years the couple and their two children divided their time between the United States and Berlin. In 1964 Heyden purchased her first tapestry loom for a commission in Switzerland, beginning a long career as a creator of tapestries. She moved back to Durham in 1966 when her husband took an appointment at the Duke University Medical Center. She assisted with the Triangle Festival of Crafts and continued to support the development of the arts in Durham.

Heyden's first important exhibit was at the Duke University Art Museum in 1972. Her work can be seen at the Durham County Library, City Hall, the Rare Book Library at Duke, and the Judea Reform Congregation. She also has work in the Gallery of Art and Design at the North Carolina Museum of Art and has exhibited her work all over the United States. Heyden left Durham in the 1990s but returned again in 2006 after a sojourn in Tessen, Switzerland, where she played with the String Orchestra of Locarno.

Hill, Samuel Washington (1909–1998)

When he was still a young man, Samuel Hill was a choir director and organist at his grandfather's church in Alabama. He received his B.A. in music with an emphasis in piano and organ at Talladega College, Alabama, and his M.A. in music and music education as well as a professional certificate from the Teachers College of Columbia University in New York. Hill came to NCCU for a brief time in 1941 and returned in 1949, remaining on the faculty until 1966. At NCCU Hill directed the university choir and took it on an annual spring tour along the East Coast and to Detroit.

Hill, Willie

Willie Hill played the trumpet in elementary school in Durham and later learned to play the acoustic and bass guitars. He played in the school bands at Hillside High, sang in his church choir, and majored in music at NCCU. When Hill was nineteen he played bass with the Communicators and wrote the hit single "One Chance," which the band recorded in 1974. In the mid-1970s he played in the Modulations for several years. Later he toured with Doug Clark and the Hot Nuts into the mid-1980s. Hill also established a recording studio in Durham, producing his own music as well as work by other artists.

Holsenbeck, Bryant (1949–)

Bryant Holsenbeck is a mixed-media artist known for installations that use recycled materials and objects from everyday life. Born in Tennessee, Holsenbeck grew up in Greensboro and earned her B.A. and M.E. from UNC-Chapel Hill. She traveled, studied basket making on Nantucket, and returned to Durham in 1976, teaching basketry around the Triangle. She served on the founding board of the Scrap Exchange in 1991, and won an Indy Arts Award (1994), two North Carolina Artist Grants (1997 and 2001), and an NEA Arts and Learning Grant. Holsenbeck has taught and traveled nationally, turning waste and abandoned objects into art. She taught art part-time at the North Carolina School of Science and Mathematics and created installations at the Durham Art Guild, the Duke History Department, and the SEEDS community garden. In February 2005 the John Hope Franklin Center for Humanities at Duke exhibited her installation "Hunting and Gathering," which used objects such as bird nests made from chopsticks to contrast human and animal migration patterns.

Hopkins, Marian Turner (1948–)

Marian Hopkins, a dancer, choreographer, and teacher, was one of the founding members of New Performing Dance Company (NPDC) in Durham, formed in 1975 under the auspices of Dance Associates of Allied Arts (now Durham Arts Council). A native of Georgia, Hopkins has a B.A. from Heidelberg College, Ohio, and an M.A. in dance from Ohio State University. She was the artistic director of NPDC during its early years and a soloist with the American Dance Festival during a program of the North Carolina Choreographers Project. Hopkins danced with one of North Carolina's first professional dance companies, the Frank Holder Dance Company, based in Greensboro. She also danced with Carolina Dancers, performing in the Triangle and New York, in the North Carolina Dance Showcase, and at the American College Dance Festival. Hopkins has taught at many schools in the Triangle and since 1979 at UNC-Chapel Hill, where she directs its Modernextension Dance Company.

House, Tom (1949–)

Born into a family of Scotch-Irish immigrants who worked at Erwin Cotton Mill, Tom House spent a great deal of his youth in Old West Durham, where he was exposed to gospel music. His father and uncles played blues and "home-grown" music. With other children he would perform for tips alongside the black musicians at the tobacco warehouses. House published poetry while a teenager and began to write and perform his own songs as a young man. He moved to Nashville in 1976 and in that year had his first on-stage musical appearance. House has released over five albums of his work. He has also collaborated with several other musicians on a number of operas. One, based on Faulkner's *Light in August*, he performed at the Faulkner Festival in the 1990s. More recently House collaborated on the writing of two song cycles based on Lee Smith's books: *Fair and Tender Ladies* and *Christmas Letters.*

Howard, Rosemary (1946–)

Rosemary Howard, dancer, choreographer, and academic, received a B.A. and a Master of Communication in performance studies from UNC-Chapel Hill and an M.F.A. in dance from UNC-Greensboro. First a member of Dance Associates of Allied Arts (now the Durham Arts Council) and then of the New Performing Dance Company (NPDC), she has been a performer and teacher at the NPDC's school, as well as a choreographer for musicals and plays for the school and for Elon University, Duke University, UNC-Chapel Hill, and community theaters. Recently she has directed performances at the Carrboro Arts Center, including *The Trojan Women.*

Hunt, Edward (1947–)

Edward Hunt was a founder of Manbites Dog Theater in 1987 and has since been its managing director and associate artistic director. Besides being the sound designer for numerous plays, he has been the co-author of four plays: *A Tune for Tommy* (2000), *Indecent Materials/Report from the Holocaust* (1990), *Hotline* (1991), and *802701* (2000).

Irwin, Kim (1947–)

Kim Irwin is a performance and visual artist who has worked with Max Below in community arts initiatives in Durham. She was born in Dayton, Ohio, and received her B.F.A. from UNC-Chapel Hill and her M.F.A. from East Carolina University. Irwin and Below have used Polaroid photographs to create installations and companion performances, such as "Childhood Stories," which have been exhibited nationally, including at the North Carolina Museum of Art in 1990 and 1999. Irwin has received seven grants from the North Carolina Arts Council for residencies and community-based arts events. A grant with Below in 1988 funded a video about change in downtown Durham. Irwin and Below have worked with the neighborhood center of the Durham Department of Parks and Recreation to create a Polaroid "Community Family Album" as part of the Alternate ROOTS Community / Artists Partnership Project. Irwin's residencies have included one at the Headlands Center for the Arts in California (with Below) and another at Miami Dade Community College. Her solo exhibition and installation "Secretaries" was exhibited nationally in the early 1990s. In 2003 Irwin received a Public Service Award from the City of New York, where she lives when not in Durham.

Keaton, Benjamin (1935–)

Benjamin Keaton holds both a B.A. and M.A. from East Carolina University and has done additional graduate work at UNC-Chapel Hill. He served on the music faculty of NCCU for seventeen years, during which he was also frequently the music director for the department of theater. He was president of the Durham Theatre Guild and maestro for the Durham Savoyards from 1982 to 2002. In addition, he has directed for the Carolina Playmakers, Jenny Wiley State Theatre of Kentucky, the Lost Colony, Opera House Theatre of Wilmington, and Opera Ft. Collins, and is the founding musical director of Long Leaf Opera. His numerous compositions include a four-movement symphony for orchestra, chorus, and soloist titled *Places, Please! A Savoyard Symphony*, based on the thirteen extant operas of Gilbert and Sullivan. He has composed the scores to a number of theater works, including three outdoor dramas with Paul Green, one with Randolph Umberger, and one with Mitchell Douglas, as well as the score to *Remembered Nights* for the 125th anniversary of Thalian Hall at UNC.

Kitchen, Nicholas (1968–)

A native of Durham, Nicholas Kitchen is a classical violinist with an already long and notable career. His mother, a violinist, was his first teacher. He then studied with Giorgio Ciompi in Durham, attended the Curtis Institute, and pursued graduate study at the New England Conservatory of Music. With three friends from Curtis he formed the Borromeo Quartet.

A stellar soloist and chamber musician, Kitchen has performed all over the world with the most famous orchestras and chamber groups. He has recorded the entire solo violin works of J. S. Bach, and made dozens of other recordings. He is also artistic director of the Cape Cod Chamber Music Festival and a frequent guest soloist at other festivals in the United States and abroad. He has received a Presidential Scholar in the Arts Award and the Albert Schweitzer medallion for artistry. Kitchen plays a Stradivarius violin, purchased for him by the A. J. Fletcher Foundation.

Kong, Ellen

The artist and ceramicist Ellen Kong was born in Hong Kong. She has a B.F.A. from Taiwan Normal University and an M.F.A. from UNC-Greensboro. She also studied at the Penland School of Crafts and the Idyllwild School of Music and the Arts. Using skills she learned when she studied painting, she has refined the technique for Raku-fired and smoke-fired clay through airbrush, masking, collage, and glazing. Her preferred form is the sculptural kimono for which she writes haiku. She was the featured artist in the Tenth Anniversary Art Exhibition of Toyama, Japan, and she has received commissions from Duke University Medical Center, the Columbia Museum of Art in South Carolina, UNC-Greensboro, Wachovia Bank in Chapel Hill, and Eisai in Research Triangle Park. She is the author of *The Great Clay Adventure* (1999) and *Experience Clay* (2003) and has received awards from both national and international organizations. She taught at Durham Academy for many years.

Kremen, Irwin (1925–)

Irwin Kremen, born in Chicago, is a longtime artist and psychology professor at Duke. He received a B.A. from Northwestern University, an M.A. from the New School for Social Research, and a Ph.D. from Harvard University. Kremen, who became a professor emeritus in 1992 after almost forty years of teaching at Duke, has been a fellow at the university's Institute of the Arts since 1982, and is a self-taught artist. His first show, of collages, was at the National Museum of American Art of the Smithsonian Institution in 1978 and his work has since been displayed nationally. The Duke University Art Museum, the Rose Art Museum at Brandeis, the Museum of Fine Arts in Houston, and the Wichita Museum all hold permanent collections of Kremen's works. In 2004 ACA Galleries in New York held "Three in One: Collage Painting Sculpture," a mixed-media exhibition of Kremen's work. In 1998 he received the Sam Pagan Award for outstanding contributions to fine arts in North Carolina. Kremen also works in metal, which he includes in collages that he creates with the unusual method of Japanese paper fasteners as opposed to glue.

Lee, Elizabeth

Elizabeth Lee, a dancer, choreographer, teacher, and writer, was formerly a dance critic for the *Durham Herald* (1978–87). Born in New York, she moved to Durham in 1965 and obtained her B.A. from Duke University and a Ph.D. in comparative literature from UNC-Chapel Hill. She spent a number of years performing and writing about dance while teaching at local colleges and universities. She studied dance with Carol Richards, with Suzanne White Manning, and at the ADF school, and performed with Carolina Dancers at UNC-Chapel Hill. She now lives in Alexandria, Virginia, and works as a painter.

Lee, Phil (1951–)

A contemporary of the folk musician Tom House and the country musician Don Schlitz, Phil Lee is a native of Durham who started his music career early in life. As a teenager in the 1960s he played drums for Homer Briarhopper and the Daybreak Gang. The band was broadcast on morning television from Raleigh—early enough for Lee to make it on time to class at Durham High School. Working at the station exposed him to a number of country music legends who performed live on the morning show. Lee left Durham in the 1970s for New York, where he played in a band. Later he worked with Jack Nitzsche, Neil Young's manager, in Los Angeles before returning to Durham in the 1980s. While in Durham, Lee wrote and performed his own music. He subsequently settled in Nashville, where he continues to write and perform. Lee has released at least two albums of his own music under the Shanachie label.

Lentz, Elizabeth (1946–2003)

Elizabeth Lentz was born in Atchison, Kansas, and began studying art in high school with Walter Yost, a regionally known watercolorist, and Fred Anderson, a master craftsman. She chose social work as her first vocation and later studied art at the Chicago Art Institute and the Museum School in Boston. She earned an M.F.A. in 1984 from the University of North Carolina at Greensboro. At UNCG she studied painting with Peter Agostini, Andrew Martin, and Richard Fennell. After graduation she taught drawing, painting, color theory, and design at North Carolina Central University. At NCCU she met and mentored Beverly McIver, a shining star in American painting. Her work has been shown at the Lilly Library

at Duke, the Duke Institute of the Arts, Rutgers University, Morehead Gallery, the Greenhill Center for North Carolina Art, and the Durham Art Guild.

Lilly, Rowena (1942–)

Rowena ("Ronnie") Lilly, a native of Asheville, received a B.Ed. from UNC-Chapel Hill and made her career in the Durham public schools as an arts education coordinator. Beginning in 1963 as a student teacher, she went on to teach at the Durham School of Design (at Lowes Grove School), at the same time studying pottery with Dorothy Davis and at the Penland School of Crafts.

As an arts education coordinator, Lilly helped Janice Palmer and Ella Fountain Pratt set up the Creative Arts in the Public / Private Schools (CAPPS) program at the Durham Arts Council (DAC). More recently she has overseen the transformation of the former Durham High School into the Durham School of the Arts, an arts magnet school. She was also instrumental in implementing the public school Summer Arts Program at DAC during the early and mid-1980s. Lilly has received awards from the North Carolina Arts Education Association, DAC, and the *Independent Weekly*.

London, Edith (1904–1997)

Edith London was an abstract artist and founding member of the Durham Art Guild. Born in Berlin, she married the physicist Fritz London in 1929 and studied art in Paris for three years before coming to the United States in 1939 when her husband accepted a professorship at Duke. She taught in Duke University's art department from 1955 to 1969 and was a founder of the Three Arts Club, a women's group devoted to art, music, and literature.

London's collages and paintings were displayed in 1983 in "Painting in the South, 1964–1980" at the Virginia Museum of Fine Arts in Richmond and can be found in many galleries and private collections. She received the North Carolina Awards in the Fine Arts in 1988. In 1992 the Durham Art Guild and Durham Arts Council sponsored a sixty-year retrospective of a hundred of her paintings, hosted by Lee Hansley, and in 1995 she received a Women of Achievement Award from the Durham YWCA. Her work is in the permanent collection of the North Carolina Museum of Art. "Her Joyful Affirmation" hangs at the main branch of the Durham County Public Library. In 1998, to commemorate its fiftieth anniversary, the Durham Art Guild ran a limited edition serigraph print of one of London's fabric collages.

Lopez-Barrantes, Rafael (1951–)

Rafael Lopez-Barrantes, a native of Madrid, was a founder of the Archipelago Theatre in 1990 and became a member of the Duke theater studies department in 1991. Before coming to the United States he taught voice and theater in France, Spain, Italy, Norway, and Germany. He has written and directed plays for Duke and the Archipelago Theatre. He was also the founder in 1997 and is the present CEO of Celebrations Inc., which designs special event productions such as the Pavarotti Gala for the North Carolina Opera Company and the 50th Jubilee Gala for the North Carolina Museum of Art; the company has won five designing awards. Since 1997 Lopez-Barrantes has taught at the American Dance Festival.

Loudermilk, John D. (1934–)

A singer and songwriter, John Loudermilk was born in the Erwin Mill village in Durham, in a house near Knox and Ninth streets. His earliest musical influence was his neighbor Ernest Moon, an employee of the mill. As a teenager delivering telegrams in West Durham, Loudermilk would hear Moon playing a gut guitar on his porch.

Loudermilk began playing the drum for the Salvation Army but also learned a variety of other instruments, including the guitar. During a long and prolific career he has written and recorded country, rock, and pop music, but his fame rests with his compositions. His work has been recorded by stars such as the Everly Brothers, Johnny Ferguson, Sue Thompson, and George Hamilton IV. Besides "A Rose and a Baby Ruth," his most popular hits have been "Sittin' in the Balcony," "Tobacco Road," and "Indian Reservation."

Manbites Dog Theater

Manbites Dog Theater was founded by Jeff Storer and Edward Hunt in 1987 to produce new and challenging theater, to nurture developing theater artists and groups, and to strengthen the state's theatrical community. A professional, nonprofit company, it bought its own building at 703 Foster Street, which opened in 1998 with a performance of Chris Morris's *Blue Roses*. Altogether Manbites Dog has staged over eighty productions, including many local and world premières. Besides its own productions, such as Larry Kramer's *The Normal Heart* (1988) and Arlene Hutton's *Last Train to Nibroc* (2000), it hosts an Other Voices Series, presenting work by guest companies and artists. Examples include Little Green Pig's production of *The Cherry Orchard* (2006), with an African-American cast, and *piece~meal* (2005), by both hands theatre. It has also produced the Don't Ask Don't Tell Festival of Queer Performance, which has included Tim Miller's *My Queer Body* (1994), Romulus Linney's *Oscar Over Here* (1994–95), and a workshop production by Holly Hughes of *Preaching to the Converted* (1998–99). The company occasionally conducts Puzzlehunt, a community event that includes downtown performances as part of the clues to the puzzle. It has also presented live music performances by local and regional musicians, and hosted work by visual artists in its lobby gallery.

The Mary Duke Biddle Foundation

Continuing practices learned from her grandfather and her father, Mary Duke Biddle (1887–1960) chartered her namesake foundation in 1956. Born and educated in Durham, she traveled between homes in Durham and New York City before marrying and residing in Irvington-on-Hudson, near her beloved theater and opera in New York City. In 1936 she decided to return to Durham, perhaps the most fortunate decision for the support of the arts in the history of the city. Her public and anonymous support for the arts sustained limited efforts and launched new initiatives at the maturing Duke and North Carolina Central universities and throughout the city.

The foundation institutionalized lifelong interests of its founder in charitable, educational, and religious activities, with special emphasis on children and the arts. Half of its annual income is distributed to Duke University and the remainder goes to nonprofit, tax-exempt organizations in North Carolina and New York.

By choice, the foundation makes many of its grants to small, community-based organizations with limited resources. Mary Duke Trent Jones, the current chairwoman, notes that "these types of projects offer tremendous opportunities for the organizations themselves and the people they serve. Planning and executing small projects helps organizations increase their strength and effectiveness, and gives them the experience they need to conduct larger efforts." In just over fifty years the foundation has distributed a little over $30 million in grants. In 2005, a typical year, it made thirty-two grants to institutions in Durham. Through the years grants have supported students, artists-in-residence, authors, emerging artists, performances, exhibitions, celebrations, museums, historic sites, educational programs, and cultural programs in medicine. The headquarters of the foundation have always been in Durham.

McAuliffe, Jody (1954–)

Jody McAuliffe, a member of the Department of Theater Studies at Duke University since 1988, has directed over fifteen plays, including Molière's *The Miser* (1989), Maria Irene Fornes's *Mud* (1990), Neal Bell's *McTeague* (1994), and Strindberg's *The Father* (1996). She has also adapted and directed six works for the stage, notably Don DeLillo's novels *Mao II* (2003) and *Libra* (1990). In addition she has translated and directed Leonid Andreyev's *The Idea* (1993) and *He Who Gets Slapped* (1991). Altogether she has directed over seventy plays, not only at Duke and Manbites Dog Theater but in Los Angeles, New York, San Diego, San Francisco, and New Haven, and at the Sundance Institute in Utah. McAuliffe directed Marlane Meyer's *The Mystery of Attraction* at South Coast Repertory in 1999 and a video, *My Man Ray*, which she produced, adapted, and directed for the Directing Workshop for Women at the American Film Institute, Los Angeles, in 1988.

McConahay, Shirley Frey (1940–)

Shirley McConahay, a specialist in soft sculpture, is a native of Indiana with a B.A. from Transylvania University in Lexington, Kentucky, and an M.A. from Southern Connecticut State University in New Haven. She has completed numerous private and public commissions and exhibited her work extensively in the Triangle. Carolina Designer Craftsmen Guild and Duke University have recognized her work with awards. McConahay has been active in the Durham Arts Council (DAC) Creative Arts in Public / Private Schools (CAPPS) program and taught inner-city children. She has also taught soft sculpture for the Durham Housing Authority and the North Carolina Correctional Institution for Women. Her primary activity currently is teaching sewn art to indigenous people throughout the Americas for Art for Indigenous Survival, a nonprofit international organization based in Durham.

McKinney, Florentina

Florentina McKinney, potter and copper enamelist, moved to Durham when her husband joined the Duke faculty in 1958. She took workshops at Arrowmont Craft Center, studying with Helen Morel, and courses at the University of South Carolina and in Athens, Georgia. In 1968 she opened a small consignment craft shop at Lakewood Shopping Center called Florentina's and invited several craftsmen to join her, there being no other outlets for crafts in Durham. She was a partner in Craft House as well. McKinney was instrumental in founding the Carolina Designer Craftsman Guild (CDCG) in 1970. After her death in 1990, the Florentina McKinney Award was established for CDCG in 1996 to be "presented in memory of a founding member of the Guild, in celebration of the artistic spirit."

McPhatter, Clyde Leslie (1932–1972)

Clyde McPhatter was one of the influential greats in the R&B world in the 1950s and 1960s. As a child he sang in the choir at Mount Calvary Baptist Church in Durham, where his mother was an organist. When he was twelve his family moved to New York City, and he joined a gospel singing group that toured and competed regionally. In 1950 he launched his career in R&B with a hit performance during amateur night at the Apollo Theater. He sang with the Dominoes for several years before forming his own group, the Drifters.

May, Nancy Tuttle (1940–)

Born in Greensboro, Nancy Tuttle May, a painter of abstract works on canvas and paper, has lived and worked in Durham since 1969. She received her B.S. from Wake Forest University in 1961 with additional studies in Italy, France, and Taos, New Mexico. Her early works were impressionistic watercolors. She received a grant from the National Endowment for the Arts in 1976 and participated in the Visiting Artist Program of the North Carolina Arts Council from 1976 to 1980. Galleries throughout the United States show her work, and her paintings are in private and corporate collections worldwide. May has taught the business of art to emerging artists at Duke University, the North Carolina Museum of Art, Durham Arts Council, and North Carolina public schools and community colleges.

Medler, Gene (1948–)

Gene Medler, a dancer and choreographer, founded and directed the North Carolina Youth Tap Ensemble in 1982 along with an adult tap dance company. He is the director of the annual North Carolina Rhythm Tap Festival and has taught in many places locally, including Elon University, Duke University, and Meredith College, as well as at the American Dance Festival, the Ballet School of Chapel Hill, and the St. Louis Tap Festival in Missouri. Medler has performed with the Squirrel Nut Zippers, soloed in Duke Ellington's *Nutcracker* and in *David Danced* at Duke Chapel, and performed in a duet with the tap dance legend Brenda Bufalino at the World Dance Festival in New York. He has received grants from the Durham Arts Council, the North Carolina Arts Council, and the Orange County Arts Commission, as well as the "Tar Heel of the Week" award from the *News and Observer*, the "Indy Award" from the *Independent Weekly* in 1998 for contribution to the arts, and an award from the North Carolina Dance Alliance for his continuing commitment to dance in North Carolina and his resounding achievement as a dance artist. Medler was featured in the magazine *Dance Teacher Now* in March 1998 and may be seen in the PBS special "JUBA, Master of Percussive Dance."

Menapace, John (1927–)

The photographer John Menapace, born in Pennsylvania, moved to Durham from New York City in 1956 as the designer and production manager for Duke University Press. Already an avid photographer, he continued to expand his education by studying at Black Mountain College near Asheville and by "wandering about looking at other people's work." He taught classes at Penland, UNC-Chapel Hill, and Duke University and has exhibited frequently throughout the country. In 1980 he was awarded a Southeast Seven Fellowship from the National Endowment for the Arts and the Southeast Center for Contemporary Art. A fellow photographer has called him "the father of art photography in North Carolina."

Menchú portrait

The Menchú portrait is in the reception area of El Centro Hispano, a Latino organization on West Main Street. A low relief of wood and pastel measuring 48 by 72 inches, it depicts the Guatemalan activist Rigoberta Menchú, winner of the Nobel Peace Prize in 1992. The portrait was commissioned by El Centro Hispano and sponsored by the North Carolina Arts Council. Richard Goldberg was the lead artist, who worked with eighteen youths from El Centro Hispano and See-Saw Studio to complete the portrait.

Michalak, M. Victor (1923–1979)

Victor Michalak, a faculty member and the first full-time stage designer at Duke University, arrived in Durham in 1950. In all he directed twenty plays at Duke as well as scenes for Studio Opera in conjunction with the music department. He was also active in the community, directing plays for the Durham Theatre Guild—Agatha Christie's *Witness for the Prosecution* (1957), Ira Levin's *Critic's Choice* (1965), and Pirandello's *The Pleasure of Honesty* (1965). Michalak also directed summer stock in Michigan and, in North Carolina, *The Lost Colony* and *Horn in the West.*

Milroy, Sandy Miller (1939–)

Sandy Milroy, a weaver, earned a B.A. from Wellesley College and pursued additional studies at NCSU, Penland, Haystack Mountain School of Crafts in Maine, and Arrowmont School of Arts and Crafts in Tennessee. She moved to Durham in 1962, began working at Straw Valley for Bob Black and Ormond Sanderson, and became friends with Vivian Dai, with whom she studied weaving with Noma' Hardin in Greensboro and took part in a Scandinavian study tour. Milroy taught weaving at Allied Arts and became an early member of Triangle Weavers. From 1974 to 1982 she and her husband traveled and lived in Zambia, Aberdeen, Scotland, and the Lake District in England. During this time she pursued a career in textiles, teaching classes and workshops. She received a fellowship from the British Crafts Council and had a solo show in Cumbria, United Kingdom. In North Carolina she was a founding member of the Carolina Designer Craftsmen Guild and taught at the Durham Arts Council, the Duke University Craft Center, and the Montessori School for Children. Currently she teaches children's classes and works as a painter and collage artist in Chapel Hill.

Minnis, Paul

Paul Minnis is a realist painter and potter. A native of Pennsylvania, he received a B.A. and M.A. from Pennsylvania State University and then studied pottery at the Rochester Institute of Art. He first taught painting in the art department at East Carolina University (1957–73), later becoming a professor in the ceramics department and its chairman. After settling in the Triangle in the 1970s he taught many ceramicists in Durham and was a founding member of Carolina Designer Craftsmen Guild. He also conducted workshops and classes at Penn State, the Corcoran School of Art in Washington, D.C., and UNC-Wilmington. From 1973 to 1980 he owned and operated Minnis Pottery, which manufactured clay bodies and chemicals for schools, universities, and individuals from Maine to Texas.

Since 1973 Minnis has painted primarily in oil and watercolor. His paintings have been commissioned by IBM at Research Triangle Park, North Carolina National Bank, Central Carolina Bank, the *News and Observer*, Capital City Broadcasting, Northern Telecom, and American Airlines at the Raleigh-Durham airport. His paintings are also in the collections of the North Carolina Museum of Art, Duke University, and Meredith College; his pottery is in the collections of the Mint Museum in Charlotte, the North Carolina Museum of Art, and the Greenville Museum of Art, as well as is in many private collections.

Morgan, Jacqueline Erickson (1941–)

Born in Puerto Rico, Jacqueline Morgan received a B.A. from the College of Notre Dame in Maryland and then came to Durham in 1971. She was an important figure in dance during the period of cooperation and creative growth in the 1970s among studios, professional dancers, and teachers in Durham and Chapel Hill. She danced with Dance Associates, a company and school sponsored by Allied Arts (later the Durham Arts Council) and started the Day for Dancing to raise funds for dance groups. She was also the administrative director for New Performing Dance Company and school. For twelve years she was on the board of directors of the Durham Arts Council.

Morris, Chris (1955–)

Chris Morris, affiliated since 1994 with the Duke University Program in Drama (now the Department of Theater Studies), has directed *The Changeling* (by Thomas Middleton) and *Gint* (by Romulus Linney, 2003) at Duke. A member of Actors Equity, she has appeared in a number of plays at Duke, Archipelago, and Manbites Dog Theater. She is also a member of the Voice and Speech Training Association and has been a dialect coach for productions at Duke, Manbites Dog Theater, NCSU, Peace College, and the Alabama Shakespeare Festival. In 1998 she wrote and starred in *Blue Roses*, based on the life of Tennessee Williams's sister Rose, at Manbites Dog in a co-production with Archipelago. It was voted the best play of 1998 by both the *News and Observer* and the *Spectator*. The play was produced in 1999 in Portland, Oregon, and in the following year at the Tennessee Williams Center at the University of the South in Sewanee, Tennessee.

Mueller, Julia Wilkinson (1915–1977)

A native of Des Moines, Julia Mueller was a musician and academic whose principal instrument was the viola. She earned a B.M. from the Eastman School of Music of the University of Rochester in 1936, an artist's diploma from the same institution in 1939, and an M.A. from the State University of Iowa in 1942.

Because she played both viola and violin, she was always in demand by musical groups. While a student, she played in the University of Rochester Philharmonic. From 1939 until 1941 she played with the North Carolina Symphony and from 1942 to 1945 with the National Symphony.

After Duke University recruited her for its music department in 1939, she taught courses in music literature and history as well as instruction in viola and violin. She was also chairwoman of the department from 1969 until 1973. She served as concertmistress of a variety of local symphony groups and played viola in the original Ciompi Quartet.

Mumford, Eugene (1926–1977)

Eugene Mumford, one of the original Internes, began as a gospel singer before taking up R&B. In the 1950s he joined the Larks as their lead singer. Originally organized in Durham as the Jubilators, the group moved to New York in the fall of

1950 and recorded under a variety of names. After the group disbanded in 1952 Mumford joined the Dominoes and sang the lead on two of their big hits recorded in 1957. He went on to a solo career, and before his death sang with the Ink Spots.

Myers, Martha (1925–)

Martha Myers, a dancer, choreographer, teacher, and writer, was dean of the American Dance Festival from 1969 to 2000. During this period her influence on dance locally and internationally was profound. She was director of ADF Workshops for Professionals and ADF/New York Choreolab, and co-director of its Young Composers and Choreographers Program. She was a pioneer in the application of dance somatics and body-mind principles to choreography, dance training, and coaching and introduced both to the ADF summer curriculum. A founding member of the International Association of Dance Medicine and Science (IADMS), she has written on body therapies for *Dance Magazine*. Myers has been the resident choreographer for the Williamstown Theater Festival in Massachusetts and the Eugene O'Neill Musical Theater in Waterford, Connecticut. Before joining ADF she originated, wrote, and narrated the first PBS series on dance in 1961 and has done on-camera work for television. She is the Henry B. Plant Professor, Emerita, at Connecticut College.

Myers was appointed to ADF's Balasaraswati/Joy Ann Dewey Beinecke Endowed Chair for Distinguished Teaching in 2002. Her numerous awards have included the first honorary certification in movement analysis from the Laban Institute of Movement Studies; a Lifetime Contribution Award from the Connecticut Arts Commission, 1991; and the Connecticut Dance Alliance Award, 2000. She has received honorary degrees from Manhattanville College in 2004 and Virginia Commonwealth University in 2006.

Nash, Willie (1937–1999)

A native of Asheville, Willie Nash moved to Durham in 1958 to attend NCCU and study art. After three years he interrupted his studies to join the Air Force, and served for four years. In 1965 he returned to NCCU and earned a B.A. in fine art. In the years that followed his life was colored by a career as a medical illustrator, a sign painter, a teacher, and an administrator at various institutions in the Triangle.

Having worked in watercolors while growing up, Nash changed his painting medium to oil after studying art at NCCU. His paintings, characterized by a documentary realism and a vibrant sense of color, were informed by his research into the experience of black America. His subjects covered a wide range: little children playing ball, a family in a living room decorated for Christmas, black cowboys, guns and all, farm scenes with women working in the field, black musicians, and physicians. Among his paintings that are admired in Durham and the Southeast are *Fargo Street*, a tribute to family life, and *Daily Bread*, which shows an elderly couple seated at a table, saying grace over a loaf of bread.

Nash went on to teach art at NCCU, and much of his work reflects the influence of campus life. Nash loved to do portraits and felt that "if you couldn't do people, you couldn't do." His portrait of NCCU's president, Alphonso Elder, hangs in the NCCU student union. Nash's prints for college fraternities and sororities, featuring silhouetted figures and Greek insignia, have become a staple of those organizations' merchandise.

Nash displayed his paintings in galleries throughout the United States and his prints at street fairs in Durham. His prints of black family life and of historical figures have been in demand throughout the Southeast. Several of his more than three hundred paintings depict biblical scenes with black characters, such as his painting of the Last Supper. Adrienne Witherspoon, a former NCCU art student and friend, has described Nash as wanting "to reinforce a positive self-image in art for African-Americans, because there was so little available [when he started painting]. And he made it affordable."

New Performing Dance Company

New Performing Dance Company was formed in 1975 by the Dance Associates of Allied Arts (now Durham Arts Council). Rosemary Howard, M'Liss Dorrance, and Marian Turner (now Hopkins) directed the company until 1978, when Lee Wenger (now Lee Vrana) became artistic director; she led the company for the next seventeen years, developing it into a modern dance troupe. During those years the company performed in Durham and Washington and received funding from the Durham Arts Council and the touring program of the North Carolina Arts Council. Dancers and choreographers long associated with the company included Bruce Vrana, Clair Osgood, and the late Ron Paul. The company was disbanded in 1995.

Newton, Bill (1938–)
Newton, Joyce C. (1943–)

Bill and Joyce Newton are both potters. He crafts jug faces and she makes functional pottery and small fountains. Bill, a native of North Carolina, has studied at a number of workshops, at Arrowmont School of Arts and Crafts in Gatlinburg, Tennessee, and with Brad Tucker at Cedar Creek Pottery in Creedmoor. He was president of the Clayworks Pottery Guild. Joyce, Pennsylvanian by birth, creates functional porcelain pottery. She too has pursued clay studies with Brad Tucker, at Arrowmont School, and at workshops, particularly with Mark Hewitt and Ian Currie.

Noland, William (1954 -)

William Noland is a sculptor, photographer and experimental documentary filmmaker. After receiving a B.A. from Sarah Lawrence College, he spent two years as assistant and apprentice to the British sculptor Sir Anthony Caro. An associate professor of Visual Art in the Department of Art, Art History and Visual Studies at Duke University, he is the recipient of a National Endowment for the Arts Visual Artist Fellowship in Sculpture, a Fulbright Scholar Award in Photography, and a Josiah Charles Trent Foundation Grant for video. He has exhibited his sculpture and photography nationally and internationally, including twenty solo exhibitions. He was an editorial advisor and contributing photographer for the award-winning journal of writing and photography, *DoubleTake*, from 1995 to 2004. His video work has screened in a number of venues, including the Full Frame Documentary Film Festival in Durham, North Carolina, the Ann Arbor Film Festival in Ann Arbor, Michigan, and the Athens International Film & Video Festival in Athens, Ohio

Oberski, Jay (1970–)

Jay Oberski, actor, director, and founder of Shakespeare and Originals, is the co-author of two plays: *Ein Kleiner Kowboy* (2000, with words from Rilke) and *Life, Love, Cows* (2001, from stories by Chekov), both of which he directed at Manbites Dog Theater. A lecturing fellow in the Duke University Department of Theater Studies since 2000, he is perhaps best known to audiences in Durham as an actor, having appeared in many productions with Manbites Dog, Archipelago Theatre, and Shakespeare and Originals. In 1995 he acted in *The Toy Garden* at La Mama in New York and in 1997 he acted in three plays at the Moscow Art Theatre (American Studio).

O'Brien Atkins Associates

The O'Brien Atkins architectural firm was founded by William L. O'Brien Jr. (1939–), John Atkins III (1943–), and Belton Atkinson (1939–) in 1975 and now comprises eighty-five persons. Its first project was designing the home of the UNC basketball coach Dean Smith. Its practice now includes projects all over the United States and as far away as Ireland. Clients have included major national and international firms in Research Triangle Park: the MCI network and administrative complex, the GlaxoSmithKline corporate headquarters and operations facility, fifteen office buildings for Cisco Systems, the National Science Headquarters, Sprint's administrative headquarters, and the new Raleigh Convention Center. O'Brien, a native of Greensboro, has been the hands-on project manager for all the firm's architectural projects. His primary role has been to assure quality control of all construction documents before they leave the office and to maintain the same quality in the construction phase of each project. Atkins, a native of Durham, has served as president and CEO and managing principal of the firm. Atkinson, also from Durham, has been secretary-treasurer of the firm and is in charge of architectural drawing and the documentary phase of construction.

Olson, Julie (1953–)

Julie Olson, a native of Washington state and a long-time resident of Durham, makes hinged boxes and functional pottery as well as other objects such as lamps and books. She studied at Olympic College, Bremerton, focusing on design, print making, and pottery, and at the Penland School of Crafts. She also received private instruction in pottery, metalwork, and book making. Olson has taught advanced pottery at NCSU Crafts Center. Her awards include an Award of Excellence from the Carolina Designer Craftsmen Guild, Cedar Creek Pottery, and the Orton Cone Box Show Purchase Award.

Ormston, Katherine (1907–1995)

Trained in journalism, Katherine Ormston worked for the Literary Guild in New York before moving to Durham to be treated by Walter Kemp-
ner on the Rice Diet plan. She settled permanently in Durham and in 1950 became executive secretary at the North Carolina Heart Association. Later she worked at the Kempner Foundation, editing its journal. Ormston was a devotee of early music who played the recorder, taught classes in the instrument at the Arts Council, participated in performance groups with her students, and established the Triangle chapter of the American Recorder Society, with which she remained active until her death.

Palmer, Janice (1935–)

A native of Texas, Janice Palmer earned a liberal arts degree from the University of Texas and moved to Durham in 1967 with her husband, Richard Palmer, who taught chemistry at Duke. She began teaching art classes at the YWCA and Allied Arts Council and helped to form the Council for the Creative Arts in the Public Schools (CCAPS), later part of the Durham Arts Council. With money from the federal Changing Education Through the Arts program (CETA), Palmer helped to develop artist residencies in Durham schools. At the request of Dr. James Semans of Duke Medical Center and with funding from the National Endowment for the Arts, she became the founding director in 1978 of Cultural Services, with the mission of bringing art to the Duke hospitals. Palmer served with the organization for more than twenty years.

Duke was a pioneer in the arts-for-health movement. A longtime advocate for the arts in Durham, Palmer made contacts and raised money to place artwork in patients' rooms and public spaces, often buying local pieces. The Cultural Services Committee also established gardens, performances, journal-writing programs, and poetry readings for patients and staff, and advised planners on the designs of new medical buildings. Palmer retired from the directorship in 1999, but has continued to stay active in the arts-for-health movement through the Society for Arts in Health Care and by working with the Medical Center development office to raise an endowment for the Cultural Services Office. Palmer received the first North Carolina Arts for Health Award in 2006.

Pendergraft, Norman E. (1935–)

Norman Pendergraft, a native of Durham, received a B.A. in music and an M.A.T. from UNC-Chapel Hill, where he also studied musicology, and joined the NCCU faculty in 1966 as an associate professor of art. He pursued a Ph.D. in comparative arts at Ohio State University and completed all but a dissertation. In 1976 he was appointed director of the NCCU Art Museum, which was formed from what was then known as the art gallery. Under Pendergraft's leadership the collection grew to include more than two hundred works of art and came to be considered one of the finest collections of African-American art in the United States. Pendergraft is nationally known as a specialist in the field, and NCCU's collection contains some of the best sculptures, paintings, and prints by black artists from Africa, America, and the Caribbean. The permanent collection includes works by the sculptor, printmaker, and painter Elizabeth Catlett; the dancer, costume designer, performer, and painter Geoffrey Holder; the nineteenth-century expatriate artist Henry O. Tanner; and other classical masters such as Robert S. Duncanson and Edward M. Bannister. Among its early-twentieth-century masters are such names as Richmond Barthe, Robert Blackburn, Jacob Lawrence, William H. Johnson, Aaron Douglas, Romare Bearden, Selma Burke, Norman Lewis, and Charles White. Contemporary artists include Juan Logan, Barkley Hendricks, Minnie Evans, Sam Gilliam, and Kerry James Marshall.

In Durham Pendergraft built a reputation as a man committed to the community that he served. Like Catlett, an internationally known artist who taught art in Durham's public schools, and Dr. James E. Shepard, founder of NCCU, he considered it his responsibility to take art into the community and liked to bring the black community beyond NCCU's walls to the art museum. At his retirement in 1997, Dr. Patsy Perry, provost and vice chancellor for academic affairs at NCCU, described Pendergraft's community impact on the visual arts in Durham and the Art Museum's place in the heart of NCCU: "He brought the community to the museum. He had this wonderful sense of how to involve small children, teens, university students, community people and university faculty and staff members. His exhibits featured work from public school system children. He was able to have such a rich, rich blend of all these groups."

Peterson, Ronan (1973–)

Ronan Peterson, a potter, was born in North Carolina and earned a B.A. in anthropology and folklore at UNC-Chapel Hill in 1996. These interests led him to further studies at the John C. Campbell Folk School, Brasstown, where he began his work in ceramics. He apprenticed with David Vorhees and Steven Forbes-deSoule before attending the Penland School of Crafts, where he completed a two-year intensive work exchange program, studying with internationally known artists and craftsmen. He currently teaches at Claymakers as well as other pottery centers in the Triangle. Peterson has received an Emerging Artists Grant from the Durham Arts Council and an Emerging Artists award from *Ceramics Monthly*. He receives numerous private commissions for his functional earthenware pottery, and his work has been featured in several books and magazines.

Phelps, Ruth Seifert (1920–)

The daughter of a founder and organist of the Pittsburgh Symphony Orchestra, Ruth Phelps has been steeped in music from birth. She studied music at the Carnegie Institute of Technology (B.A. and B.M.) and the Juilliard School (diploma in organ), as well as pursuing graduate degrees at Middlebury College, the University of Zurich, and Ohio State University. Besides her long service from 1961 to 1976 as the organist and choir director at the Duke Memorial Methodist Church in Durham, she has taught music and German language and literature in many places, including at Middlebury College, Ohio State, Elon University, and Duke University. She has given many recitals and participated in chamber groups, playing the piano, clavichord, and organ.

Pinckney, Nancy

Nancy Pinckney, a dancer, choreographer, and educator, is an assistant professor at NCCU and director of the dance program. When the American Dance Festival moved to Durham in 1977, the NCCU group was used in a pilot outreach program with Chuck Davis as its artistic director. Now the group performs at exhibitions and attends workshops on tour. In 1982, with Inez Howard of Norfolk State University, Virginia, Iantha Tucker of Morgan State University, Baltimore, and the Historically Black Colleges and Universities Association, Pinckney established the Black College Dance Exchange. She was responsible for NCCU's participation in the International Conference of Blacks in Dance. She has also choreographed for plays for the NCCU Drama Department.

Pizzaro, David (1931–)

Pizzaro, a native of Mt. Vernon, New York, began his career in music as a chorister in the Cathedral Choir School in New York City in 1945. After graduation from Yale, where he studied organ and harpsichord (with Ralph Kirkpatrick), he spent two years as an exchange student in Germany, studying with Michael Schneider. Later

he studied the organ with Norman Coke-Jephcott and Marcel Dupré. Pizarro was the organist and choir director of St. Philip's Episcopal Church in Durham from 1957 to 1964. During that time he was on the music faculty at NCCU and a visiting lecturer at UNC-Chapel Hill. He also organized the Durham branch of the American Guild of Organists.

Pizarro's musicianship and demanding standards produced exceptional concerts for the Durham community. He was enabled to do this by taking advantage of available musician's union funds to pay professional musicians for charitable and church performances. He raised the bar for church music in Durham.

On leaving Durham, Pizarro served St. Stephen's Church in Providence, followed by an appointment as senior organ instructor at the Longy School of Music in Cambridge. He finished his professional career as the organist of the Cathedral of St. John the Divine in New York City. He is a fellow of Trinity College of Music, London, and an associate of the American Guild of Organists.

Poole, Charlie (1892–1931)

Born in Randolph County, Poole and his family moved to Haw River in Alamance County after the turn of the century. At the mills Poole learned to play banjo. In 1920 he joined with his wife's brother Posey, a fiddler, to form the North Carolina Ramblers. He and his group, all musicians from the textile mill communities of the Piedmont, were influential in the development of string band and country music. They established a musical tradition that was picked up by others, including those from Durham's mill community. The band had a highly disciplined and well-rehearsed style of playing, and Poole was considered a master of the banjo. He recorded from 1925 to 1931 and sold over a quarter of a million copies of his music. His band set the standard for much of the string band and bluegrass music that followed. His only son, James "Dunk" Clay Poole (1912–), followed in his father's footsteps.

Prange, Sally Bowen (1927–2007)

Sally Prange, a native of Indiana, earned her B.A. in 1949 from the University of Michigan. She studied ceramics with Grover Cole, Eloise Scholes, and Paul Soldner, and in workshops of the American Crafts Council. She has specialized in porcelain since 1970, reflecting her interest in China's ancient Song Dynasty. Her interest in the natural sciences, especially aquatics and geology, has influenced her pottery forms. She was one of the first ceramicists in North Carolina to create altered rims and sculptured vessels.

Prange's work is found in an impressive array of international collections, including the Victoria & Albert Museum in London, the Museo Internazionale Della Ceramiche in Italy, and the Tajami Technical School in Japan, and the private collections of Princess Anne of Great Britain and Queen Noor of Jordan, as well as a number of museums in North Carolina. She has taught workshops at the Penland School of Crafts, Arrowmont School of Arts and Crafts in Gatlinburg, Tennessee, and the San Jose Museum of Art in California. Articles about her work have appeared in various publications including *Ceramics Review*.

Pratt, Ella Fountain (1914–)

For over forty years Ella Fountain Pratt has been a vital force in bringing dance, dance appreciation, and many of the other arts to Durham. A graduate of Mississippi State College for Women (now Mississippi University for Women), Pratt was a dancer herself and taught dance at Sullins College in Bristol, Virginia, and at Durham's YWCA after she and her husband moved to Durham in 1940. She was among the group that founded the New Performing Dance Company. She began her long career at Duke University as director of stu-

dent activities and in 1969 was appointed director of Duke's Office of Cultural Affairs, where she directed, coordinated, and produced arts performances and exhibitions. The list of major artists she brought to Duke and Durham is long and stellar.

Pratt retired from Duke in 1984 and went directly to the Durham Arts Council (DAC), where she currently directs the Emerging Artists Program. For helping to launch that program the DAC's Lifetime Service Award was created in her honor. In 1980 she received the Fannie Taylor Award for Distinguished Service to the Performing Arts from the Association of College, University, and Community Arts Administrators. With financial support from the association, the Mary Duke Biddle Foundation, the First Presbyterian Church, and the DAC published *I Am Ella Fountain Keesler Pratt: An Oral History*, edited by Alicia Rouverol with a foreword by Reynolds Price. The book was presented during a weekend celebrating Pratt's achievements, along with the première of *A Fanfare for Ella Fountain*, by the North Carolina composer Scott Tilley.

Pratt, Vernon (1940–2000)

Vernon Pratt, a native of Durham, painted in a predominately geometric abstract style. He received a B.F.A. (1962) and M.F.A. (1964) from the San Francisco Art Institute and pursued additional studies at Duke University and UNC-Chapel Hill. In 1964 he joined the Duke Department of Art and Art History, where he taught design and painting as an associate professor of the practice of art. He also taught at Carolina Friends School, as an artist-in-residence at UNC-Charlotte, and at Allied Arts and was an active participant in the Durham Arts Council and Durham Art Guild. He created the Education Wall, a project of Artworks in State Buildings, on the exterior of the Education Building in Raleigh, as well as the sculpture for the building that houses the Durham Arts

Council. Pratt's work is in many collections, including that of the Rochester Institute of Technology, New York. His awards included residence grants from the Virginia Center for Creative Arts, a purchase award from the R. J. Reynolds Corporation, an award from the National Endowment for the Arts, and professional development grants from the Duke Institute of Arts. He was also named an outstanding professor at Duke. Besides his artwork, Pratt's passion was to play jazz on the saxophone.

Preiss, Andrew (1959–)

Andrew Preiss, a sculptor and furniture designer who works in metal, was born in Durham. He attended Duke University and obtained a B.A. in 1991. While at Duke he studied sculpture with William Noland and painting with Vernon Pratt. He creates sculptures and designs for public and private spaces on commission and has had his own studio, ARP Design Studio, since 1999 in the Liberty Arts building on Foster Street. Preiss's commissions include a set of gates at the George Watts Hill Pavilion and work for the Bryan Center at Duke University, Durham City Hall, the American Tobacco Historic District, Duke Gardens, and restaurants such as Café Parizade and George's Garage. He also creates functional items such as lighting, seating, and tables.

Price, Reynolds (1933–)

Born in Macon in Warren County and raised in Raleigh, Reynolds Price has lived his adult life in Durham and Orange counties. He is a James B. Duke Professor of English at Duke University and a prize-winning novelist, essayist, poet, dramatist, and translator of the gospels—twenty-five books in all.

Among Price's most successful novels is his first: *A Long and Happy Life*, which was adapted for the stage and produced at Duke in 1976, and later published as *Early Dark*. His other plays include *August Snow*, given its première in 1985 at Hendrix College in Conway, Arkansas. *August Snow* is the first play in a trilogy that also includes *Night Dance* and *Better Days*. All three plays were workshop productions at Duke in 1987 and given their première as a group at the Cleveland Playhouse in 1989. Price's sixth play *Full Moon* has been produced at Duke, in Jackson, Mississippi, and in San Francisco.

Pridgin, Samuel Lee (1910–)

Samuel Pridgin grew up in Durham and worked at the Durham Hosiery Mill. As a boy he learned basic chords on the guitar from his father and spent time watching the Reverend Gary Davis play on the streets, studying his technique and incorporating it into his own playing. Known as Starvin' Sam, Pridgin was a lifelong musical associate of Hash House Harvey Ellington. They played together in the Swingbillies and the Tobacco Tags and developed a medicine show act, which they performed as late as the 1980s.

Pringle, Jim (1943–)

Jim Pringle, a potter and native North Carolinian, moved to the Triangle in 1971. After receiving a B.S. from NCSU and an M.F.A from East Carolina University, he pursued further studies at the New York State College of Ceramics at Alfred University. He was one of the organizers of the Carolina Designer Craftsmen Guild, based in Raleigh. Examples of his work are in the collection of the Smithsonian Institution.

Pyne, George Clinton, Jr. (1914–1996)

George Pyne, a native of Petersburg, Virginia, was educated at Virginia Polytech Institute, where he received a B.S. in 1936. He secured a position with the firm of Atwood and Weeks Architects and Engineers in Durham in 1937 as an architectural draftsman and remained there for the next six years. During his military service (1942–46)

Pyne worked as an architectural engineer with the U.S. Air Force, building air fields. With the invasion of Italy, Pyne was sent to southern Italy to build an air field in the historic Greek city of Paestum. During construction, when Etruscan underground tombs were unearthed, Pyne stopped construction and called in Italian historians. The site yielded the first Etruscan remains in southern Italy, including four hundred tombs.

After the war Pyne returned to the H. Raymond Weeks firm as a licensed architect. The firm became Harris and Pyne Architects and Engineers after the death of Weeks in 1960. With Wilton E. Harris, who had worked with Atwood and Weeks as a structural engineer for many years, Pyne created a building design team of high quality, which continued for another thirty-six years. Projects included classroom additions to Duke Memorial Methodist Church, an eight-story women's dormitory at NCCU, a science building at Durham High School, and Chewning and Lowes Grove middle schools.

For his service to the arts over years of civic involvement in the Durham Art Guild, the Durham Arts Council, the North Carolina Museum of Art, and the Historic Preservation Society of Durham (HPSD), HPSD awarded him the Bartlett Durham Award in 1991. In addition, he and Mrs. Pyne were recognized for their years of work in historic preservation by the renaming of the HPSD annual preservation award as "The George and Mary Pyne Historic Preservation Award."

Randall, Dale B. J. (1929–)

Dale Randall is a professor of English and of the practice of drama at Duke University and was the interim director of the Program of Drama from 1991 to 1992. His play *Patient on the Table* was produced at World Premières in 1992. In 2001 he was associate director and dramaturg for the Duke mainstage production of *The Changeling* (by Thomas Middleton and William Rowley), and

he was dramaturg for a number of other productions, including *Last Train to Nibroc* at Manbites Dog Theater. Randall has also appeared in a number of script-in-hand productions.

Reardon, Kenneth J. (1910–1994)

Kenneth Reardon, a native of Norwood, Massachusetts, was educated at Boston University (1935) and learned his craft of dramaturgy on the job, working with the Repertory Theater in Boston. After service in the Second World War he came to Duke University in 1947 to teach in the English department and head the Duke Players. In his first season at Duke he directed *The Male Animal* (James Thurber and Elliot Nugent), *Angel Street* (Patrick Hamilton), and *The Late George Apley* (John P. Marquand and George S. Kaufman), all of which were performed in Page Auditorium. In the following year he directed all three mainstage productions with William H. Hardy. Hardy, who was then teaching engineering at Duke, himself directed two workshop productions, *Julius Caesar* and *Tartuffe*, and went on to become a novelist, teacher of script writing at UNC-Chapel Hill, and director of the outdoor drama *Unto These Hills*.

From 1949 to 1950 the Duke Players were given the Branson Building on East Campus to renovate as a theater. Reardon and Joseph Wetherby made extensive alterations to the space to create an arena theater, the first in the area. It opened in the summer of 1951 with a Play Production class doing Molière's *The Miser*.

In his twenty years as director of Duke Players Reardon directed forty-five plays, ranging from *Richard II* to *Look Back in Anger* (John Osborne), *Desire under the Elms* (O'Neill), and *The Zoo Story* (Albee). In addition he oversaw the innovative series "Scenes from Opera" in conjunction with the Music Department, which ran from 1960 to 1965. Reardon founded the South East Theater Conference and was also in the community, directing plays for the Theater Guild, giving talks on drama to many local clubs and organizations, and teaching classes in drama for both Allied Arts and YWCA programs. In 1968 he resigned as director of Duke Drama, but he continued teaching at Duke until his retirement in 1980.

Reinhart, Charles (1930–)

Charles Reinhart, president and director of the American Dance Festival, has dominated and promoted dance in America for decades. After graduating from Rutgers University in 1952 and pursuing graduate studies at the University of Copenhagen from 1956 to 1957, he worked as a producer, manager, festival director, consultant, and administrator in the arts. Reinhart was appointed director of ADF in 1968 and in 1977 moved the festival from the Connecticut College campus to Duke University.

From 1996 to 2003 Reinhart was an artistic director for dance at the Kennedy Center in Washington, sharing the position with his wife Stephanie until her death in 2002. He also worked as a producer for the New York City Center Spring Dance Festival (1969–73), the ANTA Theater at the City Center for Music and Drama (1968–73), and the Dance Repertory Season at the Billy Rose Theatre. For the National Endowment for the Arts he developed and was the national coordinator of the Dance Touring Program (1967–78) and the dance component of the Artists-in-Schools Program (1970–81). In 1966 he helped to implement the Cultural Presentation Program for the U.S. Department of State and in the early 1970s he joined the advisory committee of the Asia Society Performing Arts Program. Among the internationally famous dance companies he has managed are the Paul Taylor Dance Company, Meredith Monk / The House, the Glen Tetley Dance Company, the Don Redlich Dance Company, the Lucas Hoving Dance Company, and the Donald Mc-Kayle Dance Company. The French government named him an Officier dans L'Ordre des Arts et des Lettres in 1986 and a Commander of Arts and Letters in 2002. Other awards and honors include Dance/USA's honors for Lifetime Achievement in Dance in 1994; the Capezio Dance Award in 1996; an award from *Dance Magazine* in 2003; an Emmy for the PBS series *Free to Dance*, which aired in 2001; and an honorary degree from Duke University in 2003.

Reinhart, Stephanie (1944–2002)

An arts administrator and tireless advocate of dance the world over, Stephanie Reinhart directed the American Dance Festival with her husband Charles. She was educated at the University of Wisconsin and George Washington University and in 1974 attended the Harvard University Summer Institute in arts administration. She joined the National Endowment for the Arts in 1969 and subsequently administered its dance and education programs and helped to plan and develop the artists-in-schools program. She was also a member of the Dance Notation Bureau's professional advisory committee and co-chairwoman of the World Dance Alliance's committee for promoting the dance. With her wide administrative experience, she was an invaluable addition to ADF, which she joined in 1977 as director of planning and development. In 1993 she became co-director with her husband of ADF and received a Fulbright research grant to study the history of Argentine modern dance. She and her husband became artistic directors for dance at the Kennedy Center for the Performing Arts in 1996. The two received many awards in recognition of their importance to the world of dance. Reinhart lectured widely on American modern dance and arts administration, and her essays appear in several dance books. The ADF/Stephanie Reinhart Fund for New Works and Scholarship was established in her memory in 2003.

Riddell, Richard V. (1950–)

Richard Riddell, a native of Rochester, Minnesota, joined Duke University in 1992 as the Mary D. B. T. and James H. Semans Professor of the Practice of Theater and to head the Drama program. In 2001 he became the first chairman of the newly organized Department of Theater Studies, which he was instrumental in establishing. In his first year at Duke he directed *Our Town*, and later restructured the series *World Premières* as the New Works Festival, which invited students, faculty, and staff to submit one-act plays for production. He encouraged collaboration with other departments, resulting in co-productions of *Carousel* with Hoof 'n' Horn and the music department (1997) and *Helen* with the classics department (2000). He reinstated Theater Previews in 1996 with *Kudzu: A Southern Musical* and reestablished contact with Emanuel Azenberg as a producer and teacher. He also led a two-million-dollar fund-raising campaign to enlarge theater, classroom, and office space for Theater Studies, which opened in the fall of 2003. He resigned as chairman the same year.

Riddell is an expert in lighting design and worked with over forty professional productions between 1980 and 2001 in such places as Ford's Theater in Washington, the American Repertory Theater in New York, the La Jolla Playhouse in California, the Guthrie Theater in Minnesota, and the Oregon Shakespeare Festival. In addition, he has designed lighting for fifteen operas for the English National Opera, the Santa Fe Opera, the Houston Grand Opera, the Kentucky Opera, the Alte Oper Frankfurt, and the Netherlands Opera. Among the many awards he has won for his lighting designs are a Tony Award, Drama Desk Award, and Joseph Maharam Award in Design for *Big River* (William Hauptman and Roger Miller) in 1985.

Riley, Laura Ames (1952–)

Laura Riley, a mixed-media and dimensional artist, was born in Concord, Massachusetts, grew up in Connecticut, and while still in high school began her art studies with Fred Schall, a designer, painter, dioramist, and assemblage artist who has been a major influence on her work. She also studied with George Baer. She attended the Worcester Museum School of Art, affiliated with Clark University, where she graduated (1973) with a double major in painting and sculpture. After moving to Miami she studied print making with Shirley I. Green at the Metropolitan Museum and Art Studio at the Biltmore in Coral Gables. In 1992 she moved with her family to Chapel Hill, and for ten years she worked in her studio in the old Venable Tobacco Company building in Durham, which at the time was a haven for artists and a hive of offices of small businesses.

During these years Riley moved from print making to dimensional art, which incorporates drawing and sculpture as well as photography, sound, and light in three-dimensional space. Although dimensional art by its nature is usually temporary, permanent forms of her work have also been commissioned for the Coconut Grove Bank in Miami and the Sterling Regency I building in Cary, where she worked with the architects to create sculptural art that flanks the main entrance. She has also had many commissions for temporary installations.

In 2004 an Emerging Artists grant from the Durham Arts Council enabled Riley to work in bronze at Liberty Arts in Durham to create permanent and outdoor sculptures. She also works as a conservator of paper art.

Roberson, Ruth (1931–)

Ruth Roberson, a native North Carolinian, received a B.S. from East Carolina University in 1953. She began quilting in Durham in 1976 and taught at the Duke University Crafts Center while writing a monthly column about quilting for the *News and Observer*. In 1977 she was one of the founders of the Durham Quilters Guild (later the Durham/Orange Quilters Guild). While attending an Earthwatch Expedition in Alabama with the folklorist Jane Sapp, she learned how to document quilts. In 1983 she became director of the North Carolina Quilt Project, which documented ten thousand quilts made in North Carolina before 1976.

Roberson's main interest has been in women's lives and quilting as part of their lives. Consequently the North Carolina Quilt Project gathered information about the owners and makers of the quilts as well as documenting the quilts' histories, construction, and designs. The project received financial support from the North Carolina Arts Council, the National Endowment for the Arts, the North Carolina Quilt Symposium, and the Z. Smith Reynolds Foundation. Project co-sponsors included the North Carolina Quilt Symposium and the North Carolina Museum of History, which held a quilt exhibition in 1988 and holds the project's records. The project culminated in the publication of Roberson's book *North Carolina Quilts*, published by the University of North Carolina Press.

Rowles, Ann (1947–)
Ann Rowles, a sculptor, was born in California, grew up in North Carolina, and received her B.A. in 1969 and M.F.A. in 1990 from UNC-Chapel Hill. She also studied art at UNC-Greensboro. From 1975 to 1995 she worked in Durham. She has taught sculpture and drawing at UNC-Chapel Hill, NCCU, and Western Carolina University. Her awards include a Visual Artist Fellowship from the North Carolina Arts Council, the Triangle Arts Award in Visual Arts presented by the *Independent Weekly*, and an Emerging Artists Grant from the Durham Arts Council. She has exhibited widely in public and private ven-

ues and her work is in collections in California, Georgia, Massachusetts, New York, North Carolina, and Virginia. Currently she lives in Atlanta, where she is a studio artist at the Atlanta Contemporary Art Center.

Salim, Yusef (1930–)
The jazz musician Brother Yusef Salim was born in Baltimore and grew up in a musical household where local artists played regular jam sessions. He took up the piano at an early age and became a jazz musician. In Baltimore from the 1940s to the 1960s he played and recorded with a number of influential artists, including Leo Parker. He moved to Durham in 1974 and opened a nightclub and restaurant where a number of local and national jazz artists performed. While the club is no longer in existence, Salim continues to perform in the area.

Sanderson, Ormond
Sanderson, a native of North Carolina, works with enamel on metal as well as ceramics. Trained as a musician, with a B.M. and M.M. from the University of Michigan, he later studied with Gerome Kamroski and Peter Ostuni. In 1958 he left teaching and settled in Durham with Bob Black, a potter, to become an artist full time, settling on land belonging to his uncle. The two established a studio and used rooms in the old farmhouse to exhibit and sell pottery, calling their enterprise Straw Valley. They encouraged other artists and craftsmen throughout the area in the development and appreciation of crafts.

Sanderson has exhibited his work widely, including at the American Pavilion of the 1964 World's Fair, the Museum of Contemporary Crafts in New York, and leading museums and universities. His work is in private collections as well as in the Phillips Gallery, the Everson Museum of Art in New York, and at the Royal House of Monaco. He has received awards from the Mint Museum in Charlotte and the Southeast Exhibition of Craftsmen in Atlanta.

Santana, Carlota (1941–)

The dancer and choreographer Carlota Santana began her career performing with the Maria Alba Company with José Molina, Roberto Cartagena, and Rosario Galán. She instituted the company's arts-in-education program, which integrated Spanish dance into school curricula. With Roberto Lorca Flamenco in 1983 she founded Vivo Carlota Santana, a dance school and flamenco company. Since 1997 the Maria Alba Company has been based in both New York and Durham, where it has received support from the North Carolina Arts Council's Arts-in-Education program as well as the Durham Arts Council, the City of Durham, and the Barrie Wallace Fund for the Arts of the Triangle Community Foundation.

Santana is on the faculty at Duke University and has also taught at New York and Long Island universities. Her company has performed in Durham at the American Dance Festival, in New York at Lincoln Center, the Joyce Theater, and the New Victory Theater, and in Colombia and Spain. It commissions and performs new flamenco story-ballets and recently gave the premières of *Federico*, *Navidad Flamenca*, *Bailaor/ Bailaor*, and *Mano, Mano*. In recognition of Santana's commitment to creating new works and developing young dancers and choreographers, *Dance Magazine* designated her "the keeper of Flamenco."

Sartor, Margaret (1959–)

Margaret Sartor, a photographer, graphic designer, editor, and author, graduated in 1981 from UNC-Chapel Hill. She moved to Durham, where she is now a visiting lecturer in public policy studies at the Terry Sanford Institute of Public Policy at Duke University and a research associate at the Center for Documentary Studies. She is the editor of *What Was True: The Photographs and Notebooks of William Gedney* (with Geoff Dyer), *Their Eyes Meeting the World* (by Robert Coles), and *Gertrude Blom: Bearing Witness* (with Alex Harris). Her youthful diaries, shaped for publication as *Miss American Pie*, were published in 2006. She is the recipient of numerous awards, including a North Carolina Visual Artists Project Grant. Her photographs have been published in books, magazines, and journals throughout the United States and are in public and private collections, including those of the Birmingham Museum of Art in Alabama, the Museum of Fine Arts in Houston, the Ogden Museum of Southern Art at the University of New Orleans, the Mead Art Museum at Amherst College, the North Carolina Museum of Art, and the Rare Book, Manuscript, and Special Collections Library and the Center for Documentary Studies at Duke University.

Saville, Eugenia (1914–2006)

Eugenia Saville taught in the music department at Duke University for thirty years before retiring in the 1970s. She earned an M.M. at Columbia University and was an accomplished pianist and musicologist, with a special interest in the music of Giovanni Carlo Maria Clari. Saville wrote *Italian Vocal Duets of the Early Eighteenth Century* and many articles for scholarly journals. Her special contribution to musical life at Duke was to establish and lead the Duke Madrigal Singers, made up of singers from the student body and the community. The group gave regular concerts and won many awards.

Scrap Exchange

The Scrap Exchange is a nonprofit organization whose mission is to promote creativity, environmental awareness, and community through the reuse of materials. The organization collects clean reusable materials from industries, businesses, municipal sources, and individuals and distributes them through the Creative ReUse Center in downtown Durham. Chris Rosenthal and a board of directors began the Scrap Exchange in 1991. Rosenthal had worked for a similar program in Australia called "The Reverse Garbage Truck." The Art Gallery at the Scrap Exchange shows works by artists who create artworks with the reused material. There is also a traveling creative arts program that goes to fairs and festivals throughout the Southeast. Locally the Scrap Exchange participates in the Bimbe Festival, Earth Day, and Downtown Durham's Culture Crawl, and offers workshops for teachers and children.

SeeSaw Studio

SeeSaw Studio is a free, after-school design and business program for motivated and creative Durham youth from thirteen to twenty-one years of age. It was founded in 1998 by Stephen A. Wainwright, James B. Duke Professor Emeritus of Zoology at Duke University. He based his idea for the organization on the Kazuri Bead Company in Nairobi, which gave employment to women without hope. SeeSaw Studio provides workshops and apprenticeships that focus on design, entrepreneurship, art, and life skills, and addresses the lack of opportunities for career training for low-income youth and teens with chronically high dropout rates. Apprentices work on commissioned projects for community clients and on retail products of their own design as well as SeeSaw's own line of FunKtional products. They create floating silkscreen banners, painted metal sculpture, low-relief woodcarving, and fiber wall hangings. SeeSaw Studio has received grants from the National Endowment for the Arts, the North Carolina Arts Council, the Governor's Crime Commission, and the Kellogg Foundation, and matching funds from the Mary Duke Biddle Foundation for artists' residencies.

Shakespeare and Originals

Shakespeare and Originals was founded in 1999 by Jay Oberski to present "actor-powered Shakespeare and original work by Triangle playwrights." Oberski directed David Turkel's *Crimson & Clover* (1999), *King Lear* (1999), *Ein Kleiner Kowboy* (2000), *Life, Love, Cows* (2001), *Prufrock* (which Oberski adapted from T. S. Eliot's poem, 2002), and *Love's Labors Lost* (2002). Other productions include Michael A. Smith's *A Mouthfulla Sacco & Vanzetti* (2000) and *Hurricane Salad* (2002), Lissa Brennan's adaptation of *Lysistrata, Loose Lips Sink Ships* (2003), and John Justice's *Two Sams* (2003). Most of these plays were produced at Manbites Dog Theater.

Shakur, Sadiyah (1946–)

The dancer, choreographer, and teacher Sadiyah Shakur is the founder and artistic director of Collage, a youth dance company based at the Hayti Heritage Center. Founded in 1985 and now a program of the Durham Arts Council's dance school, it performs African, Caribbean, jazz, and modern dance, and hip-hop. A native New Yorker with a degree in education, Shakur was one of the original members of the Chuck Davis Dance Company in New York before coming to Durham with the group in 1978. With an Emerging Artist Grant from the Durham Arts Council, Shakur studied dance and song in Africa. Collage has performed at the Brooklyn Academy of Music, Exploris Museum in Raleigh, and the North Carolina School of Science and Math.

Sharpe, Lois (1953–)

Lois Sharpe, a potter, works in porcelain, using a barnacle glaze she developed herself. Born in North Carolina, raised in Durham, and trained as a nurse at the Watts Hospital School of Nursing, she soon shifted her interest to pottery. She studied ceramics at the Penland School of Crafts and in numerous workshops and was a founding member of Clayworks Pottery Guild. She supplies galleries from Maine to the Virgin Islands that continue to commission her work. Sharpe teaches at the Durham Arts Council.

Shatzman, Merrill (1956–)

A native of New York, Merrill Shatzman is a print-maker, graphic designer, and artist who moved to Durham in 1985. She received her B.F.A. in 1978 from the Rhode Island School of Design and her M.A. and M.F.A. in 1981 from the University of Wisconsin. She taught at Sonoma State University and California State University in Long Beach before arriving at Duke University in 1985, where she is now an associate professor of the practice of visual arts. Shatzman has also taught at the Southeastern College Art Conference in Carrboro.

Shatzman's abstract work primarily involves printmaking techniques such as etching, woodcut, lithography, and silkscreen but also incorporates drawing and painting media. Her many awards include the Missouri Springfield Art Museum Purchase Award at the Prints U.S.A. Exhibition in 2003. Shown nationally, her work appears in the Boston Public Library and in numerous museums, including the National Museum of American Art in Washington, the Brooklyn Museum of Art, the Fogg Art Museum at Harvard, the Grunwald Center for the Graphic Arts at the University of California, Los Angeles, and the Mint Museum in Charlotte.

Shepard statue

The larger-than-life statue of James E. Shepard (1875–1947), founder and president of the National Religious and Training School and Chautauqua, later North Carolina College, is located prominently on the campus of the institution now known as North Carolina Central University. Commissioned by the James E. Shepard Memorial Foundation, the statue was dedicated by the Prince Hall Grand Lodge Free and Accepted Masons of North Carolina and unveiled by Shepard's confidant and friend James T. Taylor and his granddaughter Carolyn Smith Green on June 1, 1957.

The artist who created the sculpture, William Zorach (1887–1966), was born in Lithuania and immigrated to the United States in 1891. Growing up in Ohio, Zorach studied at the Cleveland Art School before going to New York City and then Paris. He and his wife, Marguerite, were among the avant-garde in American painting, both having been represented in the famous New York Armory Show of 1913. Zorach turned to sculpture in 1917. First influenced by cubism, he later developed a personal, restrained, dignified style influenced by Egyptian and Greek sculpture. Many of his works deal with the theme of love and devotion. Among Zorach's works are *Mother and Child* (Metropolitan Museum of Art), *Spirit of the Dance* (Radio City Music Hall), and *Benjamin Franklin* (Post Office, Washington, D.C.).

Simonetti, Vincent (1944–)

A native of New Jersey, Simonetti received his training in tuba and conducting from the Manhattan School of Music. He was a student of William Bell and Joseph Novatory, among other notable tuba players. He played with a number of ensembles and opera orchestras before moving to Durham in 1967 to join the North Carolina Symphony, with which he remained until its move to Raleigh in 1975. From the start, Simonetti was involved in Durham's broader musical community; he founded the Durham Symphony in 1976 and served as its conductor for eight years. With tuba as his lifelong love, he started a business selling tubas and euphonia the same year he co-founded the Durham Community Concert Band.

Success in this endeavor led him to establish the Tuba Exchange—the only store of its kind in North Carolina, which buys, appraises, and sells historic brass instruments.

Smith, Andre Raphael (1962–)

A graduate of Hillside High School and a student of Clarke Egerton, Durham native Andre Smith received an M.A. from Yale University, where he began studies in conducting. He received a diploma in conducting from the Curtis Institute of Music and an advanced certificate in orchestral conducting from Juilliard. He made his début with the New York Philharmonic in 1999 and went on to numerous guest-conducting appearances with the Cleveland and Chicago orchestras, among others. He is assistant conductor of the Philadelphia Orchestra.

Smullin, Frank (1943–1983)

A native of Massachusetts, Frank Smullin was a noted sculptor, draftsman, and computer artist who in later years called himself an "analytic constructivist." For four years before his death he produced computer-aided tubular sculptures, but primarily he worked in wood, using a chainsaw and chisel for his reliefs, and drew fine figurative drawings. Smullin received his B.A. in 1965 from Harvard College; his B.F.A. from Boston University in 1968; and his M.F.A. from the City University of New York in 1970. He pursued additional studies at Skowhegan School of Painting and Sculpture, Maine. He joined Duke University in 1972 and was sculptor-in-residence and instructor in the Art Department as well as a fellow of the Institute of the Arts. With Stephen A. Wainwright, a zoologist, and George Pearsall, an engineer, he taught the course "Structures" at Duke. He was a visiting artist at Sculpture Space in Utica, New York, and at the Center for Advanced Visual Studies, MIT. Smullin's work has been shown widely here and abroad.

Solow, David (1961 -)

David Solow, a native of New Jersey, studied at Duke University, Columbia University, and the North Carolina School of the Arts before completing the creative writing program in poetry and a B.F.A. at UNC-Chapel Hill. He is the recipient of many grants and fellowships, most recently an Art Omi Residency, a North Carolina Artist Fellowship, and a Kohler Arts/Industry residency. His work has been exhibited at universities, museums, and galleries throughout the United States.

Sprinkle, William Van Eaton (1906–1965)

William Sprinkle was the son of a Methodist minister in Mockville, North Carolina. After earning his undergraduate degree at Duke University, he completed the architecture course at Yale University in 1928. For two years he worked without pay for an architectural firm in New York, painting watercolors to earn his keep. In 1930 he returned to Durham to work for the architect Howard Haines, gaining experience in residential design and church facilities. Sprinkle opened his own office in 1934 and completed a number of commissions for Duke. Among them were four rustic log cabins in the woods for the law school dean, who was convinced that the best way for students to learn law and social responsibility was as Lincoln had done, in a quiet and simple setting. *Time* magazine called the complex, completed in 1938, "an architectural, if not intellectual, wonder for U.S. higher education."

From 1934 to 1941 Sprinkle designed many fine residences for local professionals. He joined the U. S. Army Engineers during the Second World War and, with the rank of captain, worked with British Army and Navy engineers to design and plan the construction of prefabricated harbors to be used for invasions of Europe. These harbors were vitally important to the success of war operations and to the eventual Allied victory. After the war Sprinkle resumed his practice, designing public and private buildings, including many substantial residences in Durham. In 1950 he hired Dorris Stanley, the first female draftsperson to work in an architectural firm in North Carolina. Stanley, born in 1926 and raised in Farmington, Maine, graduated from the University of Maine in Orono in 1948 with a degree in psychology, taking some drafting classes because she enjoyed them. She settled in Durham in 1950, and while looking for work was told that a local architect needed a draftsperson. Sprinkle offered her the job and she found her calling. She commented, "The first day of work, when I put pencil to the paper, I thought I had died and gone to heaven." After Sprinkle's death Stanley continued to design residences until her retirement in 1989.

Stevens, Billy (1952–)

A rock-and-roll musician from Illinois, Billy Stevens arrived in Durham in the 1970s to attend Duke University, where he majored in comparative religion. He ran a radio show for many years and in the late 1970s was an owner with the jazz artist Yusef Salim of the Sallam Cultural Center. As part of his radio show, he developed a program on the history of rock-and-roll and its blues origins. Over time he expanded the program into a history of popular American music and its African and European roots. From 1986 he took this program on tour around the world under the sponsorship of the Department of State's U.S. Information Agency. In the early years of the new century Stevens obtained an M.A. in southern studies from the University of Mississippi; he remains involved in Durham's music scene.

Stevens, Cici (1956–)

Cici Stevens is a sculptor whose installations highlight the interrelatedness of the natural world and the industrial environment. She is particu-larly interested in the process of decay—the changes in structures over time and the "unbuilding" of natural forces like oxidation, freezing, and condensation. In 1983 she received a B.S. degree from the University of Wisconsin, Madison, in her native state. Since settling in the Triangle in 1989 she has seen her works shown throughout North Carolina and has received commissions from ArtQuest, the Greenhill Center for North Carolina Art in Greensboro, and Durham County Mental Health, among others.

Storer, Jeff (1953–)

Jeff Storer, since 1982 a member of the Duke University Department of Theater Studies (originally the Program in Drama), is also the artistic director of Manbites Dog Theater, which he co-founded in 1987. Between the two positions Storer has directed over seventy productions. The more notable for Duke have included *Carousel* (in collaboration with Hoof 'n' Horn and the Music Department, 1996), *Darker Face of the Earth* (2000), and *Cloud Nine* (2003); and for Manbites Dog, *Execution of Justice* (1994) and *How I Learned to Drive* (1998). He has also directed plays for the Public Theater and Circle Repertory Theater (both in New York), Rollins College in Florida, Boston University, the Dallas Theater Center, and the Paul Mellon Arts Center in Pennsylvania. In addition, Storer is the co-author of nine plays: *Heat Lightning* (1986); *The Occasional Waltz* (1986); *Deadline at Dawn* (1987); *Indecent Materials / Report from the Holocaust*, (1990); *Hotline* (1991); *Walking Miracles* (1997); *802701* (2000); *A Tune for Tommy* (2000); and *Plays Well with Others* (2001). All were produced at Manbites Dog Theater and directed by Storer. *Indecent Materials* also played at the Public Theater as part of the New York Shakespeare Festival (2000).

Summer Theater at Duke

Summer Theater at Duke was founded by John Clum in 1972 as a supplement to the training that students received as well as a much-needed boost to theater in the area. In the first year Clum directed all three plays: *A Thurber Carnival*, *What the Butler Saw* (Joe Orton), and *Under Milkwood* (Dylan Thomas). Scott J. Parker, in 1971 appointed technical director for Duke Players, became technical director for summer theater and by 1973 sometimes director, including of *Spoon River Anthology* (Edgar Lee Masters), *Private Lives* (Noel Coward), *When You Comin' Back, Red Ryder?* (Mark Medoff), and *Loot* (Joe Orton). The series used guest actors who belonged to Actors Equity and many guest directors, including Richard S. Mogavero, William Shawn Smith, John Younger, Kevin Patterson, Brenda Mezz, and Linda Wright. From 1978 to 1981 Richard Aumiller shared direction of the series with Clum, directing two of the four plays each season. Subsequent guest directors included Ed Hill and Jeff Storer, who directed *Man of La Mancha* (1983) and *Old Times* (1984). Other notable productions include *The Lion in Winter* (1975), the première of Reynolds Price's *A Long and Happy Life* (1976), *Design for Living* (1980), and an opera by Robert Ward, *Claudia LeGare* (1981), all directed by Clum. The theater closed in 1984.

Summers, Marie (1933–)

Marie Summers, a North Carolinian, is a potter who works in clay. After graduating from UNC-Greensboro she worked with several well-known potters, including Karen Karnes and Michael "Mick" Casson. At first she worked on the wheel, making functional pottery, but she now creates pieces by hand. She has had numerous private commissions and received awards and prizes for her work. Although retired, she still crafts sculptural pieces and works occasionally with small groups, teaching clay work as a means of self-discovery.

Tate, Grady (1932–)

Grady Tate, a jazz trumpeter, drummer, and singer, started singing at the age of four at church and in school. He picked up the drums at the age of five and taught himself how to play. A graduate of Hillside High School, he studied music under "Shorty" Hall. It was during his time in the Air Force in the early 1950s that he learned to play jazz drums. After returning to Durham he received a degree from NCCU in the late 1950s. He then moved to Washington, D.C., where he taught in the high schools and resumed his music career, later joining the faculty of Howard University.

Throughout his musical career Tate has played and recorded with a number of well-known musicians, including Stan Getz, Sarah Vaughan, Lena Horne, and André Previn. He spent six years on Johnny Carson's "Tonight Show" playing drums and has received recognition for his jazz and blues singing. Tate has returned to Durham in recent years to participate in jazz concerts at NCCU and the Hayti Center. He has also appeared with the jazz singer Nnenna Freelon, also a native of Durham. A dynamic drummer and singer, Tate in recent years has focused on jazz singing, and at the age of seventy released a vocal CD.

Terry, David (1962–)

The artist and illustrator David Terry, a native of Tennessee, received a B.A. in 1982 from the University of the South in Sewanee, Tennessee, and two M.A.'s in 1989 from Middlebury College in Vermont and Duke University, and pursued additional studies at the University of Virginia and Oxford University. He has lived and worked in Durham since 1987. Terry's work is drawn or painted solely in pen and ink on paper, with tinting done in watercolor and gold inks. He has completed many published book covers and numerous privately commissioned works. His drawings and illustrations have appeared in newspapers and magazines throughout the United States, including the *Oxford American*, the *Washington Post*, the *News and Observer*, and *Southern Exposure*. He also completed advertising commissions for Senator John Edwards's presidential campaign in 2004, National Public Radio, the National AIDS Memorial, the Cathedral of St. John the Divine in New York, Whole Foods, Barnes & Noble, Duke University, and the North Carolina Museum of Life and Science. He was awarded an Emerging Artist Grant from the Durham Arts Council.

Terry, Sonny (1911–1996)
McGhee, Brownie (1915–1986)

Sonny Terry was born in Greensboro as Saunders Terrell and was blind by the age of sixteen as a result of two injuries. At an early age he learned to play the harmonica from his father and developed a distinctive "whoopin'" style. Blind Boy Fuller, whom he met in 1934, persuaded Terry to move to Durham, where they performed as a team. They recorded together from 1937 until Fuller's death in 1941. By that time Terry had met Brownie McGhee, a musician from Tennessee, after J. B. Long, the manager of a department store, brought them together for a recording session. Developing a partnership that lasted into the 1970s, they moved to New York in 1942 and became the first blues artists to tour in Europe in the 1950s; they influenced a new generation of British musicians, who emerged as famous rock musicians in later decades.

Tetel-Hanks, Joan (1934–)

Joan Tetel-Hanks is a creative drama and sociodrama specialist with B.S. and M.S. degrees from the University of Wisconsin. She has done additional work there in management skills and techniques, and in cultural resources management. Since settling in the Durham area she has been involved in many civic efforts related to the development of the arts. During her tenure in the Durham school system (1965 to 1970) she brought creative and socio-drama to four middle schools, helping students interact with those of other races.

From 1991 to 2001 Tetel-Hanks developed and managed an innovative program at the Duke University Medical Center. It has trained actors to portray patients in a variety of situations and with a variety of diseases to help medical students, residents, nurses, and physician assistants learn to interact with sick people and diagnose diseases. Tetel-Hanks designed the cases, wrote the scripts, and recruited and coached the actors. She has written numerous articles and produced videos on aspects of this work.

Theater Previews

Theater Previews, originally known as Broadway Previews and sponsored by Duke University for the Duke, Durham, and Triangle communities, was designed to present non-reviewed early tryouts of plays and to provide internships for drama students at the university. Many of the early shows were produced by Emanuel Azenberg, a noted Broadway producer who was instrumental in starting the series in 1998. Since 1998 the shows have been produced in collaboration with commercial and other nonprofit professional producers. The first season had two shows produced by Azenberg: *Long Day's Journey into Night* (Eugene O'Neill), with Jack Lemmon and Kevin Spacey, and *Broadway Bound* (Neil Simon), with Linda Lavin and Jason Alexander. Productions in the following seasons were, in 1987, *A Month of Sundays* (Bob Larbey), with Jason Robards and Patricia Elliot, and *An Eve-*

ning with Waylon Jennings; in 1988, *A Walk in the Woods* (Lee Blessing), with Sam Waterston and Robert Prosky, and *My Heart Belongs to Daddy* (Laury Marker and Nelsie Spenser), starring the authors; and in 1989, *Metamorphosis* (an adaptation of Kafka's story by Steven Berkoff), with Mikhail Baryshnikov and Madeleine Potter, *Moonlight and Valentino* (Ellen Simon), with Robert Duncan and Sarah Fleming, *The Circle* (Somerset Maugham), with Rex Harrison and Patricia Conolly, *Artist Descending a Staircase* (Tom Stoppard), with Stephanie Roth and Harold Gould, and *The Merry Wives of Windsor, Texas* (adapted by John L. Haber), with Charles Antalosky and Ollie O'Shea.

The number of productions each year decreased in the 1990s. In 1990 Avner Eisenberg wrote and starred in *Avner the Eccentric*. Productions in the following years were, in 1991, *Lucifer's Child* (William Luce), with Julie Harris; in 1992, *1492* (Christopher Bishop with Ben Shelfer), with Leroi Freeman and Robert Cuccioli; in 1993, *Laughter on the 23rd Floor* (Neil Simon), with Nathan Lane, Mark Linn-Baker, and Randy Graff; in 1998, the musical *Kudzu* (Jack Herrick, Doug Marlette, and Bland Simpson), with Nicole Bradin and the Red Clay Ramblers; in 1999, *Eleanor: An American Love Story* (Thomas Tierney, Jonathan Bolt, and John Forster), with Anthony Cummings and Anne Kanengeiser; in 2000, *Birdy* (William Wharton), with Robert Hogan, Michael Pitt, and Grant Show; in 2001, *A Thousand Clowns* (Herb Gardner), with Tom Selleck; and in 2002, *Paper Doll*, with F. Murray Abraham and Marlo Thomas. The producing director for Theater Previews is Zannie Voss, a member of the Department of Theater Studies.

Since 1989, through Theater Previews the university has sponsored Professional Workshop Productions. These have included *Oscar Over Here* (Romulus Linney), directed by Jeff Storer at the Manbites Dog Theater; *Those Women* (Nor Hall,

Ellen Hemphill, and Sam Piperato), co-produced by Archipelago Theatre, with Chris Morris and Cynthia Mitchell; *Dream True: My Life with Vernon Dexter* (Tina Landau); *References to Salvador Dalí Make Me Hot* (Jose Rivera); and *Hortensia and the Museum of Dreams* (Nilo Cruz).

Trovillion, Nancy (1952–)

Nancy Trovillion, a native of Florida and 1975 graduate of Converse College in South Carolina, got her start in dance with the National Endowment for the Arts. In 1979 she moved to Durham and the next year she became administrative director of the American Dance Festival. While with ADF she became involved with local dance, taking classes with Lee Wenger Vrana's New Performing Dance Company and with local dancers and choreographers in ADF's North Carolina Choreographers Project, creating and performing new work. She is currently the deputy director of the North Carolina Arts Council.

Tucker, Bradley F. (1952–)

Bradley Tucker, a potter and a native New Yorker, obtained a B.A. in English from Atlantic Christian College (now Barton College) in Wilson in 1976. He pursued additional studies in pottery production at Montgomery Technical College, apprenticed with Sid and Pat Oakley at Cedar Creek Pottery, and studied at the Penland School of Crafts. He opened his own studio at Cedar Creek Pottery in 1982, where he continues to create functional stoneware fired with wood ash glazes in a gas kiln. His work has been exhibited and is in several permanent collections at home and abroad, including those of Louisburg College, the North Carolina Museum of History, the Odyssey Center for Ceramic Arts in Asheville, the North Carolina Pottery Center, and the collection of *Ceramics Monthly* in Columbus, Ohio. Tucker has received an Emerging Artists Grant from the Durham Arts Council. Several publications have featured his work, including *Functional Pottery*, by Robin Hopper; *Wheel-Thrown Ceramics*, by Don Davis; *The Ceramic Design Book*, by Chris Rich; and *Ceramics Monthly*.

Twaddell, William Powell (1879–1949)

William Twaddell, a musician, choir director, and composer, was born in Philadelphia to Jacob and Nancy Freeman Twaddell. He began his career in music as a choirboy and received his training in Philadelphia and New York City, concentrating on organ and church music. He worked as an organist and choir director in Philadelphia and then in Bridgeport, Connecticut; Rye, New York; and Baltimore, Maryland before settling in Durham in 1922. There he served a series of churches—Temple Baptist, First Presbyterian, and St. Philip's Episcopal—raising the standard and appreciation of church music in the area. Perhaps his greatest influence was in the pubic schools, where he was director of music. Year after year he developed award-winning choruses, inspired many talented students to pursue careers in music, and introduced generations of students to the appreciation and enjoyment of good music. A notable student was Lucille Brown (later Browning), who became a star of the Metropolitan Opera. The Durham Chamber of Commerce honored Twaddell with its award for his "splendid and unique services in enriching the cultural life of the city."

2 Near the Edge

L. D. Burris and Carol Childs (also known as Keval Kaur Khalsa), dancers and choreographers, formed the Durham dance company 2 Near the Edge in 1992. It explores the new and exotic in dance, performing locally and nationally. Burris and Childs combine poetry, drama, and music with dance in entirely new ways. For example, their production "Bring Me Your Breasts" features the poet Jaki Shelton Green and the composer John Hanks; "Inwardly Mobile" presents four dancers, two in wheelchairs. The company has performed at the American Dance Festival (ADF) and throughout the United States and abroad. It has received grants from the North Carolina Arts Council, the Durham Arts Council, the Duke University Institute of the Arts, the Duke University Office of Community Affairs, and Alternate Roots in Atlanta.

Childs, with an M.A. in dance from Ohio State University, also teaches jazz, modern dance, and dance composition as an associate professor of the practice of dance at Duke University. She has performed with the Limón Company, Clay Taliaferro, and many other independent choreographers in the United States and Europe. Burris, a former marine, was a founding member of the African American Dance Ensemble and a performer and choreographer in ADF's three-year program "The Black Tradition in American Modern Dance." He is an adjunct faculty member at Meredith College and is the founder of the Triangle Center for Contemporary Dance.

Umberger, Randolph (1942–)

Randolph Umberger, a faculty member at NCCU in theater, holds a B.A. and an M.A. in dramatic art from UNC-Chapel Hill, where he was a Shubert Foundation Fellow in playwriting. After earning a Ph.D. in theater literature and criticism from Tulane University he joined the faculty of NCCU in 1967 and chaired the department from 1970 to 1975. He is the author of two North Carolina outdoor dramas, *Strike at the Wind*, now in its twenty-fifth season in Pembroke, and *The Liberty Cart*, which ran for thirteen years in Kenansville. He is the author of a dozen other plays and novels, and his adaptation of Zora Neale Hurston's novel *Mules and Men* won the American College Theater Festival Award of the Kennedy Center for the Performing Arts in 1991. Umberger has directed over one hundred college and professional productions, including productions for Carolina Playmakers, the Opera House in Wilmington, and the Jenny Wiley State Theatre of Kentucky. He has directed the Durham Savoyards and was a founder and artistic director of the Long Leaf Opera. A recipient of numerous teaching awards, Umberger has also lectured at Furman University, the North Carolina School of the Arts, Pembroke University, UNC-Chapel Hill, and Duke.

Vaughan, Caroline (1949–)

Caroline Vaughan is a fine arts photographer. She was born in Durham, North Carolina, graduated in 1971 with a B.A. from Duke University where she was a co-founder of the student photographic publication *Latent Image*, which printed volume 23 in March 2003. After studying with John Menapace, production manager of Duke University Press, she studied at the Penland School of Crafts in 1970 and 1974. After graduating from Duke, during 1971-72 she participated in a program of intensive study with Minor White at M.I.T. She was the only female among his seven students for that academic year—and received what was to be her must influential instruction in the technical and spiritual nature of her chosen art form. While at M.I.T. she was invited by Polaroid Corporation to participate in the Young Artists Program for several years. In 1977, Vaughan was nominated by a panel of photographic experts from Europe, North America, and Australia as one of forty-three promising young photographers and listed in the Time-Life publication *Photography year 1977*.

She received an Emerging Artist Grant from the Durham Arts Council, Project Funding from the Documentary Center in 1990 and again in 2002 to fund portrait projects, the most recent "Personal Disruptions," a coming of age of the college students during the time of the Vigil at Duke. The North Carolina Arts Council awarded Vaughan a Visual Arts Fellowship in 1990. In 1996, Duke University Press published a mid-career retrospective of her work, *Borrowed Time: the Photographs of Caroline Vaughan*. In 2005 she was included in the book *Quartet: Four North Carolina Photographers*, published by Safe Harbor Press. Ms. Vaughan has published and exhibited nationally and her work is collected in numerous museums, including the Addison Gallery of American Art, Andover, Massachusetts; the Amon Carter Museum, Fort Worth, Texas; the Gregg Museum of Art and Design, Raleigh, North Carolina; the Polaroid Museum Collection, Cambridge, Massachusetts; and the North Carolina Museum of Art, Raleigh, North Carolina. Most recently she taught as a first year instructor in 2007 at the Penland School of Crafts. After working twenty-five years at Duke in the Development Office, Ms. Vaughan retired in 2007 to continue her photographic career full time.

Vega Metals

Francis Vega (1959–), a Cuban who settled in Durham in 1981, and his partner Neal Carlton have had a major impact on the Durham arts community in design and cooperative work with other artists through their business Vega Metals. Established in 1987, it represents collaborative teams of full-time artists and blacksmiths. Examples of Vega Metals work include the design and crafting of the iris fountain in Duke Gardens, one of the gates to the George Watts Hill Pavilion of Durham Central Park, over three hundred linear feet of mirror-polished solid bronze railings in the North Carolina Legislative Building, the metalwork for Edward J. Debartolo's Biltmore Square Mall in Asheville, and many other public and private commissions throughout the state and nation. Among the artists the firm has assisted are Edwin White, Bill Noland, Don Drumm, Irwin Kremen, and Frank DePasquale. Vega Metals has received a number of awards, including several from the National Ornamental and Miscellaneous Metals Association in McDonough, Georgia.

Vrana, Lee Wenger (1946–)

Lee Vrana, a dancer, choreographer, and educator, was born in New York and received a B.A. in dance from Sarah Lawrence College. After earning advanced degrees in education and administration, she moved to Durham in 1975 and joined the New Performing Dance Company (NPDC) while it was still Dance Associates of Allied Arts (now Durham Arts Council). She remained with the company as its artistic director from 1978 to 1995. She received artist fellowships from the North Carolina Arts Council and participated in its touring program, performing in Durham and Washington. Vrana was director of education at the DAC for ten years before moving to the Durham public school system, where she was a curriculum specialist for ten years at the Durham School of the Arts. She is now the assistant principal at Hillside High School.

Walker, Tim (1954–)

Tim Walker, a native of Texas, is a photographer and builder of furniture and architectural pieces with leather. He received his B.A. from Duke University in 1976 while living in Durham from 1972 to 1992. His work is in many private collections and in the Mint Museum in Charlotte. He has been active with the Durham Arts Council and in regional art planning consortiums. While in Durham, Walker received an Emerging Artists Grant from the Durham Arts Council. He now lives in Miami.

Ward, James A. (1915–)

An architect and draftsman, James Ward earned a degree from Wofford College in mathematics, worked five years during the Depression as a draftsman in the offices of architectural and engineering firms, and served for three years in the U.S. Army, all experiences which he found extremely useful for his very long and productive professional career. A native of Forsyth County

and a 1948 graduate of NCSU, Ward finally embarked on his career as an architect and engineer with Marion Ham's firm in Durham. There he remained for sixteen years, designing schools, churches, residences, and commercial projects.

In 1964 Ward became associate architect at Duke University and in the next year he moved up to the top slot; in 1967 his responsibilities were expanded to include physical planning. During his service the university adopted the policy of using the original construction material of Hillsborough stone for all future buildings on West Campus, after an unfortunate interim of construction with alternative materials. He retired from his university positions in 1984.

Ward's early connection with the Howard Haines firm, which the Methodist Church had selected to build all rural churches in North Carolina, led to his second career. In 1984 the Duke Endowment, which supported rural Methodist churches, designated him the architect in the design and renovation of these churches. He retired a second time in 2004.

For his long and outstanding service, Ward received awards from the Methodist Conference and the Duke Endowment. Despite his busy career, Ward found time to serve as a Durham county commissioner, planning director for the City of Durham, and chairman of the building committee for Durham Regional Hospital.

Ward, Robert (1917–)

The composer Robert Ward was born into a musical family and from early childhood sang as a boy soprano with family members and church choirs. He earned a B.A. in music from the Eastman School of Music in 1939 and then joined the faculty of Queens College in New York. When war intervened he joined the Seventh Army's regimental band and for five years led army bands, taking morale-building music to Okinawa and Korea before he returned home to complete his music studies. After receiving a diploma from the Juilliard School in 1946 he held several faculty positions, including at Juilliard.

In 1957 he turned to business and to music editing and publishing when he joined the Galaxy Music Publishing Company and Highgate Press. While there he developed the administrative experience and know-how that served him well when in 1967 he became chancellor of the North Carolina School of the Arts. He retired from the chancellorship in 1974 but continued as a faculty member and composer-in-residence. In 1979 he joined the music faculty of Duke University, where he taught composition until his retirement in 1987.

Throughout his career Ward always put his compositional work first. This concentration has resulted in a prodigious amount of music, including works for orchestra, band, piano, and chorus; perhaps his best-known work is *The Crucible*, an opera based on the play by Arthur Miller for which he won the Pulitzer Prize. He continues to compose and live in Durham.

Weinstein, Emily (1955–)

Emily Weinstein, a painter, was born in Newburgh, New York, and has lived in Europe and the United States. She earned her B.F.A. from Virginia Commonwealth University in 1978 and studied at the West Surrey College of Art and Design in England and the Académie Charpentier in Paris. Now living in Durham, Weinstein has started two art businesses: Pet and People Portraiture, and Murals by Many. Her murals can be seen around Durham: the "Eno River" mural on the Old Penny Furniture Building on Morris Street, "The Arts in Durham" at 401 Foster Street, and a mural next to Lakewood Shopping Center that depicts the Hayti area's heritage, completed with local children. Weinstein has published three collections of her art, *Cat Book*, *Dog Book*, and *Moon Book*, a journal, and paintings of the moon's phases. She does commissioned portraits of both pets and people. Weinstein has had solo shows across North Carolina and Virginia, including a display of her moon paintings at the Durham Arts Council in 1999.

Weiser, Conrad (1939–)

Conrad Weiser, a potter, works in porcelain, stoneware, Raku, and earthenware. Born in North Carolina, he received his B.A. from UNC-Chapel Hill and his M.F.A. from the Universidad de Guanajuato, Instituto Allende, Mexico. He has studied with several potters including Val Cushing at Alfred University in New York and Albert Levy at the Instituto Allende, and with the sculptor Robert Howard at UNC-Chapel Hill. He was director of the North Carolina State University Craft Center until he retired in 1993. He also taught at the Duke University Crafts Center until it closed in 2004 and at the Durham Arts Council. Former students include Jim Lux and Charlie Pritchard.

Wells, Barbara

Barbara Wells, a weaver, first arrived in Durham in 1966. She is a registered nurse and holds a B.S. in nursing from Johns Hopkins University. During a year in Sweden she became interested in weaving, which she began to study with Sandy Miller (now Milroy) when she returned to Durham in 1972. She pursued additional studies at the Penland School of Crafts, and with Sharon Keech and Silvia Heyden in Durham. She weaves with wool, silk, and other fibers in original designs and has exhibited widely. She has received many private commissions for her work in Durham, St. Louis, and Chicago. Currently, she weaves afghans, shawls, and other commissioned works.

Wetherby, Joseph C. (1910–1976)

Joseph Wetherby came to the Duke University English Department in 1947 as a teacher of speech and related courses. He became involved with theater by directing *Ghost Train* in 1949 and by working with Kenneth Reardon on designs to change Branson, an engineering building, into Branson Theater. He was best known at Duke for his prize-winning debate teams; in 1976 the team he coached won the national championship. In the community he was known for his interest in dialects. He was a long-time business manager for Savoyards and was producer or stage director for three of its productions: *The Mikado* (1965), *Iolanthe* (1967), and *The Gondoliers* (1974). He was the Southern Regional Director of Delta Sigma Rho-Tau Kappa Alpha (the debate organization of the Southeast) from its founding in 1952 until his death. For his contributions to theatrical and allied fields he was awarded life membership in the American Educational Theater Association in 1961.

Wexler, Emily (1959–)

Emily Wexler, a basket weaver, was born in Pennsylvania and moved to Durham in 1978. She has a B.A. from Duke University and studied with Deb Nickell, Bryant Holsenbeck, and Henrietta Snipes. She has taught basket weaving at the Craft Center at Duke University and the Durham Arts Council (DAC). Wexler has received many private commissions, as well as an Extended Study Grant from DAC's Creative Arts in the Public/Private Schools (CAPPS) program. She has been an organizer at DAC's CenterFest arts festival. Currently she makes baskets and teaches at her home in Durham.

Wheeler, Nina (1955–)

Nina Wheeler, a dancer and choreographer, is the owner of Nina's School of Dance, which has been in operation in Durham since 1980. The school teaches four hundred dancers annually, and many of its dancers have gone on to careers with the Ailey School, the Juilliard School of Dance, and the American Dance Festival. Wheeler received an M.A. in dance from Dance Educators of America (affiliated with New York University) and also studied with North Carolina Dance Alliance in Raleigh, with Gus Giordano in Chicago, with Alvin Ailey in New York, and with Jose Meier at Carnegie-Mellon University. In 1993 she won the Durham Arts Council Hitchings Award for her many contributions to dance throughout the community. One such contribution is an annual presentation that she gives with her sister, the dancer Tommi Galaska, and many of her school's dancers; the presentation, "Multiple Choices for Children," benefits the Pediatric Unit at Duke University Medical Center. Wheeler is an adjunct faculty member at Elon University, where she teaches jazz dance. She also produces the Miss North Carolina Pageant.

Whiteside, Tom (1957–)

Tom Whiteside is an artist and film historian. A native of Virginia, he received his B.A. degree from UNC-Chapel Hill in 1979. His work has focused on regional film history, especially the history of such films as *The Lost Colony Film*, directed by Elizabeth Grimball, and *Movies of Local People*, directed by H. Lee Waters. He has made more than thirty experimental films and videos. Whiteside has been a visiting artist in the North Carolina community college system, an artist-in-residence at the Headlands Center for the Arts in Sausalito, California, and an arts administration fellow in the media arts section of the National Endowment for the Arts. He is the founder and director of Durham Cinematheque Outdoor Screen, which shows free vintage and documentary films.

Wilkinson, Margot (1945–)

Margot Wilkinson, a potter, works in functional high-fired porcelain. A native of Durham, she has a B.F.A. from East Carolina University. She studied with Sid Oakley and pursued further studies at the Penland School of Crafts. Her work is privately collected. She is now retired and living in Chapel Hill.

Williams, Mary Lou (1910–1981)

Mary Lou Williams, a jazz pianist, composer, and arranger, played keyboard instruments from a very young age. When she was a toddler, her mother would hold her while playing at the family pump organ, and after a time, a precocious Williams joined in. Seeing her daughter's interest, her mother gave her a broad music education, and when the family moved to Pittsburgh, Williams began classical piano lessons. Before she was ten Williams was escorted by her stepfather to play at a number of popular venues, and she came to be known locally as the "little piano girl." She played for a traveling vaudeville show by the age of fifteen, and in a jazz orchestra soon after. Based in Kansas City, the band became known for its Kansas City swing style and performed through the 1930s. In 1942 Williams relocated to New York, where she performed with artists like Dizzy Gillespie and Thelonious Monk.

After touring in Europe in the mid-1950s, Williams converted to Roman Catholicism and withdrew briefly from the world of jazz. She re-emerged in 1957 to perform with Gillespie at the Newport Festival and continued to perform in clubs in New York City. She also began writing jazz music in a liturgical form. Williams joined the music department at Duke University in 1977 and remained there until her death. In September 1983 Duke University established the Mary Lou Williams Center for Black Culture in her honor.

Wilson, Anna Ludwig (1944–)

Anna Wilson, a native of Virginia, was introduced to music at an early age through piano lessons from her mother, a professional musician. In high school she took up the flute so that she could play in the band and became a mas-

ter in the instrument. With a B.A. and an M.A. from UNC-Chapel Hill, and graduate study with Thomas Nyfenger at Yale, she has spent her adult life in and around Durham, teaching and performing throughout the area and state. She has received two emerging artist grants from Durham Arts Council, the Kathryn H. Wallace Award for Artists in Community Service (2002), and the Making a Difference for Durham Families Award (2006).

Wilson's ambition has been to bring music of all varieties to all audiences, with particular attention to those usually underserved—the infirm, the ill, the poor, and the generally disadvantaged. She has accomplished this through the Mallarmé Chamber Players, of which she was a founder in 1984. Operating under the Arts Council, she has carried out her mission with grants, donations, and support from Mallarmé subscribers.

Under Wilson's direction, Mallarmé has given many free concerts in unlikely places, in addition to its subscription concerts. The players have sent musicians into schools and summer camps, developed special materials for teachers, and commissioned new works. They have performed all over the state and in other states. More recently Wilson helped to establish the Mallarmé Youth Orchestra for exceptional children, under the direction of the violinist Yoram Youngerman.

Wilson, David (1970–)

David Wilson, a native of West Virginia, is a painter and illustrator whose main themes are family, music, and culture as they pertain to black history. After receiving his B.F.A. in 1993 from Hampton University he moved to North Carolina and lived in Durham until 1996. He was one of two North Carolina artists selected by the Triangle Transit Authority to work on the "Community Canvases." His art is to be integrated into the design of the regional rail stations planned for the Triangle. His work is in many private collections and has appeared in publications such as *Essence* and *Upscale*. He has completed artwork for the Durham County Detention Center, the North Carolina Museum of History, Hargraves Community Center in Chapel Hill, and the Nash Senior Center in Nashville, as well as the large mural across from the Hayti Heritage Center, "Hayti Remembered," with Emily Weinstein. As a graphic designer he has worked with the Chrysler Museum of Art in Norfolk, Virginia, and with Whole Foods Market in North Carolina, and created the official poster for the annual basketball tournament of the Central Intercollegiate Athletic Association in 2000. In 1999 he toured with the United States Army in Germany, presenting his work during Black History Month. Wilson has received awards and grants from the Reader's Digest Fund, Durham Arts Council, the Durham Art Guild, and the Mary Duke Biddle Foundation. He lives in Apex, North Carolina.

Wilson, Erin Cressida (1964–)

Erin Wilson was already a noted playwright when she joined the Duke University program in drama in 1995. Besides many plays, she has written radio and movie scripts. Plays and screenplays written or produced while she was at Duke include *Ten Unknown Soldiers* (one of ten musical theater pieces, 1996), *Pieces of Quilt* (four short plays with other playwrights for an AIDS fund raiser, 1996), *Hurricane* (1997), *The Bay of Naples* (1997), *The Trial of Her Inner Thigh* (1998), *The Erotica Project* (stage version 1998, radio series 1999), *I Feel Love* (2002), *Secretary* (film script, 2002), and *Brave New World* (two short plays for the September 11 memorial held in 2002). Most of these have been published. Performed widely in the United States and a few foreign countries, her plays have won a variety of prizes at the Sundance Festival, Independent Spirit, from the North Carolina Council (best new play), and at the MacDowell Colony.

Wilson left Durham in 2003 to become professor and head of graduate playwriting in the creative writing program of Brown University.

Wood, Sherri (1964–)

Sherri Wood, a native of Indiana, is a fiber artist and multidisciplinary artist who has lived and worked in Durham since 1994. She received a B.A. in 1986 from Bethany College in West Virginia, an M.A. in theological studies from Emory University in 1997, and an M.F.A. in 2004 from Bard College. She teaches at the Penland School of Crafts. Through improvisational quilts, embroidered tattoo dolls, crochet, and sewing, she explores feminine and domestic popular culture. Wood has been awarded artist-in-residence fellowships at the MacDowell Colony in New Hampshire and at Headlands Center for the Arts, a visual artist fellowship from the North Carolina Arts Council, and an emerging artists grant from the Durham Arts Council.

Woolbright, Normadiene (1953–)

Normadiene Woolbright began her career as a dancer and choreographer in her native New York after receiving a degree from High School of Performing Arts and a B.A. in dance from Herbert H. Lehman College. She was with Chuck Davis and his dance troupe while it was in New York, and since his move to Durham in 1983 and the formation of his new troupe, the African American Dance Ensemble (AADE), she has been its director of programs and tour manager. She has performed at the American Dance Festival with Jennifer Muller and at the Black College Dance Exchange with Nancy Pinckney. She appeared in the movie *The Wiz*. Woolbright has influenced a generation of young dancers through the AADE's children's unit, Alayanse, and as a dance teacher in Durham's public schools.

Wray, Julia (1933–1989)

Julia Wray, a native of Virginia, taught dance at Duke University beginning in 1955 and was the founder and director of its dance program. After earning undergraduate and graduate degrees from UNC-Greensboro she became an associate professor of dance at the Institute of the Arts and a member of its executive council. Because she had belonged to the group that brought the American Dance Festival to Duke, she became its academic liaison. In addition, she was a consultant to the Cultural Arts Division of the North Carolina Department of Public Instruction and the first president of the North Carolina Dance Alliance. Wray received the first annual Hitchings Award for Dance, which was then named for her in honor of her long contribution to dance in North Carolina. She sponsored exchange programs with the North Carolina College (now NCCU) Dance Group and enticed Clay Taliaferro, a lead dancer with José Limón, to join Duke in 1987 as professor of the practice of dance. She died weeks before the performance of Limón's *Missa Brevis* in Duke Chapel, a performance she had worked to present. Duke Dance dedicated to her memory in 1989 a mini-festival that featured dance companies from around the state, "A Celebration of North Carolina Dance in Tribute to Julia Wray."

Wynkoop, Rodney (1951–)

A native of Ohio, Rodney Wynkoop sang and played the piano in primary and secondary school. After earning his B.A. from Yale in 1973 and a master's degree in choral conducting from Yale and the University of Wisconsin, he then received his doctorate from the Yale School of Music. He worked as the director of chapel and choral music at the University of Chicago. At Duke he was an artist-in-residence from 1984 until 1989 and then became a professor of the practice of music, teaching choral conducting. In 1989 he also became the director of choral music and conductor of the Duke University Chorale and the chamber choir. Wynkoop has carried on many of the grand traditions of Duke Chapel while also conducting and directing a number of community groups, including the Choral Society of Durham and the Vocal Arts Ensemble. Among his many honors and awards are the Lara Hoggard Award for Distinguished Service in Choral Music in North Carolina.

About the Contributors

Jean Anderson, author and historian, has written extensively about the history of Durham. Her previous books include *Durham County: A History of Durham County North Carolina* and *Piedmont Plantation*.

Jim Wise is a local historian, author, and newspaper columnist. He is a favorite lecturer at Osher LifeLong Learning Institute at Duke University and the author of *Durham: A Bull City*.

Margaret Pepper Fluke is a ceramic artist and community leader who came to Durham in 1958. She was deeply involved in the restoration of the Carolina Theatre and Hayti Heritage Center. She was one of the seven women who founded Craft House of Durham Ltd. and was a founding exhibiting member of Carolina Designer Craftsmen Guild.

Jill Salinger Winter is property manager for a private historic estate and garden near Leesburg, Virginia. She has forty years' experience as a freelance editor, writer, abstractor, proofreader, and production manager for professional books, textbooks, journals, monographs, and newsletters.

Linda Belans became director of Health Arts Network at Duke University in 2003, a program that integrates arts and humanities into the life of Duke Medical Center. She is the creator and original host of the radio series *The State of Things*, co-creator of the award-winning radio series *Do No Harm*, and arts contributor to the *News and Observer*.

Nonna Skumanich is a freelance writer. She graduated from the North Carolina School of the Arts in ballet and received a law degree from the University of Washington. She is a licensed attorney with the Washington and North Carolina bars.

Randolph Umberger is a retired senior professor of theater at North Carolina Central University, where he served as chairman of the department and as division chair of Arts and Humanities I courses. He holds a B.A. and M.A. in dramatic arts from the University of North Carolina at Chapel Hill and a Ph.D. in theater literature and criticism from Tulane. He is an award-winning playwright and director and, along with Benjamin Keaton, is the founder of Long Leaf Opera.

Kate Dobbs Ariail is a freelance writer and art critic who lives in Durham. She has an M.F.A. from Syracuse University, has served on many community boards, and was instrumental in the creation of Liberty Arts.

Index

Griffith, William J., 104, 113, 138, 186
Grimball, Elizabeth, 275
Gropius, Walter, 66, 68
Gross, Gladys Estelle Peterson ("Peter"), 23, 157, 180
Gross, Paul, 157
Gross Chemistry Building, 84, 238
Grossman, Stefan, 228
Grossman, Susan E., 238
"Guardian of Generations" (Sullivan), plate 7
Guest, Romeo, 75
Guidry, Charles, 238
Guion, Maggie, 105
Gulley, Wib, 56
Guptill, Randy, 156
Gussow, Roy, 68
Gutstadt, Joe, 181

Haber, John L., 270
Hackney, Balford, 80
Hackney, George F., 239
Hackney, Sear, Keener, and Williams, 239
Hackney and Knott Architects, 239
Haines, Howard, 239, 266, 273
Halby's, 172
Halcott, John B., 10
Hall, Betsy, 104
Hall, Bill, 104
Hall, Karen, 230
Hall, Louise, 214
Hall, Nor, 270
Hall, Phillmore "Shorty," 154, 168, 169–70, 231, 268
Hall, Toni K., 110
Ham, Marion A., 239, 273
Ham Keener Williams Architects, 239
Hamilton, George, IV, 173
Hamilton, Iain, 140, 143, 149, 194, 239
Hamilton, Patrick, 259
Hamm, James W., 31, 34
Hammond, J. Samuel, 148
Hamner, W. Clay, 87
Hampton, Clyde, 134
Hampton, Lisa Harris, 187
Hanes, Frederic M., 30

Hanes Building, 84
Hanes House, 65
Hanks, John Kennedy, 141–42, 158, 239–40, 271
Hanks, Nancy, 123
Hansley, Lee, 247
Hardin, Charles, 39, 40
Hardin, Noma', 250
Hardy, William H., 259
Harlequins (band), 170
Harrell, Paula, 137
Harris, Alex, 240, 263
Harris, Ewing "Skeeter," 101
Harris, Hilda, 133, 159, 240
Harris, Jan, 240–41
Harris, Jessica, 112
Harris, Julie, 220, 270
Harris, Rennie, 122
Harris, Robin, 112
Harris, Wilton E., 26, 259
Harris and Pyne Architects and Engineers, 26, 259
Harrison, Rex, 270
Harrison, Vernon, 66, 237
Hart, Julian Deryl, 195
Hartill, Brenda, 158
Hartman-Cox (architectural firm), 94
Harwood Hall (Watts House), 13, 35, 97, 184
Haskins, Gwendolyn Tait, 133
Hatful of Rain, A (Gazzo), 219
Hauptman, William, 261
Hawkins, Jane, 156
Hayes, Afrika, 154
Hayes, Brenda, 110
Hayes, Isaac, 226
Hayes, Roland, 23, 136, 154
Hayti, 6–7, 13, 56, 274; "house parties" in, 24; theaters in, 20; urban renewal in, 76
Hayti Heritage Center. See St. Joseph's Historic Foundation / Hayti Heritage Center
Hayti Mural, 241–42, 277
Haywood, Margaret, 43, 45
Health Arts Network at Duke (HAND), 127, 218
Heart of Durham Motel, 77
Heat Lightning (Storer), 267
Heckley, E. Azalia, 22

Heckscher, William S., 214
Hemphill, Ellen, 214, 242, 270
Henderson, Fletcher, 168, 170
Henderson, J. J., 43, 241
Henderson, Lana, 215
Hendricks, Barkley, 255
Hendrix, Mildred, 145–46
Henze, Hans Werner, 159
Hepburn, Katharine, 46, 184
Heritage Square Associates, 242
"Her Joyful Affirmation" (London), 247
Herndon, Fred, 35
Herrick, Jack, 270
Herring, Herbert, 113
Herzog, Elizabeth, 222
He Who Gets Slapped (Andreyev), 248
Hewitt, Mark, 103, 253
Hexner, Jonathan, 201
Heyden, Siegfried, 242
Heyden, Sylvia, 36, 101, 103, 198, 242, 274, plate 15
Heyman, Dorothy, 101
Hicks, Bill, 176, 177
Hideaway Lounge, 172
Hill, Ed, 268
Hill, George Watts, Jr., 46, 73
Hill, George Watts, Sr., 73, 75, 81, 82, 83, 227, 230
Hill, John Sprunt, 18, 30, 61, 73
Hill, Martha, 127
Hill, Samuel Washington, 23, 133, 242
Hill, Valinda, 14
Hill, Willie, 172, 243
Hillandale Golf Course, 87
Hill Building, 61, 227
Hill Family Foundation, 81–82
Hill Recreation Center, 105, 114
Hillside High School, 23, 154, 168, 169, 190, 222, 231, 243, 273
Hines, Gregory, 112
Hinners, Melinda, 40
Hinson, Glenn, 167, 169
Hip Hop Film Festival, 235
Hispanics, 129
Historically Black Colleges and Universities Association, 256
Historical Properties Act (1966), 86

Merlino, June, 203
Merrick, John, 42
Merrick, Lyda Moore, 202
Merrick-Moore High School, 105
Merry Wives of Windsor, Texas (Haber), 270
Messiah (Handel), 27, 149
Metamorphosis (Berkoff), 270
Methodist Conference, 273
Methodist Female Seminary, 9
Metropolitan Opera, 27, 133, 142, 158, 240, 271
Meyer, Marlane, 248
Meyers, Chris, 155
Mezz, Brenda, 268
Mezzatesta, Michael, 201
Michalak, Victor, 185, 250
Middleton, Thomas, 251, 259
Mies van der Rohe, Ludwig, 66, 73
Mikado, The (Gilbert and Sullivan), 157, 275
Milburn and Heister (architectural firm), 7, 71
Miller, Arthur, 144, 274
Miller, Roger, 261
Miller, Tim, 247
Milroy, Sandy (Miller), 101, 250, 274
Minnis, Paul, 98, 101, 250–51
Minnis Pottery, 250–51
Minor, Henry H., 40, 44
Miser, The (Molière), 248, 259
Missa Brevis (Limón), 278
Miss American Pie (Sartor), 263
Miss Holeman's Private Music School, 14
Mitchell, Carol, 103
Mitchell, Cynthia, 270
Mitchell, Joseph, 137
M. K. Sullivan Dance Studio, 114
Modern Black Mass Choir, 149
Modernextension Dance Company, 243
Modernist architecture, 61, 63, 71, 73, 74, 83, 94
Modern Museum, 203, 216
Modulations (band), 172, 243
Moffett, Dave, 171
Mogavero, Richard S., 268
Moiseiwitsch, Benno, 136
Molière, Jean-Baptiste, 248, 259
Molly's Not Dead, 119

Monk, Meredith, 260
Monk, Thelonious, 168, 275
Monsieur Beaucaire (Tarkington), 23
Montessori School for Children, 250
Montgomery, Paul, 52, 171, 172
Month of Sundays, A (Larbey), 216, 269
Montreux Jazz Festival, 135
Moon, Ernest, 247
Moon Book (Weinstein), 274
Moonlight and Valentino (Simon), 216, 270
"Moor's Pavane, The" (Limón), 123, 125
Mora, Francisco, 222
Morehead Hill, 13
Morehead Planetarium, 227
Morgan, Jacqueline (Erickson), 40, 112, 116, 117, 118–19, 123, 126, 199, 251
Morgan, Richard, 199
Morris, Chris, 247, 251, 270
Morse, Robert, 220
Moses, Constance (Connie) Roy, 43, 44–45, 46, 49, 52, 170–71
Moses, Montrose J. (Monte), 45, 49, 52, 170–71
Mount Calvary Baptist Church, 249
Mount Calvary Word of Faith Church, 222
Mount Hope Finishing Company, 79
Mouthfulla Sacco & Vanzetti (Smith), 264
Movies of Local People (Waters), 275
Mozart Musicale, 8
Ms. Films, 235
Mud (Fornes), 248
Mueller, Julia Wilkinson, 25, 138, 139, 140, 141, 150, 151, 251
Mules and Men, 189, 271
"Mule Train, The" (exhibition), 213
Mumford, Eugene, 164, 172, 251–52
Mumford, Lewis, 66, 68
murals, 30, 198–99, 241–42, 274, 277
Murals by Many, 274

Murder in the Cathedral (Eliot), 219
Murray, William D., 194
Music for a Great Occasion (Ward), 144
Muti, Lorenzo, 156
Myers, Martha, 126, 127, 252
My Heart Belongs to Daddy (Marker and Spenser), 270
My Man Ray (McAuliffe), 248
Mystery of Attraction, The (Mayer), 248
Myzner, Larry, 104

NC PRIDE, 233
NC Spotlight Showcase, 236
Nanaline Duke Research Center, 84
Nash, Arthur C., 25–26
Nash, Willie, 215, 252–53
Nasher, Raymond, 201
Nasher Art Museum, 127, 184, 201, 204, 216
National Association of Schools of Theatre, 189
National Endowment for the Arts (NEA), 44, 56, 123, 199, 228, 240, 249, 250, 254, 260
National Endowment for the Humanities (NEH), 152
National Historic Districts, 45, 86
National Humanities Center, 93, 94
National Register of Historic Places, 42, 86
National Religious Training School and Chautauqua, 7, 22, 132, 265. *See also* North Carolina Central University
National Science Headquarters, 254
National Teapot Show, 223
National Theatre Company, 158
National Youth Administration, 132
Navidad Flamenca (Santana), 263
Nee Ningy Band, 177
Negro Slave Songs in the United States (Fisher), 162
"Negro Woman" (Catlett), 222
Neighborhood Taproots, 45

The text of this book has been set in Trump Mediæval, a typeface designed by Georg Trump for the Weber foundry and released between 1954 and 1960. With its crisp angularity and wedge-shaped serifs, Trump Mediæval appears carved in stone. It is a strong and forthright typeface, not unlike our city of Durham.